More Praise for *Lift*

"This book inspires insights and actions through deep exposure to the power of lift. Telling stories and solid science combine to reveal useful principles for harnessing lift. This book creates the capacity for any reader to become a positive force in life."

—Jane Dutton, Robert L. Kahn Distinguished
University Professor of Business Administration and Psychology,
Ross School of Business, University of Michigan

"Becoming a positive force, a person of influence with the courage to make a difference for the common good, is a powerful state of being and the true essence of leadership. *Lift* serves as an enabling stimulus to fully engage the brain and heart and to muster the necessary courage in meeting both professional and personal challenges. A must-read book no matter your station in life!"

—James L. Pughsley, former superintendent,
Charlotte-Mecklenburg Schools (the country's
twenty-third-largest school system)

"*Lift* is an important book but must not only be read by those in tune with its message. The art must be for even those not initially sympathetic to its message to embrace it too. Then the world will truly change." —Anthony Seldon,
Master of Wellington College, United Kingdom

"Great teams in any sport require players and coaches who are a positive influence upon those around them, and the Quinns use scientific research and practical experience to think deeply and write meaningfully about influence. *Lift* asks us tough questions about the kind of people we are and inspires us to put our answers into action for the benefit of others."

—Brian Townsend, Director of Basketball Operations,
University of Michigan men's basketball team,
and former linebacker for the Los Angeles Rams and Cincinnati Bengals

Lift

Becoming a Positive Force
in Any Situation

Ryan W. Quinn and Robert E. Quinn

Berrett–Koehler Publishers, Inc.
San Francisco
a BK Business book

Berrett-Koehler Publishers, Inc.
235 Montgomery Street, Suite 650
San Francisco, CA 94104-2916
Tel: (415) 288-0260   Fax: (415) 362-2512   www.bkconnection.com

Ordering Information

Quantity sales. Special discounts are available on quantity purchases by corporations, associations, and others. For details, contact the "Special Sales Department" at the Berrett-Koehler address above.

Individual sales. Berrett-Koehler publications are available through most bookstores. They can also be ordered directly from Berrett-Koehler: Tel: (800) 929-2929; Fax: (802) 864-7626; www.bkconnection.com

Orders for college textbook/course adoption use. Please contact Berrett-Koehler: Tel: (800) 929-2929; Fax: (802) 864-7626.

Orders by U.S. trade bookstores and wholesalers. Please contact Ingram Publisher Services, Tel: (800) 509-4887; Fax: (800) 838-1149; E-mail: customer.service@ingrampublisherservices.com; or visit www.ingrampublisherservices.com/Ordering for details about electronic ordering.

Berrett-Koehler and the BK logo are registered trademarks of Berrett-Koehler Publishers, Inc.

Printed in the United States of America

Berrett-Koehler books are printed on long-lasting acid-free paper. When it is available, we choose paper that has been manufactured by environmentally responsible processes. These may include using trees grown in sustainable forests, incorporating recycled paper, minimizing chlorine in bleaching, or recycling the energy produced at the paper mill.

Library of Congress Cataloging-in-Publication Data
Quinn, Ryan W.
Lift : becoming a positive force in any situation / Ryan W. Quinn and Robert E. Quinn.
   p.   cm.
  Includes bibliographical references.
  ISBN 978-1-57675-444-3 (hardcover : alk. paper)
  1. Positive psychology.   2. Self-actualization (Psychology)   3. Success.
 4. Interpersonal relations.   I. Quinn, Robert E.   II. Title.
  BF204.6.Q85   2009
  158.1—dc22   2009008896

First Edition
14   13   12   11   10   09   10   9   8   7   6   5   4   3   2   1

To Jane Dutton and Kim Cameron,
two pioneers in the scholarship of the positive
who have lifted us to higher and more meaningful levels of life

contents

A Positive Force in Any Situation

On August 18, 1941, Officer John Gillespie Magee, Jr. of the Royal Canadian Air Force took a new airplane, the Spitfire Mk I, on a test flight.[1] Magee had received his wings as a pilot only two months earlier. As he flew the Spitfire up to new heights of 33,000 feet, he felt inspired to write a poem that has now become the official poem of both the Royal Canadian Air Force and the British Royal Air Force. Short films have been created with this poem as a basis. In its entirety or in part, the poem can be found in songs, on headstones, in presidential addresses, in museums, and in eulogies. Some have even used it as a prayer.

High Flight[2]

Oh, I have slipped the surly bonds of earth
    And danced the skies on laughter-silvered wings;
Sunward I've climbed, and joined the tumbling mirth
    Of sun split clouds—and done a hundred things

You have not done—wheeled and soared and swung
    High in the sunlit silence. Hov'ring there,
I've chased the shouting wind along, and flung
    My eager craft through footless halls of air.
Up, up the long, delirious blue
    I've topped the windswept heights with easy grace
Where never lark, or even eagle flew.
    And, while with silent, lifting mind I've trod
The high, untrespassed sanctity of space,
    Put out my hand, and touched the face of God.

It is hard to read this poem without feeling at least a bit of the exhilaration that Magee must have felt. These momentary thoughts and feelings inspired words that continue to move others generations after his death. Magee's experience and the poem it generated have "slipped the surly bonds of earth" and "done a hundred things" because Magee "trod the high, untrespassed sanctity of space" with a "lifting mind." If Magee's experience could generate this kind of impact, what impact might we have on those around us if we were also to slip the surly bonds of earth with a lifting mind?

This is a book about how we lift others by lifting our own hearts and minds. When we do this, we become a positive force, whatever our situation may be. Like Orville and Wilbur Wright, who used physical science and practical experience to build the first airplane, making it possible for Magee to rise above the bonds of earth, we can also use social science and practical experience to rise above the constraints of everyday life and lift the people around us.

The metaphor of heavier-than-air flight frames our discussion of how people can become a positive force in any situation. There are many parallels between how airplanes harness the force that makes flight possible and how we can harness the force that makes us a positive influence. The force that pushes a solid body upward through the air is called "lift." We can understand and harness a similar force, which we also call *lift*, in our social lives.[3] In other words, like people who use the aerodynamic force of lift to move upward in space, we can also use the social–psychological force of *lift* to move ourselves and others up to greater heights of achievement, integrity, learning, and love, becoming a positive force in any situation.

In this book we use the word "lift" in two ways. First, lift is influence, an uplifting effect we have on others. Second, *lift* is a psychological state, a temporary pattern of thoughts and feelings in which we are (1) purpose-centered (we have a purpose that is not weighed down by needless expectations); (2) internally-directed (we have a story of how our personal values will guide our actions); (3) other-focused (we feel empathy for the feelings and needs of others); and (4) externally-open (we believe that we can improve at whatever it is we are trying to do). When we experience these thoughts and feelings, we feel uplifted and lift the people around us.

We need to experience *lift* in order to lift others, but the pressures of daily living often drag us out of lift and into more normal states. Normal states are states in which we (1) seek comfort; (2) react automatically to the world around us; (3) focus on our own needs and feelings; and (4) believe that there is little we can do to improve. When this happens, our influence on others is nowhere near as positive as it is when we experience *lift*. Sometimes it is quite negative. And sometimes it can be hard for us to experience *lift* again.

Our purpose is to present four questions that we can use to help ourselves experience *lift* and become a positive force in any situation, and also to use scientific research to explain why asking and answering these questions lifts us and the people around us. The questions are

1. What result do I want to create?

2. What would my story be if I were living the values I expect of others?

3. How do others feel about this situation?

4. What are three (or four or five) strategies I could use to accomplish my purpose for this situation?

These questions are simple, but their power is in their very simplicity. We considered each word carefully, comparing it against scientific research. For example, the question "How do others feel about this situation?" may seem to be simply reminding us to consider the perspectives of others. As we discuss in chapter 8, however, simply considering others' perspectives is often not enough to help us experience empathy for them. It is important to focus on how other people *feel*, not just on their point of view. And research suggests that including words like "others" and leaving out words like "how would I feel" are also important for different reasons.

Scientific research, then, gives us insight into why *lift* is important, what the characteristics of *lift* are, how our psychological states influence others, and how to formulate questions that capture the nuances required to move ourselves from a normal state into *lift*. Asking and answering these questions is not the only way to experience *lift*. In fact, when we teach people about *lift*, almost everyone can remember times when they have experienced it. Those experiences have usually been unexpected, though. Another advantage of using science to develop these questions, then, is that these questions give us a way to experience *lift* intentionally, in any situation. We ourselves have used them in many situations.

We introduce the science behind *lift* in chapter 2 and continue throughout the remainder of the book. The book is rich in scientific detail, but we do not describe all of the science that is relevant (there is too much to share), and we try to make the science that we do share as practical and engaging as possible. Therefore, in addition to using science to explain how we can experience *lift* and why *lift* has a positive influence on the people around us, we also illustrate how *lift* works by sharing stories from our own lives and from the lives of people we know.[4] We take you into corporate offices where executives make decisions that affect thousands of lives and into living rooms where people make decisions that affect their children. We take you into community organizations where people work to help others and into the library where we study alone. We take you onto the basketball court and into neighborhoods, on television shows and into the classroom, into the marketplace and on the front lawn. We take you to all of these places for two reasons. One reason is to illustrate how these questions can be used in *any* situation: we designed these questions to be broad in scope. The other reason is to help this book reach a wide audience. We want it to be interesting and useful to managers leading their people, parents rearing their children, philanthropists helping their beneficiaries, professionals serving their clients, and anyone who cares about influence.

Whether you are a manager, a parent, a philanthropist, a professional, or anything else, our goal has been to make this book as useful, interesting, and accessible to you as possible. One other thing we have done to make it as useful as possible has been to write personal application pages at the end of chapters 1, 4, 6, 8, and 10. Each of these pages contains a list of practical ideas to help you in asking and answering the four questions.

If, as you try to apply these concepts, you discover additional practices that help in applying the concepts, we would love to receive your input. Please share your experiences with us, and any insights you come up with, at http://www.leadingwithlift.com/stories. Insights like these could then continue lifting others.

chapter 1

Lift: A Positive Influence and a Psychological State

A Different Kind of Power

Ron, a colleague of ours, became a bit of a legend in his company after only a few months of working there. Like many of the executives in Ron's company, Ron got projects done well and on time. Unlike many of these executives, Ron had an unusal effect on the people he worked with. People loved working together when Ron was involved, even if they began their projects disagreeing with each other. Some executives managed to push their projects through in spite of problems and disagreements. Some executives managed to work well with people but did not accomplish quite as much. Ron, however, managed to move people harmoniously toward exceptional results. He became one of the most influential people in his company.

One day Ron walked out of a staffing meeting and said something that surprised his co-workers. The meeting had occurred at the end of a long week in a stuffy, windowless room. Ron, and everyone else in the group, felt grumpy. They discussed whether people from other units in the business should be moved into Ron's department. Ron did not want anyone else to be transferred in. He argued his point and he won. It seemed like a normal business meeting. When Ron walked out, though, he told his co-workers, "I have given my power away."

Ron's co-workers could not believe him. After all, not only was he one of the most influential people in the company, he also got what he wanted out of the staffing meeting. How could he have given his power away? Even Ron could not answer this question, but he knew something had changed in that meeting, and he knew his ability to influence other people had also changed as a result.

Influence is a topic that most people care about. Managers want their people to give their best effort to the strategic changes they are implementing, employees want their managers to listen to their side of the story, parents want their children to do well in school and make good choices, a woman wants her friend to stop dating a man that she thinks is bad for her, a baseball coach wants a player to change his batting stance, a doctor wants her patient to follow her advice, a man wants his neighbor to cut down a tree that is growing into his yard, and so on. Most of us can understand the desire to be more influential. When we struggle to get people to do what we want them to, we use rational arguments, appeals to duty, rewards, punishments, or any number of other tactics to try to persuade them.[1] If we succeed, we often feel satisfied.

Ron had succeeded in persuading others, but he did not feel satisfied. He struggled to explain what he was feeling. He knew that there was something more constructive, more effective, than simply getting other people to do what you want. The tactics he had used in the staffing meeting may have gotten him what he wanted, but Ron began to see that he had also created "collateral damage"—people felt hurt and relationships had suffered. He had left people feeling weighed down rather than lifted up. The problems that led to the staffing meeting in the first place might reemerge, or he may have even created new problems. Ron realized that although he had wielded influence in that meeting, the influence was not as positive as he wanted it to be—and he wanted to be a positive influence.

Influence is positive when it (1) invites people toward purposes that (2) meet the needs of the people involved (3) in ways that increasingly reflect their highest personal and social values and (4) adapt to changing circumstances over time. Our reasons for defining positive influence in this way will become clearer as we go along. For now, it is useful to note that even though Ron had trouble explaining what had changed, he could sense that his influence was not as positive as it had been before. The problem was not just his results. Something had also changed inside him. As he struggled to explain what had changed, all he could say was, "I was in a different place."

Psychological States

Ron learned later that the "place" he was in was a psychological state. A psychological state is the current, temporary condition of our mind—the pattern of thoughts and feelings we experience at a given point.

A person's psychological state can be simple or complex. A simple psychological state, for example, could be described by a single emotion, such as "happy" or "sad." A complex psychological state can include many thoughts and emotions at the same time. For example, if a teenager receives an invitation to take the last spot on the school soccer team as a result of a good friend having been kicked off the team, then that teenager's psychological state might involve a complex blend of happiness over the good news, a resolve to succeed, concern for the friend, fear of the challenge, and guilt for accepting.

Scientists study psychological states to understand what states people experience, what leads people to experience particular states, and how particular states influence other people. This last question is particularly important. As researchers come to understand the answers to that question, they are discovering that our psychological states can influence other people in surprising and sometimes even dramatic ways.

Bill, a colleague of ours, told us a personal story that is a good example of this. Bill and his mother had not been getting along, let alone enjoying each other's company, for a long time. In any situation, Bill knew what his mother would say, what his response would be, and how the argument would unfold. He did not like it, yet he could not stop himself.

Bill went to a retreat and ended up working with a counselor. The goal was to improve his relationship with his mother. After much effort, Bill began to feel more positively toward his mother. By the end of the retreat he was anxious to see her. He reports the following experience:

> I took a deep breath and walked into the kitchen. I saw her before she saw me. I thought about the sacrifices she made and how much I loved her. She turned and looked at me. She opened her mouth. My stomach tightened and I thought, "Here it comes." She paused and smiled. Then she went on with what she was doing. I was stunned. That was not what she was supposed to do. I was different and now she was different. From then on the relationship totally changed. I never said a word, but I was different, and somehow she sensed it.[2]

Bill's relationship with his mother changed without Bill's saying a word because Bill was in a different psychological state. At the retreat, he had worked hard to consciously appreciate her positive characteristics and the sacrifices she had made over many years. This less angry and more loving orientation was probably communicated in his facial expression, his posture, and in other nonverbal ways. These nonverbal signals of love and appreciation provided Bill's mother with a new set of cues to interpret. When people receive unexpected cues from others—particularly unexpected emotional cues—they have to make sense of those cues in new ways.[3] Thus, without saying a word to his mother, Bill began to construct a new relationship. He changed the relationship by changing his psychological state.

Our psychological states influence others in at least four ways:

1.   Our facial expressions, body language, and tone of voice send new and unexpected cues that people interpret and react to in new and different ways.

2. The emotions that are part of our psychological states are contagious. In other words, people often unconsciously mimic, and then adopt, our feelings.[4]

3. Psychological states sometimes lead us to make different decisions or act in different ways than we would if we had been in a different psychological state, and other people are influenced by these decisions and actions.[5]

4. When we take different actions and perform them in different ways, we also generate different results—results that may be more effective, more creative, higher-quality, or more beneficial. People pay attention to and try to make sense of unusual or extraordinary results.[6]

Ron, for example, had experience with all of these forms of influence. When Ron felt positively, his co-workers had to make sense of his positive feelings—especially when Ron was able to look at things positively during difficult times. The energy he brought to his activities was contagious and lifted others. Because of how he felt toward others, he might listen carefully in situations where others would feel compelled to argue their points. And because he achieved exceptional results, people wanted to learn from him or be a part of his team.

Our psychological states influence other people, then, and their psychological states influence us. This means that we humans are not independent creatures. We are relational beings.[7] Who we are at any time depends on who the people around us are, and who they are depends on who we are. We weave our relationships in the stories we tell and act out with others. Our psychological states are the sum of who we are in a given moment as we play out the stories of our lives. The psychological state that Ron experienced in the staffing meeting affected how he experienced himself and acted as a manager, a co-worker, and a friend. It also affected how positively other people experienced themselves in similar roles. We are constantly influencing and being influenced by others, and the state we are in affects the quality of influence that flows between and among us.

Our purpose, however, is not just to point out that our psychological states influence others. It is to propose that there is a specific psychological state that, if we experience it, will make us a positive influence on those around us in any situation. We call this state *lift*.

Learning to Lift With Mason

Lift is a psychological state in which a person is purpose-centered, internally directed, other-focused, and externally open. To understand each of these characteristics, we share a story about Ryan and his son, Mason. This story illustrates both what *lift* is and what it is not. Ryan begins this story in a normal psychological state, but then changes and experiences *lift*.

> **RYAN:** Shortly before my son, Mason, turned six years old, he and I fell into an unhealthy pattern: Mason would do something wrong, like provoke his sister or refuse to clean up. I would tell him that I would put him in "time out" if he did not obey. He would scream something like "I hate you! I wish you weren't part of our family! Go away and never come back!" I would then try to calm Mason down and explain to him that he should clean up or leave his sister alone. I explained why "time out" was the consequence for his action. In response, however, Mason would just scream more and sometimes even hit me. Often, I would have to pick him up and take him to his bedroom kicking and screaming. I had no idea how to break this pattern.
>
> One reason Mason and I were unable to break out of this pattern was that I was treating Mason's behavior as a problem: I did not like Mason's tantrums and I wanted him to behave the way he had before. His old behaviors were comfortable for me, and I was *comfort-centered*. This desire to stay comfortable is a characteristic of a normal psychological state. In my desire for comfort, what had not occurred to me was the possibility that perhaps Mason was behaving differently because of the changes that had happened recently in his life, such as starting kindergarten. If his circumstances were different, that meant that

my circumstances were different as well. Trying to make people behave the same way in new circumstances is often not the most appropriate way to influence them.

Eventually, I decided to become more *purpose-centered* with Mason. This focus on purpose is one characteristic of *lift*. Instead of trying to make Mason behave as he had before, I asked myself what result I wanted to create regarding his choices and consequences. I decided that my purpose was to help Mason learn how to make responsible choices of his own volition. Once I made this decision, I was no longer interested in whether Mason was behaving in a way that I was comfortable with. Instead, I was wondering how I could help Mason learn to make responsible choices.

As I thought about this, I realized that Mason was already making many responsible choices. He often made responsible choices, for example, when he was clear about what the consequences of his choices were in advance. He was also better at making these choices when my wife, Amy, or I had spent quality time with him that day. On the basis of these insights, I changed the way I interacted with Mason. I tried to anticipate opportunities for Mason to make decisions—such as when bedtime was approaching or when it was time to clean up—and then I made a point of helping him understand, in advance, his options and the consequences of each option. Then I would let him make his own decisions. I also made an explicit effort to spend more quality time with Mason.

My efforts to help Mason understand his choices and consequences and to spend more time with him improved the situation somewhat. Mason appreciated the time I spent with him and in some cases made better choices. But, there were still times when I was not able to anticipate his decisions ahead of time, when he made poor choices even when he understood the consequences, or when I was not able to spend as much time with him as I would have liked. In situations like these, he threw tantrums when he had to do many of the things I asked him to do.

As I thought about the interactions in which Mason would throw tantrums, I noticed another pattern: many of Mason's tantrums occurred when my requests interrupted what he was doing. If he was building with his Legos or playing a game when I asked him to do something, I expected him to put those things aside and do it. Yet, if I was involved in an activity and Mason interrupted me, I would expect him to wait until I was done with my activity before I did what he asked. I expected him to show respect to me, but I was not doing the same for him. I failed to show him respect because I was *externally directed*. External direction is a characteristic of a normal psychological state. When people are externally directed, they let circumstances (such as the need to get Mason to clean up or to go to bed) drive their behavior instead of their values (such as respect for others' time and activities).

When I realized that I was being externally directed, I decided that I would become *internally directed*. Internal direction is a characteristic of *lift* in which people experience the dignity and integrity that comes with exercising the self-control necessary to live up to the values that they expect of others. In Mason's case, I became internally directed by showing him and his activities the same respect that I wanted from him. For example, when it came to interrupting his activities, I would ask him how much time he needed to finish what he was doing, and then ask him to do the chore that I wanted him to do after he was done. As I showed Mason this increased respect, his tantrums decreased significantly.

One day while I was making dinner for Mason and his sister, Katie, I offered to read Mason a book. Mason was excited and said yes. When I put the meal on the table, though, Mason started hoarding the food, leaving Katie without. Katie started to cry. I asked Mason why he was hoarding the food. I tried to help him understand his choices and the consequences that would result from each choice. Even so, he just screamed at me, saying that he would not be my friend anymore. I was shocked by the intensity of his reaction. I was planning to spend time with him. I was trying to help him see his choices and consequences. I was trying to show him respect. I did not know what to do. In spite of all of my efforts, Mason was screaming again. Bewildered and exasperated, I almost told Mason to stop immediately or I would put him in time out.

When I was about to threaten Mason with time out, I felt *self-focused* and *internally closed*. Focusing on ourselves and closing ourselves to feedback are characteristics of a normal psychological state. When we are self-focused, we are concerned only with our own needs, feelings, and wants. We see other people as objects that either help us or impede us in our goals. In my case, Mason was an object that was preventing me from my goal of showing that I was a good father.

When we are internally closed, we ignore and deny feedback, such as the feedback that I was getting from Mason that all my efforts to show that I was a good dad were not working. We ignore or deny feedback out of fear that the feedback says something about our worth as human beings. Because of this fear and the frustration I felt, my first instinct was to get angry.

In my anger, I was about to threaten Mason with a time out. Before I did, however, I remembered my purpose: to teach Mason how to make responsible choices. I also remembered that in my previous efforts with him, there were times when I thought I was doing the right thing and yet I was not showing him the respect I wanted him to show me. I had been at least somewhat wrong in those situations. Just as I was about to react, I caught myself and considered the possibility that I might be wrong here as well. As I opened myself to that possibility, I also opened myself up to what Mason was feeling, and to what his needs might be. I became *other-focused*.

A focus on others' needs and feelings is a characteristic of *lift*. When we are open to other people's feelings and needs, we empathize with them and feel impulses to be compassionate. When I became focused on Mason, I realized that Mason's screaming was rather extreme. He must be hurting, I felt, to have such an extreme reaction. Maybe his lashing out was the only way he knew to deal with some pain he felt inside. And if Mason was hurting inside, then I wanted to know why. I was no longer interested in proving I was a good father. Instead I wanted to understand why Mason might be hurting. And once I wanted to find out why Mason was feeling hurt, my desire to avoid feedback disappeared as well. Instead, I wanted feedback so that I could learn why Mason was feeling this way. Instead of being internally closed, I became *externally open*.

Openness to external cues—to feedback—is also a characteristic of *lift*. When we are open to these cues, we learn, grow, and adapt ourselves to the situation unfolding before us. In my experience with Mason, my focus on purpose, my commitment to act respectfully, my empathy, and my desire to learn from feedback created an entirely new situation. And because I was in a new situation, paying attention to new cues, the unconscious, automatic part of my brain began noticing new patterns in those cues and coming up with new responses faster than the controlled, conscious part of my brain. In other words, I began to have a feeling—an intuition—about what I should do.[8] My intuition was to read to Mason anyway.

My conscious reaction to this subconscious intuition was to think that reading to Mason was a crazy idea. Why would I want to reinforce his bad behavior? Somehow, though, it felt like the right thing to do, so I took a chance. I sat down and asked Mason if he would still like me to read to him.

My question to Mason was honest. It was not an attempt to bribe him into letting Katie have her share of the food. I could make more food for Katie or find another way to make her happy if I needed to. If Mason said yes and listened to the story without sharing the food, I would have found another solution for Katie. I was acting on how I genuinely felt at that moment.

When I offered to read the story to Mason, he melted. He got out a piece of paper and wrote, "I am sory. I am your frend. I want to be your frend." He handed me the paper. I told him that of course we were friends. Mason threw his arms around my neck and burst into tears. Then he let Katie have her share of the food. I read him the book while they ate their dinner.

I am not sure why Mason responded the way he did. I suspect that Mason, who was not even six years old at the time, could not have explained it himself. Perhaps he felt guilty because he knew what he was doing was wrong but he was scared to admit it.

Perhaps he wanted to feel he had control over his own life, and once he knew he had control he no longer felt a need to exert it. Perhaps he simply needed to feel loved. Perhaps it was all of the above.

On the basis of the scientific research that we will discuss throughout this book, I believe that Mason wanted to change because I connected with him on a fundamental level that took into account his deepest feelings and helped him work through those feelings in a purposeful, respectful way—even if neither of us could put those feelings into words. What I know for sure is that in a normal psychological state, my intuition was to punish Mason. When I experienced *lift*, however, my intuition was to read to him. And by acting on that intuition, I changed my relationship with my son. Offering to read to Mason was only a part of what inspired Mason to change. Offering to read a book, or to do any nice thing, may not inspire change in another situation. In fact, in another situation I might have had an intuition to punish Mason for his behavior. The intuition was less about what I did and more about who I was.

In the weeks and months following this event, Mason's tantrums disappeared almost completely. He still did things from time to time that I wished he would not do, but his behavior improved and so did mine. I still sometimes act in ways that are comfort-centered, externally driven, self-focused, or internally closed, but I am learning how to experience lift more often. As I do, Mason tends to be lifted by my efforts as well.

Lift, as illustrated in the story of Ryan's relationship with Mason, is the name of the psychological state in which a person is (1) centered on purpose, (2) directed by internal values, (3) focused on the feelings and needs of others, and (4) open to external cues that make learning, growth, and adaptation possible. We use the word "lift" to describe both this psychological state and the effect that this psychological state has on others. In other words, people who experience *lift* tend to lift others as well through their thoughts, feelings, actions, and results. When we experience lift, we become a positive force in the situations we encounter. We are unlikely to lift others without lifting ourselves, and we are unlikely to lift ourselves without lifting others.

We lift others in the situations where we experience *lift*, but situations change and people often change with their situations. New circumstances often pull us out of *lift* and into more normal psychological states, where we focus on problems rather than purpose, react to our circumstances rather than use our values to drive our behaviors, dwell on our own agendas rather than empathize with others, and avoid the feedback that could enable us to learn and grow. When we do, we weigh people down rather than lift people up. The circumstances of everyday life create strong pressures to pull us back into normal states, even after the most uplifting of experiences. Scientific research and practical experience, however, teach us what we can do to lift ourselves and others once again. Using this research as a base, we offer four questions that we can use to lift ourselves and others, becoming a positive force in any situation.

Four Questions

Ron struggled to explain his claim that he had given his power away, but he was unable to do so. He knew things intuitively that he could not explicitly explain. A few weeks after the meeting, though, Ron attended a training program for business executives titled "Leading the Positive Organization." In this program he learned about an area of research called positive organizational scholarship (POS). POS is research that examines the best of organizations and the best of human behavior in organizations.[9] It is similar to positive psychology, in which researchers seek to understand positive emotions, strengths, and virtues, and how human strengths can contribute to better communities.[10] The professors and participants discussed topics such as how to create a culture that helps organizations and their people thrive, tools for fostering high-quality emotions and relationships in the workplace, ways to energize the organization, and new ways to think about positive leadership. Ron learned about *lift* while attending this program.

The concept of *lift* had a particular impact on Ron because he recognized the psychological state from his own experience: *lift* was the "place" that he was no longer in and the "power" that he had given up. He also recognized that the reason he had experienced *lift* so much in his work before the staffing meeting was that a series of difficult life events had pushed him to rise to the occasion and be his best self. This realization worried him: what if he could experience *lift* only when critical circumstances called him to do so? What about the rest of his life and work? Given this concern, Ron felt particularly empowered when he learned that there were four questions, developed from scientific research, that could help him experience *lift* in any situation:

1. **What result do I want to create?** (When people answer this question they become less comfort-centered and more purpose-centered.)

2. **What would my story be if I were living the values I expect of others?** (When people answer this question they become less externally directed and more internally directed.)

3. **How do others feel about this situation?** (When people answer this question they become less self-focused and more other-focused.)

4. **What are three (or four or five) strategies I could use to accomplish my purpose for this situation?** (When people answer this question they become less internally closed and more externally open.)

Our purpose in writing this book is to give you these questions. When people ask and answer these questions, they tend to move out of a normal psychological state and into a state where they lift themselves and others. There may be other questions people can ask, other methods people can use, or other circumstances people can encounter that will also help them experience *lift*. We know, however, from science, from our personal use of these questions, and from others' use of these questions that these questions are particularly powerful for creating *lift*.

When Ron learned that he could experience *lift* by asking and answering a simple set of questions, he began using them to make sure that he experienced *lift* as often as possible. For example, after learning about *lift*, Ron was supposed to attend a meeting in which he and his co-workers would have to make decisions about how employees would be paid. These decisions were more complicated than usual because Ron's company had just been acquired by another company. The two companies had different forms and procedures for paying people, but there were no directions about how to coordinate these forms and procedures. In fact, the forms and procedures were just one of many problems caused by the acquisition of Ron's company. There were no instructions for dealing with any of these problems, and Ron's boss—who was his company's contact with the other company—was afraid to ask for directions. Ron worried that all these problems would make the compensation meeting a frustrating waste of time.

Ron prepared himself for the meeting by asking himself the four questions. The agenda for the meeting was to decide how to pay employees, but this agenda was problem-focused, given the companies' conflicting procedures and lack of direction. When Ron asked himself the first question, he decided that the result he wanted to create was to come up with an approach for working with the new company regarding how to pay employees that people in both companies could stand behind and work on together.

Ron then asked himself the second question, determined not to react automatically and get frustrated with people while he was in the meeting. When he did, he realized that the value he expected his boss to live was candor: he wanted his boss to have a straight conversation with the people in the other company so that they could find out what they needed to know. As a result, he decided that he should speak to his boss with as much candor as he expected his boss to speak with when he met with people in the other company.

When Ron asked himself the third question, he stopped seeing his boss (and others in the meeting) as either tools to help him achieve his goals or as obstacles preventing him from achieving his goals. Instead, he empathized with the pressure that his boss probably felt in approaching the people in the company that had just acquired theirs. Because of this empathy, he wanted to support his boss as well as to be frank with him.

When Ron asked the fourth question, he stopped worrying about what feedback he might get for taking initiative in the meeting, or what feedback he and his co-workers might receive from the other company. Instead, Ron was open to using many different strategies for developing new approaches to paying employees, and was eager to learn what approach might be the best.

When Ron entered the meeting, his boss began to work through his agenda, suggesting that the group make the best decisions it could with the information it had. Ron asked if he could stop the meeting. He asked if the group could discuss what it needed to achieve that afternoon. He suggested that the group try to come up with an approach for paying employees that would work out well for both the companies and their employees in the long run. As the group discussed these suggestions, Ron's boss remembered new and relevant information that he had learned from the other company but forgotten to share. This helped the group adapt and specify more clearly what additional information they needed to move forward. Once they were clear about what they needed, Ron's boss agreed to ask the managers in the other company for more information. When he talked to the managers from the acquiring company, the conversation went well. They were impressed by the clarity and objectives that Ron's boss came to them with.

Before Ron's boss brought their questions to the managers in the other company, Ron and his colleagues had believed that the managers from the acquiring company displayed a demeaning attitude toward them. After Ron's boss talked to these managers, however, the feeling changed. Employees from the acquiring company began to invite people from Ron's company to help them in planning the integration of the two companies.

Ron was thrilled by this experience and others like it. He now uses these four questions on a regular basis. He is increasingly purpose-centered, internally directed, other-focused, and externally open, lifting himself, his co-workers, and his organization.

Anyone can do what Ron did. Social science and practical experiences help us understand how people can lift themselves and others, how people can experience this more often, why asking these four questions can change a person's psychological state, and how one person's psychological state influences other people. Our first step in learning the answers to these questions begins with a history of the science behind *lift*, an explanation of where the word "lift" comes from, and an explanation for why the four characteristics are all necessary for a person to lift themselves and others. This step of the journey occurs in chapter 2.

➤ Practices for Applying the Principles of Lift

The swirl of daily life sometimes makes it a struggle to pause and ask oneself the four questions or to remember what they are. Here are some suggestions:

1. **Identify critical activities and schedule a preparation time.** One of our colleagues decided that one type of activity in which he feels it is particularly important to be a positive influence are his meetings at work. He went through his calendar and scheduled ten minutes before every meeting to ask himself the four questions. We can use the same principle in any recurring activity. If you have trouble identifying activities in which extra preparation would be useful, the electronic assessment and development tool at the website: http://apps.leadingwithlift.com/assess/ can help you figure this out.

2. **Put a coin in your shoe.** Another way to remember to pause and ask the four questions is to create a spontaneous reminder. You could put a coin in your shoe and ask the four questions whenever you feel the penny move. You could also

wear a bracelet, a ring, or tie a string around your finger. If you own a personal digital assistant, you can also set up the assessment at http://apps.leadingwithlift.com/assess/ to send you reminders.

3. **Pay attention to tense emotions.** If we feel strong, tense emotions like anger or fear, and we are not facing any physical danger, then there is a good chance that our influence in that situation will not be positive. Strong, tense emotions are often a good signal for telling us when we should stop and ask the four questions.

4. **Give other people permission to call you out.** If it is hard to be a positive influence in particular types of situations, and there are people you trust who are often involved in those situations, tell them about your desire to be a more positive influence there. Give them permission to ask you to pause in such a situation if they think that you are not being a positive influence. This technique can help you be more accountable for the influence you have on others. It can help other people feel that it is okay to learn from mistakes because of the example you are setting.

5. **Print the four questions on an index card.** If you have trouble remembering the four questions, print them out on a card and carry them with you in a wallet or purse, or tape them onto your computer or refrigerator.

6. **Use a mnemonic.** We can also use mnemonics to remember the questions, such as

> **L** ist strategies: "What three (or four or five) strategies could I use to accomplish my purpose?"
>
> **I** ncrease integrity: "What would my story be if I were living the values I expect of others?"
>
> **F** eel empathy: "How do others feel about this situation?"
>
> **T** hink of results: "What result do I want to create?"

L egacy: "What result do I want to create?"

I f . . . : "What would my story be if I were living the values I expect of others?"

F eelings: "How do others feel about this situation?"

T actics: "What three (or four or five) strategies could I use to accomplish my purpose?"

chapter 2

The Science, History, and Metaphor of Lift

BOB: In my second year of college I became increasingly depressed. When I realized what was happening, I decided to find some direction in my life. I started by trying to determine my major. Despite months of agonizing, I made little progress.

One day I was walking across campus when a question struck me: "What is the most meaningful thing you have ever done?" I knew the answer instantly. During my life, I'd had a number of opportunities to help other people make significant and positive changes in their personal lives. These experiences were the most meaningful things I had done. A moment passed. Then something inside me said, "Major in change."

That was a great answer. The only problem was that there was no major in change. I wrestled with this problem and eventually approached my education differently. I became proactive. I read books that were not assigned, went to public lectures, and took classes from many fields that I thought would help me understand change. My formal major eventually became sociology, but I graduated with a body of knowledge about how to help people change. Then I went to graduate school and focused on this same question as it related to groups and organizations. I studied change, taught change, and helped people and organizations make change. As I did these things, I became interested in questions of human effectiveness. Why are some organizations, groups, and people more effective than others? Why are some people more effective in wielding positive influence than others?

Ryan developed similar interests. In our research, teaching, and professional practice we learned that one of the most central and overlooked principles for lifting others is that our psychological states have an enormous impact on the people around us. Through our research, practice, and teaching, we developed a framework for understanding the principles that govern the process by which people experience *lift* and become a positive influence. This research and application is analogous to the research and application that Orville and Wilbur Wright conducted to achieve heavier-than-air flight by harnessing the aerodynamic force of lift.

Four Principles for Harnessing Lift

Orville and Wilbur Wright began their quest to develop a manned, sustainable, heavier-than-air flying machine in 1896.[1] We share their story not only because their discovery process was similar to ours, but also because the principles they used to harness aerodynamic lift are analogous to the principles that can be used to harness the psychological state of lift. Their story is a useful metaphor, which we draw on both in this chapter and throughout the book.

The Wright brothers' quest to develop a heavier-than-air flying machine started while they were running a small chain of successful bicycle shops. During this time they heard that Otto Lilienthal, a German engineer who built and successfully flew manned gliders, had died while flying one of his gliders. Lilienthal's death was a shock to the world because Lilienthal—"the flying man"—had been studying aeronautics for more than two decades, had amassed extensive experimental data in his "lift tables," and had made two thousand brief flights in sixteen different glider designs. The Wright brothers wondered why a man as knowledgeable and experienced as Lilienthal had died. They were also restless to expand their work beyond their bicycle shops.

The Wright brothers' research into aeronautics began in earnest in 1899, when they requested all the information that the Smithsonian Institute could provide to them on flying and began devouring materials on the topic. They learned that to build a machine that could harness the power of lift, the machine would need all of the following:

1. Forward *motion*

2. *Air*

3. *Properly designed wings*

4. Flight controls—that is, a means of *adapting* to flight conditions

Scientists had discovered the first two principles centuries before the Wright brothers began working on the problem: if the particles of a fluid substance like air move over the top of an object at a faster rate than the particles moving under the bottom of the object, then the particles under the bottom of the object put pressure on the object, lifting it upward.

Lilienthal had worked extensively on the third principle, compiling data on how different wing designs would generate different degrees of lift. Lilienthal's problem, however, came from trying to adapt to the changes that occurred in the air. Airplanes need to achieve a degree of stability while in the air, but the circumstances in the air often change. Airplanes, then, must adapt to these changes. Lilienthal tried to solve this problem by literally moving his body around on the glider. Moving one's body around on the surface of a glider is an unreliable means of adapting, so this was where the Wright brothers began to focus their attention.

Many of the scientists and enthusiasts who were working on the problem of flight at the same time as the Wright brothers thought that flying machines would achieve stability by having stable designs. They believed this because they did not think that humans could adapt to changes in wind currents swiftly enough. The Wright brothers thought differently, though, because of their experience with bicycles. Bicycles are unstable and yet remain controllable. On the basis of this experience, the Wright brothers believed that a flying machine could also be unstable and yet controllable. To make such a machine, they needed to create controls that would allow a pilot to adapt to wind-current changes along three dimensions: raising one side of the aircraft while lowering the other, raising and lowering the nose of the aircraft, and turning the nose of the aircraft right or left. The problem was figuring out how to create these controls.

Four Lenses on Organizational Effectiveness

BOB: We can relate to how the Wright brothers felt. For example, when I finished graduate school and took my first job as an assistant professor, the hot topic in my field was organizational effectiveness. Organizational scientists realized that effectiveness was more than just one measure of performance, but they did not agree about which measures they should use or how organizations could become effective. Like the Wright brothers, who requested literature to read from the Smithsonian Institute, I had been devouring the research literature on organizational effectiveness. I could tell that something was missing from the research: the people who were studying effectiveness all seemed to be using different definitions of what effectiveness was. Also like the Wright brothers, I knew that we needed to reframe the problem. The Wright brothers realized that scientists were making a mistake by trying to create airplanes that were stable by design. I realized that people were making a mistake by trying to impose their own definitions onto organizational effectiveness.

The Wright brothers found the inspiration they needed to solve one of the problems for controlling an unstable aircraft when Wilbur was absent-mindedly twisting a rectangular, cardboard, inner-tube box. As he twisted it, he realized that the box retained its stiffness from side to side. If that was true with a cardboard box, then it would also be true with the wings of a biplane. If one set of wings met the oncoming air at a different angle than the wings on the other side, then each side of the wings would experience a different degree of lift, banking the aircraft to one side or the other and enabling the pilot to maintain balance and to turn the aircraft. The Wright brothers built a large model aircraft with this design and flew it like a kite in the summer of 1899. To their delight, the model responded to their controls immediately and exactly, suggesting that a full-size aircraft might do the same.

BOB: My colleague John Rohrbaugh and I had an insight that reframed the problem of organizational effectiveness in a way that was similar to the Wright Brothers' reframing of the problem of controlling an unstable airplane. In a conversation with John, I explained that everyone studying organizational effectiveness was using different definitions and measurements. John replied, "Instead of studying organizational effectiveness, why don't you study how people perceive organizational effectiveness?" This idea had never occurred to me. But like Wilbur twisting a cardboard inner-tube box and coming up with an idea that nobody else had thought of, this new question enabled John and me to come up with an entirely new perspective.

John and I got excited as we discussed this question. We realized that the effectiveness of an organization depends on who is judging that effectiveness. That meant that we should study the people who study organizations. This would help us see if there were any patterns in all of the different claims about what effectiveness was. If there were patterns, then we would be able to have a much more informed conversation about what makes an organization effective. To study how people perceived effectiveness, John and I[2] identified the criteria of effectiveness that we found in the research literature (such as "Profit," "Quality,"

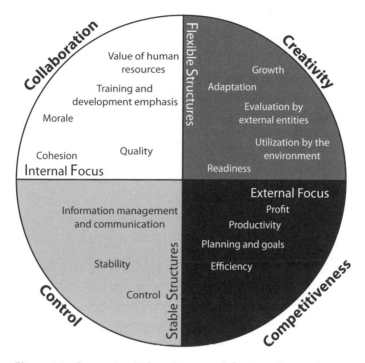

Figure 2.1. Competing-Values Framework for Organizational Effectiveness

or "Growth," as shown in Figure 2.1). We asked experts to rate how similar they thought each criterion was to each of the others. Analyzing these ratings, we found that all of the criteria could be mapped along two dimensions. One dimension (the vertical line in Figure 2.1, labeled "Flexible Structures" by the top half and "Stable Structures" by the bottom half) describes how flexible or stable the structure of an organization is. The second dimension (the horizontal line in Figure 2.1, labeled "Internal Focus" by the left half and "External Focus" by the right half), describes the degree to which an organization focuses on internal or external issues. When we lay these two dimensions on top of one another, they create four quadrants, or four broad lenses through which we can understand an organization's effectiveness: competitiveness, collaboration, control, and creativity.

1. **The Competitiveness lens** defines effectiveness in terms of how productive and competitive an organization is, using criteria such as profit, goals, and efficiency.

2. **The Collaboration lens** defines effectiveness in terms of how collaborative and developmental an organization is, using criteria such as morale, quality, and training.

3. **The Control lens** defines effectiveness in terms of how reliable and accountable an organization is, using criteria such as information use, stability, and control.

4. **The Creativity lens** defines effectiveness in terms of how adaptable and innovative an organization is, using criteria such as adaptation, growth, and utilization.

Using these four lenses, we can identify the underlying values in anyone's approach to organizational effectiveness and tell him or her how to approach the analysis in a more complete way. For example, we find that researchers who study topics related to effectiveness tend to use many criteria from one lens (such as the competitiveness quadrant), a few criteria from the two lenses next to the first lens in the model (such as the control and creativity quadrants), and no criteria (or almost none) from the opposite quadrant (such as the collaboration quadrant). In other words, most researchers are systematically biased in their beliefs about effectiveness. They exhibit favoritism for the values represented by one quadrant and prejudice against the values represented by the opposing quadrant, even though values in all four quadrants are positive.

We find that most people, without knowing anything about this framework, behave just like the researchers who have studied organizational effectiveness. They apply negative labels to values in the quadrants that are on the opposite side of the framework from the values they prefer. For example, people who favor competitive values tend to call collaborative values "soft" or "unproductive," whereas people who favor collaborative values tend to call competitive values "cutthroat" or "selfish." Because of this tendency, we call the framework created by these four lenses the "Competing-Values Framework" (CVF). Like the Wright brothers after trying their ideas out with their model glider, we had a new technology to help lift people and their organizations to higher levels of effectiveness.

Becoming Scientists

Heartened by successful trials with their model glider, the Wright brothers spent the year between the summer of 1899 and the summer of 1900 building a full-size glider designed for manned flight. They employed the research and experimentation of the people who preceded them but also introduced a number of their own innovations. In addition to designing wings that could "warp" (or twist like an inner-tube box), they also moved the high point of the arc in the wings toward the front edge of the wings and mounted an elevator (a movable horizontal surface) to the front of the glider to help counteract upward or downward pitching. They went to Kitty Hawk, North Carolina to test their full-size glider because of the strong, steady winds, wide open spaces, and sandy landing surfaces there. They first tested the glider a number of times as a kite, and then flew it as pilots a few times. By the time their stay in Kitty Hawk for the summer of 1900 was complete, the Wright brothers were pleased to learn that many of their designs, including the warping wings, the arc, and the elevator, worked well. The glider did not achieve as much lift as they had hoped it would, but it had flown for at least three hundred feet.

The amount of lift generated seemed to be the only problem with the aircraft the Wright brothers had designed. So, using tables that Otto Lilienthal had created for predicting how much lift a wing would generate, the Wright brothers increased the size and curvature of their wings. They had high hopes for their return to Kitty Hawk in 1901. The results, however, were disappointing. The new glider not only had problems with lift, it also had problems with its controls—both the elevator and the wing warping. The Wright brothers reduced the arc of the wings; this helped somewhat, but the glider still crashed and Wilbur was thrown into the glider's elevator mechanism, receiving a black eye and bruises. After that, baffled by these results, the brothers flew their glider only as a kite, and on the train ride home to Ohio, a dejected Wilbur said that he did not think that people would learn to fly in his lifetime—perhaps not even in a thousand years.

When the brothers arrived home in Dayton, Ohio, there was a letter waiting for them from Octave Chanute, a civil engineer, inviting them to Chicago to speak to the Western Society of Engineers. This was an intimidating request. The Wrights had done one thing that no one else had—compared actual flight data with Lilienthal's experimental data. However, their flight data did not match the experimental data, and they were not sure why. What would they say to a body of learned scientists?

Just before Wilbur left to give his speech to the Society, he and Orville built a wind tunnel out of a soap box and ran some preliminary experiments, which convinced them that Lilienthal's tables were wrong. Wilbur gave his talk, which was received well, and on returning to Dayton he and Orville made a fundamental change in their approach to harnessing lift: they transformed from practitioners—well-read enthusiasts who were trying to build a flying machine—into scientists, systematic empiricists who were trying to understand fundamental principles for harnessing lift. Throughout the winter of 1901 and 1902 they created a better wind tunnel, built as many as two hundred different model wing shapes to test, measured lift and drag more accurately, and ran experiments using these measurements. They created more accurate equations and tables and designed a new glider based on them. As a result, in the summer of 1902, their new glider responded well to its controls, flew more than seven hundred times and sometimes farther than six hundred feet, allowed them to land safely, and enabled them to develop the most advanced piloting skills in the world. By transforming from practitioners to scientists, they built a fully controllable aircraft.

Becoming a Practitioner

Like the Wright brothers with the glider from the summer of 1900, we were thrilled with the possibilities that the CVF presented. It turned out to be even more useful than we thought it would be. It improved our understanding of organizational effectiveness, but it also helped us clarify our understanding of leadership, organizational life cycles, organizational culture, presentations, innovation, value creation, and management skills.[3] We also discovered that other scholars with no knowledge of the CVF were developing frameworks that were very similar to it. For example, Paul Lawrence and Nitin Nohria later found that humans have four biologically determined drives (for bonding, learning, acquiring, and defending) that map perfectly onto the quadrants of the CVF.[4] Shalom Schwartz found that cultural values across societies can be mapped onto two dimensions that are nearly identical to the two dimensions of the CVF.[5] Katherine Benziger identified four thinking styles that are similar to the CVF quadrants and mapped them to activation in the four quadrants of the human brain.[6] In his review of the anthropological literature of cultures across the earth, Alan Fiske identified four models people use for relating to others that are similar to the quadrants of the CVF.[7] And philosopher Ken Wilbur's *A Theory of Everything* posits that the whole universe can be summarized in a four-quadrant framework that maps nicely into the CVF.[8] We are not so ambitious in our own claims, but we do believe that this converging evidence suggests that there is something fundamental about the CVF.

Social scientists have not been the only ones to get excited about the CVF. Others often come to us as well. They tell us their problems, tell us what they think the solution should be, and express frustration over the fact that their solution is not working. When this happens, we often draw a picture of the CVF and show them how the solutions they are proposing fall into only two or three of its quadrants. Then we suggest that they try a solution that incorporates values from one of the missing quadrants. More often than not, people understand their omission, see new solutions, and return to work feeling energized about the possibilities.

BOB: I was thrilled with the opportunities the CVF gave me to help people and organizations change their cultures, develop their leaders, and make strategic decisions. I also learned how to help people do this themselves. One of the things I learned was that in order to help people change, I often had to change myself as well. Similarly, I learned that if people wanted their organizations, communities, or families to change, they would also need to change themselves. I developed a number of insights into this phenomenon, and eventually decided that I should write a book about it. When I tried to write the book, though, I could not. Every time I sat down to write it, I failed.

At this point, I felt like the Wright brothers after the failure of their glider in the summer of 1901. In contrast to the Wright brothers, however, my personal transformation had to occur in the opposite direction. Rather than transform from a practitioner to a scientist, I had to transform from a scientist to a practitioner. As I struggled to write a book about the things I was learning, I realized that I was writing a book to help others change, but I was not changing myself. I was trying to write this book academically and scientifically, which was not likely to be interesting or accessible to the people that I was writing the book for. I was afraid to write the book in a way that would be interesting and accessible for practitioners because I was worried about what my academic colleagues would think of me. Eventually, I realized my problem, gathered the courage, and wrote the book in the way that I knew it should be written.

The result for me, as for the Wright brothers, was profound. I named the book *Deep Change*.[9] After it was published I began to be flooded with letters from people telling me how the book had changed their lives or requesting help with their lives and organizations. The lessons I had been learning since the day I decided to major in change were beginning to come together.

From a Controllable Glider to Powered Flight

Things began to come together for the Wright brothers as well, as they moved from developing a fully controllable glider to developing a powered aircraft. Between the summer of 1902 and December 1903, the Wright brothers calculated the power that an engine would need to propel their glider through the air and generate enough lift for flight. Along with adding an innovative new engine, they continued to improve the wings, designed and built propellers, and built a launching rail in Kitty Hawk for the now much heavier flying machine. Weather and technical problems provided a few setbacks, but on December 17, 1903 the Wrights made four flights in a fully controllable, heavier-than-air, self-propelled flying machine, including one flight of 852 feet for fifty-nine seconds. The Wright brothers had harnessed the power of lift.

From Deep Change to Lift

In the decade after Bob published *Deep Change*, he and his colleagues, like the Wright brothers, drew on the insights of others and a few innovations of their own to add power to the principles they were discovering. During this decade, Ryan began a graduate program and eventually became a professor of organizational behavior as well. Also during this decade, we both had the opportunity to participate in and interact with scientists in both the fields of positive psychology and positive organizational scholarship—fields that ask unabashedly positive questions about human beings and human societies. For example, in the field of positive psychology, scholars ask questions about topics such as learned optimism, authentic happiness, optimal experiences, human strengths, and positive emotions. These are unusual topics for a field that had historically focused on depression, disorders, dysfunctions, and decision errors. Similarly, in the field of positive organizational scholarship, scholars study topics such as high-reliability organizations, authentic leadership, psychological safety, high-quality connections, and organizational virtues. Both fields generate exciting insights into how we live and work.

Two concepts that come up regularly in both positive psychology and positive organizational scholarship are the topics of influence and psychological states. This literature often suggests that one person's psychological state can have a surprising influence on another person's psychological state. The psychological states that we read about (and which we described in chapter 1) reminded us of the quadrants of the CVF. We began to wonder if positive but competing psychological states could be captured by the CVF, and how these states might be integrated within people's experiences. We found that the CVF works very well for gathering and integrating these states, as shown in Figure 2.2. A purpose-centered state mapped well onto the competition quadrant because of its focus on results and achievement. An internally directed state mapped well onto the control quadrant because of its focus on the self-control required to live with integrity to one's values. An other-focused state mapped well onto the collaboration quadrant because of its focus on the feelings and needs of other people. And an externally open state mapped well onto the creativity quadrant of the CVF because of its focus on coming up with new approaches and learning from feedback. We began to share this frame-

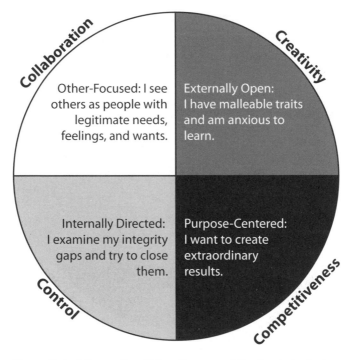

Figure 2.2. A Competing-Values Framework for Psychological States

work with others. It had a powerful impact, as the stories throughout this book illustrate.

Putting It All Together

The Wright brothers harnessed lift by creating a flying machine that could (1) propel itself forward (2) through the air (3) with properly designed wings (4) and control systems that allowed a pilot to adapt to changing conditions in the air. Our framework of psychological states helps people harness lift by showing them how to become (1) purpose-centered, (2) other-focused, (3) internally directed, and (4) externally open. Figure 2.3 shows how each of the aerodynamic principles for harnessing lift serve as a metaphor for the social–psychological principles for harnessing lift. For example, the requirement that an airplane

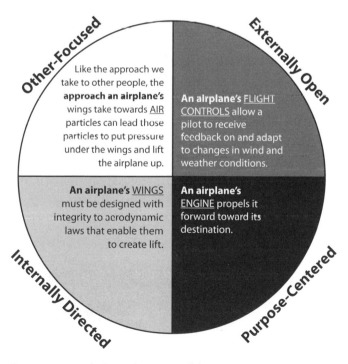

Figure 2.3. Psychological States and the Four Aerodynamic Conditions for Lift

be able to propel itself forward is a metaphor for being purpose-centered because purposes and goals motivate forward motion, or action. This forward motion must occur through air. The requirement that wings turn air particles correctly is a metaphor for being other-focused because the way a wing approaches air particles determines whether those air particles lift the wing, just as the way a person's approach, or empathy, toward other people influence how much they lift each other. The requirement for properly designed wings is a metaphor for being internally directed because internal direction is about acting with integrity to one's values, and wings that maximize lift are those in which the design has integrity to aerodynamic laws. Finally, the requirement for airplanes to have flight controls that enable them to adapt to changing air conditions is a metaphor for being externally open because it is openness to feedback that allows us to adapt to life's experiences.

Four Requirements for Positive Influence

When Otto Lilienthal tried to pilot a glider without effective flight controls, he lacked the ability to adjust to changing conditions, crashed, and died. When the Wright brothers used Lilienthal's incorrect tables to design the wings of their glider in the summer of 1901, Wilbur crashed and hurt himself. Without flight controls, properly designed wings, an engine, and air, an airplane is in danger of crashing. Similarly, when a person is not purpose-centered, internally directed, other-focused, and externally open, that person is in danger of exerting a negative rather than a positive influence.

Why are all four characteristics of *lift*—and these four characteristics in particular—necessary for a person to be a positive influence? To answer this question, imagine a real estate agent who is showing homes to a young family. If she is purpose-centered, internally directed, and other-focused but not externally open, then even though she wants to find the family a home, acts with honesty and integrity, and wants the family to be happy in their home, she will ignore or deny feedback as they go through the process, and will be less likely to learn the nuances of what the family wants. If she is not other-focused, she will not care about the family's needs and desires, getting them into the first house she can find that will make her a profit. If she is not internally directed, she will not try to live her professional values, perhaps investing less than her full effort into the project or cutting corners with the family, the sellers, the mortgage broker, or others. If she is not purpose-centered, her work will be less meaningful and focused, making the family's need for a home a problem to be solved rather than an opportunity to contribute to the lifestyle, security, and happiness of this family for years to come. Any of these omissions can diminish the positivity of her influence.

There are at least two reasons why these omissions will diminish the positivity of our real estate agent's—or anyone else's—influence. The first is that each of the four characteristics of *lift* embodies a particular type of moral responsibility. They are grounded in four of our most prominent moral philosophies. To keep this book accessible to most readers, we will not discuss these philosophies here other than to identify how each characteristic of lift is grounded in one of them. The purpose-centered characteristic, for example, is grounded in utilitarianism because of its focus on end results. The internally directed characteristic is grounded in virtue ethics because of its focus on living our values. The other-focused state is grounded in Kantian relational ethics because of its focus on seeing others' feelings and needs as valuable in and of themselves. And the externally open state is grounded in pragmatism because of its focus on learning from and adapting to particular situations.[10]

The second reason why omitting one of these characteristics from *lift* will diminish the positivity of a person's influence concerns the relationships between and among these characteristics (and the moral philosophies in which they are grounded). These relationships are at least as important (if not more important) than the characteristics themselves. The values that fall on opposite sides of the CVF are competing—or even opposing—values. In other words, in the CVF, the externally open characteristic is the opposite of the internally directed characteristic, and the results-centered characteristic is the opposite of the other-focused characteristic. But these are not opposites in the way we normally think of them.

Normally, we think of opposites in terms of "positive" and "negative." The CVF, in contrast, suggests that we can have two positive opposites. The negative opposite of humility, for example, may be arrogance, but the positive opposite of humility is confidence. Confidence is positive. But we need to keep our confidence in check with our humility, or our confidence will become arrogance. Similarly, we need to keep our own desires (the results we want to create when we are purpose-centered) in check by our concern for others (the empathy we feel when we are other-focused) or we will become self-focused, and we need to keep our focus on others in check with our purposes, or we will become comfort-centered—trying only to find comfortable solutions to problems that others define for us. The same is true for the relationship between the externally open and internally directed characteristics. It is by keeping all four of these characteristics in play that our real estate agent can be a positive influence in finding a home for her clients, and we can be a positive influence in the situations we encounter.

The CVF, and the four moral philosophies its quadrants represent, help us understand why we need four characteristics, and these four characteristics in particular, to lift ourselves and others. Like the engine, wings, air, and flight controls of an airplane, any characteristic that is left out puts us in danger of decreasing the positivity of our influence. To experience these four characteristics, however, we need to understand each individually. Thus, our next step is to examine what each characteristic consists of, why we do not experience them more often, and what effect these characteristics have on us and on the people around us when we do experience them. Social scientific research and practical experience help us answer these questions.

chapter 3

Seeking Comfort and Dwelling on Problems

BOB: I was once talking to a friend, Mindy, who was upset at the leader of a local community organization. This leader said that Mindy's son would be expelled from the organization because he had violated some of the organization's most important rules. Mindy raged on about what an unjust person this leader was. She listed things that she might do to take action against him. As I listened, it was clear that if she actually did the things she said she was going to do, she would make the situation worse. It was also clear that if I told her this, she would likely turn her anger toward me. I wondered if there was something I could say that would lift her out of this angry and vengeful state.

Mindy's reaction to her son's situation was a normal one. Good people sometimes react unproductively to negative situations. The fact that they do this relates to the first dimension of lift. Mindy was approaching the situation in a comfort-centered way, and comfort-centered approaches often lead to unproductive actions.

The alternative to a comfort-centered approach is a purpose-centered approach. Most of the time, most people are comfort-centered rather than purpose-centered. They are comfortable with a given situation. When problems disrupt—or threaten to disrupt—the situation, they try to solve those problems. Many of us spend our lives solving problems rather than finding purpose.

Problem solving itself has some productive elements. Problems tend to grab people's attention and motivate them to action. The actions that people feel motivated to take, however, may not be actions that are likely to lift either the person taking the action or anyone around that person. Mindy had a problem, for example, and that problem— like an engine on an airplane—was propelling her forward. The way in which that problem was propelling her forward, though, was unlikely to lift her, her son, or anyone else.

Building a Better Engine

The Wright brothers faced a situation that was analogous to that of our friend when the time came for them to build an engine that could propel their glider through the air. At that time, engines existed that could propel their glider forward, but none of these engines could propel the glider in a way that would harness lift. The biggest problem was that the engines that could generate enough power to propel the glider fast enough also weighed too much. The weight of these engines would push the airplanes down with greater force than the lift that these engines could help generate. To address this problem, the Wright brothers performed calculations for the power, speed, thrust, and weight of the engine they would need. They sent these numbers to the various companies that manufactured engines and asked them to build the engine they required. Ten companies responded, but none of them could make the engine—at least, not for a price that the Wright brothers could afford.

It may have been fortunate that engine companies could not produce the engine the Wright brothers needed. They were determined enough to build an airplane that they were willing to figure out how to do it themselves, using innovative ways. For example, to help meet the weight requirements, the Wright brothers developed an aluminum crankcase for their engine. It was the first time anyone had used aluminum to build an engine, and aluminum is still a standard material in airplane construction today. The Wright brothers also had the idea to create propellers as if they were rotating wings. This propeller design creates a horizontal force (or thrust), similar to the way that wings produce vertical force (or lift). The Wright brothers used a chain-and-sprocket mechanism—like the ones on their bicycles—to transfer the power from the engines to the propellers. With these and other innovations, the brothers built an engine that could propel their aircraft in a way that would generate lift.

There are many different ways to build engines, and some are better for helping airplanes achieve lift than others. If the Wright brothers had used an engine that the engine companies of their day were selling, they could not have generated sufficient lift (the aerodynamic force) to make their glider achieve flight. Similarly, there are many social and psychological "engines" that will propel a person forward, but not all of them are sufficient to generate lift. Like Mindy, who was upset about her son, people often have problems that focus their attention and propel them to action, but their forward motion does not lift them or others. In cases like these, the poor designs of our psychological "engines" tend to weigh us down rather than lift us up. In other words, the problems that move us forward are weighed down with inappropriate expectations.

Mindy's problem weighed her down with inappropriate expectations. She expected her son to continue participating productively in an organization from which he was going to be expelled. Her expectations were disrupted, she was angry with the discomfort this caused, and she invested enormous energy in trying to return things to the way they had been. When a new situation disrupts our previous expectations, though, it is often more productive to change our expectations than to try to make the world conform to our old expectations. If the expectations we have created or learned from past experience are not appropriate, either because we developed inappropriate ones to begin with or because the situation has changed, it is difficult, if not impossible, for us to harness lift without changing those expectations.

Inappropriate Expectations

To understand how inappropriate expectations weigh us down, imagine that you are an airline pilot, flying to Las Palmas in the Canary Islands. You expect to drop off your passengers, pick up new passengers, and return home. If all goes well, you should be able to complete this process without coming too close to the number of flight hours that you are limited to for the month. This is important because pilots who exceed the legal limits for flight hours in your country can be fined, lose their licenses, or even be imprisoned. As you approach Las Palmas, however, you find out that a bomb has exploded in the Las Palmas airport. You need to fly to the Los Rodeos airport in Tenerife instead to wait until the situation in Las Palmas is resolved. The extra time that these new orders add to your trip will put you dangerously close to exceeding the legal limits for your flight time this month. How would you feel?

Most people faced with a situation like this would feel anxious, stressed, or tense, and these feelings affect how you perform in both physical and mental activities. Physiologists like Timothy Noteboom and his colleagues, for example, have studied how sources of tension (like mild electric shocks) decrease the steadiness and precision with which people are able to grip a machine between their fingers and thumbs.[1] Psychologists like Mark Ashcraft and Elizabeth Kirk show that anxiety lowers people's performance on activities like math tests.[2] And neuroscientists like Bernet Elzinga and Karin Roelofs examine how increases in cortisol—a stress-related hormone—can decrease people's working memories when they engage in stressful activities like giving public, evaluated speeches with only five minutes of preparation.[3]

The ability to remain steady, be precise, and keep up one's working memory can have a significant impact on performance in many activities, such as piloting an airplane. A little bit of tension may improve performance because it activates people's nervous systems, focuses their attention, and motivates them to eliminate the tension they feel. As tension increases, though, these same biological processes can lead people to focus to the point where they lose perspective, decrease the efficiency of complex thinking, and take more habitual or more erratic action.[4]

Most of the negative effects that come with higher levels of tension can be seen in the actual story of KLM and Pan Am airplanes that were diverted from the Las Palmas airport. On March 27, 1977, these two airplanes were sent to Los Rodeos because of an explosion at Las Palmas. This explosion was not the only source of tension: the pilots on one airplane were in danger of exceeding their legal limits for flying hours, the airplanes were bigger than the Los Rodeos airport was equipped to handle, and a cloud floated onto the runway, reducing visibility. As a result, the pilots and the controllers made many mistakes that are typical when people experience higher levels of tension. Pilots focused too much on getting to Las Palmas. They struggled to process instructions, asking what they were supposed to do only a few seconds after they had received them. Controllers issued orders erratically, changing some and refusing to be questioned on others. One pilot—who had spent more time training other pilots over the past ten years than actually flying—acted habitually and authorized himself to take off rather than waiting for permission. When he did, the wheels of his airplane hit the right wing and rear cabin of the other airplane, the fuel in his own airplane ignited, and 567 of the 586 people on board the two airplanes died.

Karl Weick, an organizational scholar, used research on tension to analyze the events that occurred at the Los Rodeos airport.[5] He pointed out that people—like the pilots and controllers in Los Rodeos—usually feel tense when they expect events to turn out one way but those events turn out another way instead. Our nervous systems are designed to rally our effort and attention toward resolving disrupted expectations like these,[6] either by removing the disruption or by finding some other way to make events turn out the way we expected them to. The longer it takes to do this, the more tension we feel. In Los Rodeos, tragedy occurred largely because disrupted expectations increased tension, which lowered performance, which disrupted more expectations, and so on until it became harder and harder to restore effective coordination.

The experience of disrupted expectations, increased tension, and decreased performance is not limited to dramatic events like the tragedy in Tenerife. Mindy, our colleague, had this same experience regarding her son's expulsion. His pending expulsion disrupted her expectations and she was not able to remove the disruption. She felt anger and fear, two emotions that are high in tension. As a result, she had trouble focusing on anything else, thinking through the situation carefully, and acting constructively. In this new situation, her old expectations were like a poorly designed engine: they kept propelling her forward, but as they did so, they also weighed her, and everyone she interacted with, down.

Expectations and Problems

Disrupted expectations create a gap between the situations people expect and the situations with which they are faced. Gerald Smith, a decision scientist, points out that if we experience a gap like this, and if the gap matters to us and it is difficult to close it, then we are likely to label the gap as a problem.[7] Mindy thought of her situation as a problem, for example, because her son had been expelled from the organization in which she expected him to participate productively and happily. The pilots in Los Rodeos had a problem because they expected to fly to Las Palmas and back but were unable to do so. These gaps mattered, and they were hard to close.

Once we think of gaps like these as "problems," the "problem" label implies that the appropriate response to that gap is to solve it—to restore the situation to its expected state. Therefore, Mindy felt compelled to restore her son's membership in the community organization and the pilots felt compelled to complete the flight plan that had been disrupted.

Sometimes it is appropriate to label as a "problem" the gap that a disruption creates. This is true when it is possible, desirable, and ethical to try to restore a situation to its previous or expected state. Many situations, however, cannot or should not be returned to their previous or expected states. For example, when Mindy's son violated the organization's rules, he created a new situation. He had taken actions that had consequences, he was fully aware of those consequences, and all the other members of the organization were aware of the consequences. To restore him to his previous state would undermine both the rules and the consequences for him and for the other members. In Los Rodeos, completing the flight as quickly as possible was an unsafe expectation. Trying to solve these "problems" did more harm than good. It would have been more productive to question the validity of these expectations and to create new expectations, given the new situations that had emerged.

A Bias for Confirming Evidence

One reason why people try to restore their situations to match previous or expected situations, rather than update their understanding of the new and unfolding situation, can be seen in an experiment conducted by Mark Snyder and William Swann.[8] Snyder and Swann told the participants in their experiment that they would be interviewing another person to find out if the other person was an introvert or an extrovert. On the surface, this seems like a relatively easy task: introverts tend to be more distant and quiet, whereas extroverts tend to be outgoing and talkative. Introverts often get energized by a good book or a conversation with a single friend, whereas extroverts get energized by parties and large social gatherings. Traits like these, it would seem, should be relatively easy to discern when conversing with another person.

Snyder and Swann found, however, that the ease with which the participants in their experiment discerned a person's introversion or extroversion depended significantly on the instructions they were given. For example, rather than ask participants to "find out if that person is an introvert or an extrovert," Snyder and Swann told half of their participants that they needed to interview people to find out if they were introverts, and told the other half of their participants that they needed to interview people to find out if they were extroverts. They gave these participants no data to indicate whether the people they were going to interview were introverts or extroverts. Then they gave the participants a list of ten questions that largely made sense to ask only of people who are already known to be introverts, eleven questions that largely made sense to ask only of people who were already known to be extroverts, and five neutral questions.

Snyder and Swann asked the participants to select twelve questions from the list for their interview. On average, those who were told to find out if the person they were interviewing was extroverted selected a high number of questions designed for people that are known to be extroverted, and those who were trying to find out if the person they were interviewing was introverted selected a high number of questions designed for people that are known to be introverted. The differences in the numbers between groups was statistically significant, suggesting that people tend to look for evidence that confirms what they are looking for, rather than to look for evidence that disconfirms what they are looking for—even when there are no data to suggest that a person should look for confirming evidence.

Snyder and Swann followed this first experiment with other experiments. They had participants actually conduct the interviews rather than just pick the questions. They gave the participants data on how likely it was that the person they interviewed would be an introvert or extrovert, so that the participants would know to look for disconfirming evidence. They even offered to pay participants money for making more accurate assessments. Even so, in every case, the simple instruction to find out if a person was an introvert or an extrovert led participants to look for—and sometimes even create—evidence that confirmed the personality trait that had been mentioned in their instructions.

The tendency for people to look for evidence that confirms their expectations has been found in experiments of all kinds. For example, in one experiment, some participants were given an article to read that presented evidence for the deterring effect that capital punishment has on violent crime and an article to read that presented evidence suggesting that capital punishment does not deter violent crime. Although both articles were written with equal rigor, people hailed the article that supported their beliefs as a highly competent piece of work and were hypercritical of the article that refuted their beliefs, looking for minor flaws and enlarging them.[9]

In another experiment that occurred during the election between George W. Bush and John Kerry, scientists presented people with information about each candidate. As they read the information, the scientists monitored responses in the participants' brains using functional Magnetic Resonance Imaging (fMRI). They found that when participants were presented with information that disconfirmed their expectations, the reasoning areas of the brain were hardly activated at all. In other words, people put no mental effort into any evidence that disconfirmed their beliefs, dismissing it out of hand. In contrast, when people were presented with information that confirmed their expectations, the emotional areas of the brain were activated pleasantly. In other words, their brains rewarded them for finding confirming evidence.[10] The tendency for people to seek confirming evidence crosses all political boundaries and all domains of life.

The human tendency to seek confirming evidence is an efficient thing for our brains to have. If evidence confirms our expectations, we can continue acting the way we have been acting, and we will not have to invest the energy that is necessary for thinking consciously about what we should do differently. Our brains need to manage our actions with as little conscious thought as they can, or they would be overwhelmed with energy demands and information overload. Therefore, we create simple expectations for our experiences and act as if our expectations are correct, sometimes even when we receive overwhelming evidence that they are not. Our unconscious minds cling tightly to our expectations, searching for and even creating data that confirm those expectations and ignoring or discounting data that do not confirm them.

The tendency to seek data that confirm our expectations explains why Mindy did not realize that her anger and her intentions were unproductive. Her son's expulsion confronted her with two options. She could fight her son's expulsion, or she could change her expectations. The tendency to seek confirming evidence, however, suggests she was not likely to change her expectations. It is more comfortable to solve "problems" than it is to admit that we have inappropriate expectations. Because of this, Mindy said the organization's people and processes were unfair. She created arguments to back up her claims, and these arguments made it "obvious" to her that she should fight the leaders of the organization over her son's expulsion.

From Problem Solving to Purpose Finding

Mindy is normally a pleasant and peaceful person. She was caught in a trap that most of us get caught in. Her expectations had been disrupted and she labeled this disruption as a problem. By trying to solve the problem, she was about to create more problems. Her expectations, like the engines the Wright brothers had to choose from before they created their own, were weighing her down. Until she dropped the dead weight of her inappropriate expectations, she would not feel uplifted and would not lift others.

To drop the dead weight of her inappropriate expectations, Mindy needed to stop thinking about her situation as a problem. When people think of a situation as a problem, it implies that a person should solve the problem. Karl Weick points out, however, that if a situation can be labeled a problem, "then one could also say things like, that is an issue, manage it; that is a dilemma, reframe it; that is a paradox, accept it; that is a conflict, synthesize it; that is an opportunity, take it."[11] In other words, the labels we use determine how we see our situations, and how we see them affects how we respond to them. If Mindy was to change her expectations, she would need a different label—a different way to see her situation.

> **BOB:** As I listened to Mindy complain, I remembered a question that I read in Robert Fritz's book, *The Path of Least Resistance*.[12] Fritz argues that to move from a reactive state to a creative state, a person should ask the question "What result do I want to create?" This is a powerful question because it focuses us on results and creation, rather than on the interruptions that have disrupted our expectations. It changes our expectations, creating new purposes that are not inhibited by our existing expectations.
>
> With these ideas in mind, and after having listened for a long time, I asked Mindy, "What result do you want to create?"
>
> Mindy looked at me for a moment. Baffled by my question, she said she wanted justice and began complaining again. I listened for a few more minutes. Then I asked again, "What result do you want to create?" I got the same response. After waiting a few more minutes, I asked the question a third time. Finally, she stopped and asked, "What do you mean by that?"
>
> Mindy, like so many others we have worked with, was unable to process this seemingly simple question. People usually think that they are purpose-centered when in fact they have no idea what their purpose is. I tried to help. I said, "If you could have all of your hopes and dreams for your son come true, what result would you want to create for him?"
>
> Mindy looked at me in silence for a time. Then she slowly described how she wanted him to have a happy life, to be a responsible and productive citizen, to serve others, and so on.
>
> I asked how the actions that she was threatening to take would bring about the result she desired to create. She paused for a long time. She began to speak more softly. She said, "He has made some bad decisions; he needs to recognize that and pay the consequences."
>
> As she said this, her disposition seemed to change. The anger dissolved. She seemed more peaceful and more determined. She

had new expectations. She said she was going to go home and have a conversation with her son. As she turned and walked away, I was struck by the dramatic change. In her traumatic situation, she had stopped trying to solve the problem and instead clarified what result she wanted to create. As soon as she did, the most appropriate strategy became obvious. By asking and answering this basic question, she lifted herself into a new and more positive state and she was now more likely to lift others.

chapter 4

Becoming
Purpose-Centered

BOB: A few years ago some of my colleagues and I were appointed
to serve on a committee that was assigned to design the new
Executive Masters of Business Administration (EMBA) program for
our business school. The marketplace for EMBA programs was
already competitive, and we needed to design this program with
a high degree of excellence. In other words, this assignment
presented an opportunity to lift both ourselves and the school
by being very clear about the result we wanted to create.

I was not able to attend the first meeting of the committee.
When I arrived at the second meeting, my colleagues briefed me
on what had happened in the first meeting. They showed me their
design and asked, "What do you think?"

I said, "Would you mind closing your eyes?"

This was not a standard procedure. After some resistance, my
colleagues closed their eyes.

I asked them to envision the first graduating class. I said, "After the first graduate collects a diploma and walks off the stage, this graduate comes to you, hugs you, and says, 'Thank you, this was the most powerful educational experience of my life!'"

I told them to imagine the next person doing the same thing. So do the third and fourth. Then I told my colleagues to open their eyes. I then asked them how the program they had begun designing would generate the results they had just imagined. There was an uncomfortable silence. One of them changed the subject and the discussion moved on. I was being ignored.

The approach that Bob used to challenge his colleagues was unusual. He could have just suggested that they be more purposeful in their design. Bob had two reasons for asking them to visualize the first graduating class, though. First, he knew that his colleagues had worked hard on their design. Rethinking the purpose of the program might have required them to start designing the program again from scratch. They would be reluctant to do that. Second, he knew that people often think they are pursuing outstanding results when they are just reproducing things they are familiar with. It is not just faculty members in a university who act this way: most people choose comfort over purpose more than they realize. They design to meet expected constraints instead of to create a vision. Telling his colleagues this, however, would probably have made them defensive rather than inspired them to change their design.

A visual image can sometimes inspire people to try something new. When Bob asked his colleagues to visualize the first graduating class, however, his colleagues ignored him. The image he provided them did not confirm the quality of their program design. It suggested that they were more interested in comfort than in excellence. Like the participants in the experiments on the confirming evidence bias, they dismissed the evidence because it did not confirm their expectations.

Bob's colleagues did not ignore him because they disagreed with the vision he painted for them. His colleagues are good, competent people. Their design was a good, logical design. The design was, however, based on uncritical expectations about what an EMBA program should be.

When the dean had asked them to design an EMBA program, he created a gap between their current situation (no EMBA program) and their expectations (an EMBA program). Designing the program became a problem to be solved, not an opportunity for purpose-centered action. It was an important problem, but a problem nonetheless. They did not ask themselves what result they wanted to create; they just designed a solution for the problem as it was given to them.

Our work and lives are filled with presumed constraints that prevent us from setting and pursuing goals that we would be excited about achieving, whether we are designing a program, deciding how to enter a new market, cleaning our house, performing surgeries, or any other activity. The sociologist Harold Garfinkel used to teach this principle to his students by giving them homework assignments designed to test their assumptions about how the world works.[1] For example, he once sent his students to a grocery store and told them to try to negotiate the prices of the products. People in the United States almost never try to negotiate the prices of products in grocery stores; they expect grocery store prices to be fixed and nonnegotiable. To the surprise of Garfinkel's students, however, they found that in most cases they were able to negotiate lower prices for the products they wanted to buy than the prices that were displayed on the products. Garfinkel was well known for "natural experiments" like these, and one idea we learn from his work is that many of our expectations are often constraints that weigh us down rather than lift us up.

The expectations that Garfinkel's students had about grocery stores prices were similar to Bob's colleagues' expectations about designing an EMBA program. Before we can understand how his colleagues were influenced to question their expectations and consider a loftier purpose, though, it is useful to understand what a purpose-centered state is, and what it consists of.

The Impossible Lawn

Richard Thurman tells a wonderful story that illustrates the experience of a purpose centered state.[2] During Thurman's youth in the early 1900s, a rich woman moved into his small town. Many of the townspeople called her "The Countess." She asked Thurman to mow her lawn. On his first day, she made him mow the lawn three times before she said that he was finished. She paid him two dollars and told him that if he did the job with the same quality the next time, she would pay him three dollars. He could earn up to five dollars, and he would evaluate his own work. She told him that a job that was so good he would "have to be something of a fool to spend that much time on a lawn" was worth four dollars. A five-dollar lawn was so good it was "impossible."

Thurman resolved to earn four dollars, and tried to do so for a number of weeks. He eventually completed $3.50 jobs, but never reached the four-dollar mark. Thurman began to lie in bed each week, dreaming of completing a four-dollar job, when "one Thursday night [as] I was trying to forget that day's defeat and get some sleep . . . the truth hit me so hard I sat upright, half choking in my excitement. It was the five-dollar job I had to do, not the four-dollar one! I had to do the job that no one could do because it was impossible" (p. 109).

When Thurman realized that he "had" to do the five-dollar job, he became purpose-centered. He was not in a purpose-centered state when he was pursuing the four-dollar job, even though he had a goal to do a four-dollar job. This is a subtle but important distinction. Like the students who thought that prices in a grocery store could not be negotiated and like professors who thought that EMBA programs all looked pretty much the same, Thurman accepted the Countess's claim that a five-dollar lawn was impossible and focused on solving the problem of a four-dollar lawn. A purpose-centered state involves more than having a goal. When people are purpose-centered, they envision and pursue extraordinary results that are not constrained by previous expectations or by the expectations they receive from others. The results they pursue are energizing because they are self-chosen, challenging, and constructive. They also provide a clear definition of the situation, focusing people's attention. These are the key components of a purpose-centered psychological state. They are illustrated well by Thurman's experience.

Energizing Goals

When Thurman realized that he could mow a five-dollar lawn, he chose his own purpose rather than accept the four-dollar goal that the Countess implied was the best he could do. Before setting a goal to mow a five-dollar lawn, Thurman mowed the lawn the way the Countess had shown him. She had pressed him into service. He was being paid for his work, and the Countess had even told him he might be fired when his first few jobs met only a two-dollar standard. Rewards (like money) and punishments (like the threat of being fired) are what psychologists call *extrinsic motivators*. They motivate us, but they are outside pressures, not end results that we want to create ourselves. Goals that we want to achieve ourselves are much more energizing.

Imagine, for example, that someone asks you to play a game. This game is designed to test the flexibility of your thinking. You have a deck of cards with pictures of different shapes, numbers, and colors. An instructor asks you to sort the cards into piles that are based on particular combinations of numbers, shapes, and colors. The instructor also changes the combinations from time to time to see how quickly you can adjust. After each card, the instructor tells you if you placed it in the right pile. The challenge of this game, then, is to try to understand, recognize, and keep up with the patterns. A game like this could be a fun diversion for a few minutes.

Contrast this game with another scenario. In this case, imagine that you are playing the same game, but this time the instructor does not tell you to sort each card into particular combinations, but instead tells you that the cards need to be placed in a certain order. The instructor gives you explicit instructions for where to place each card, and then tells you if you did it right or wrong. This game, in contrast to the previous one, is not a test of your mental flexibility, but a test of your ability to follow detailed instructions.

The interesting thing about these two games is that they are designed so that the correct sequence for card placement is exactly the same in both games (for example, square, 10, blue, red, green, 9, 4, circle). The difference between the games, then, is that in the first game you get to try to figure out the sequence for yourself, and in the second game someone tells you how to do it. Which version of the game would you find more energizing?

These two games were performed in an experiment by Glen Nix, Richard Ryan, John Manly, and Edward Deci.[3] As you might expect, the energy that people felt in the first game remained high from the beginning to the end of the game, whereas the energy that people felt in the second game dropped precipitously by the end of the game. These psychologists conducted similar experiments involving word-finding puzzles and selecting classes. In each case, energy was highest when people were able to choose for themselves what they wanted to do.

Stephen Marks, a sociologist, also observed that people get energized by freely chosen purposes.[4] The energy we feel toward an activity, he said, affects how much physical energy we expend in that activity. Marks points out that, at least in developed societies where people have adequate food to eat, the physical energy we have in our bodies is plentiful for all of the activities we engage in on any normal day. The reason we sometimes do not feel energy for activities is usually not attributable to a lack of physical energy. It is because of a lack of subjective energy: we are simply not interested. When we are intrinsically interested in an activity, we not only have energy for it, but we easily translate the energy we feel into physical effort.

The energy we feel toward the activities we participate in is influenced by how positive and challenging our goals are as well as by how freely chosen they are. A positive goal is one in which a person strives to achieve outcomes such as "maintain a healthy lifestyle," "increase sales by 5 percent this quarter," or "mow a five-dollar lawn." Negative goals involve striving to avoid outcomes, such as "keep from getting fat," "avoid losing market share," or "keep the Countess from firing me." Research suggests that people experience more positive emotions when they remember experiences with positive goals than experiences with negative goals.[5] If other influences are not present to dampen one's energy, it is plausible that people will feel more energized pursuing positive goals than negative ones.

A challenging goal is one that people believe will stretch their resources and their abilities to the limit in order to accomplish it. If, for example, you were challenged to count out loud and backward from 1,528 by thirteens, you may consider this to be a challenge or you may consider it to be a threat. Joe Tomaka and his colleagues asked people to participate in activities like these.[6] The heart rate, strength of heart beats, blood vessel activity, and other physiological measures of participants who saw this activity as a challenge indicated that they were mobilizing increased energy to complete the task. When Tomaka and his colleagues compared participants who saw this activity as a challenge with those who saw it as a threat, they found that those who saw it as a challenge felt less stress and performed better than those who saw it as a threat.

Studies like these explain why Thurman "sat upright, half-choking in [his] excitement" when he decided to mow a five-dollar lawn. A five-dollar lawn was a self-chosen, positive, challenging goal. Self-chosen goals increase our energy because of our intrinsic interest. Challenge increases our energy because we need energy to generate the required effort. And positivity increases our energy because we are attracted to the desired result.

Focus and Direction

The question "What result do I want to create?" energizes people because it leads them to pursue results that are self-determined ("What do *I* want . . .") and that challenges them in positive ways (". . . to *create*?"). Creating implies doing something positive, difficult, and new rather than relying on existing expectations about what can and cannot be done. Energy alone, however, is not sufficient. People need to know how and where to exert that energy, which is why this question also focuses us on creating *results*. Self-chosen, challenging, positive goals give people results to focus on as well as energy for pursuing those results.

> **RYAN:** When I was in graduate school, I learned about goal-setting theory. The simplest version of goal-setting theory states that

people perform better when they have goals that are difficult and specific.[7] Many, if not most, of the students who earn Master of Business Administration (MBA) degrees learn this theory. Therefore I was surprised when I worked in a company run by a man with an MBA and discovered how few of our activities were directed by clear goals. For example, we seldom had any idea what the goals for our meetings were. As a result, we would spend these meetings reacting to problems rather than trying to create results we desired. Our conversations would wander. Our time could have been spent much more productively.

Not long after working at this company, I conducted a study that examined the impact of goals on people's work experiences.[8] More than one hundred scientists, engineers, technicians, and managers from Sandia National Laboratories participated in this study. I gave each of them a survey booklet and a pager. For one week, at four random times each day, I paged these people. After receiving the signal from the pager, they would take out the survey booklet and fill out a survey about what they were doing when I paged them. I asked them to rate the clarity of their goals, their concentration, the degree to which they were enjoying their work, their awareness of and responsiveness to the activity, and so forth.

One of the things I learned from this study was that goals do more than give people a result to shoot for. Goals also help people define the situation they are facing. For example, one scientist's goal was to write new software that would enable a system to test the connections among its subsystems. This goal defined his situation by helping him see that he needed to learn algorithms for testing connections between subsystems, which books or papers would be useful to him in finding algorithms, and what to look for when perusing these books and papers. Without a clear goal to define his situation he would have been less able to identify which algorithms, books, information, and other items he should pay attention to, or how to use those tools and information. He could also use his goal to judge how much progress he was making. He could tell, for example, by reviewing a book's table of contents or index whether that particular book would bring him closer to or take him farther away from achieving his goal.

Research on goal-setting is consistent with these findings. Goals direct people's actions even to the level of the movements that people's eyes make when they have a goal to assess characters' personalities in a movie.[9] Goals, then, direct people's attention and focus it on extracting relevant information and responding to that information appropriately.[10]

The goal to mow a five-dollar lawn redefined Thurman's situation, redirected his attention, and focused him on new activities. Once he realized that he should mow a five-dollar lawn, the information he paid attention to and the actions he planned to take changed:

> I was well acquainted with the difficulties ahead. I had the
> problem, for example, of doing something about the worm
> mounds in the lawn. The Countess might not even have noticed
> them yet, they were so small; but in my bare feet I knew about
> them and I had to do something about them. And I could go
> on trimming the garden edges with shears, but I knew that a
> five-dollar lawn demanded that I line up each edge exactly with
> a yardstick and then trim it precisely with the edger. And there
> were other problems that only I and my bare feet knew about.
> (p. 109)

Worm mounds, yard sticks, and trimming with an edger were all aspects of the situation that were not relevant to Thurman when his goal was a four-dollar lawn. But with the goal of a five-dollar lawn, he suddenly had new directions in which he needed to invest his energy.

The next week, Thurman set out to mow a five-dollar lawn. He ironed out worm mounds. He mowed the lawn four times—twice horizontally and twice vertically. He used an edger and a yardstick to trim the edge precisely. He smoothed sod with his hands and cleared grass out of the walkway. He worked from early in the morning until the sun began going down. Then he knocked on the door and announced to the Countess that he had mowed a five-dollar lawn.

The Countess was surprised and wanted to see "the first five-dollar lawn in history." She walked around the lawn with him, admiring what he did. When she asked him what inspired him to do such an incredible thing, Thurman had no answer. The Countess guessed:

> "I think I know . . . how you felt when this idea first came to you of mowing a lawn that I told you was impossible. It made you very happy when it first came, then a little frightened. Am I right?"
>
> She could see she was right by the startled look on my face.
>
> "I know how you felt because the same thing happens to almost everybody. They feel this sudden burst in them of wanting to do some great thing. They feel a wonderful happiness, but then it passes because they have said, 'No, I can't do that. It's impossible.' Whenever something in you says, 'It's impossible,' remember to take a careful look. See if it isn't really God asking you to grow an inch, or a foot, or a mile that you may come to a fuller life." (p. 110)

Thurman then summarized what the moral of this story was for him:

> Since that time some 25 years ago when I have felt myself at an end with nothing before me, suddenly with the appearance of that word "impossible" I have experienced again the unexpected lift, the leap inside me, and known that the only possible way lay through the very middle of the impossible. (p. 110)

The Influence of a Purpose-Centered State

When we, like Richard Thurman, create new purposes that shed the inappropriate expectations of a comfort-centered state, we lift ourselves with new ideas, new direction, and new energy. And we cannot create a new purpose for ourselves without influencing others also, often lifting them as well as us. For example, Bob knew what kind of program he wanted to create when he went to the second design meeting for the EMBA program. As a result, he knew how he wanted to respond when his colleagues asked what he thought of their design. By asking them to envision a result that he knew they would claim they wanted to create, and then asking them how their first design would bring the desired outcome, Bob revealed that they were not, in fact, designing an extraordinary program. They were simply reproducing the existing MBA program with minor modifications. Bob's colleagues, like most people, did not like to receive disconfirming evidence, so they chose to ignore him.

> **BOB:** I could understand how my colleagues felt. I—like most people—like to think that I am purpose-centered when I am really just solving problems. I know how hard it can be to shed inappropriate expectations, so I chose to remain purpose-centered but patient. I mostly remained quiet, only occasionally asking questions. The questions were radical, but I asked them quietly and respectfully. For example, at one point my colleagues mentioned grades. I asked, "Why are we having grades?"
>
> One of my colleagues patiently explained what grades were and why we needed them. I nodded. Later, we talked about books. I asked why we were using books. I received a less patient response. One of my colleagues said, with some anger, "Because without books, we would overwhelm Document Processing."
>
> Document Processing is an administrative function that makes course packs full of readings and case studies. We use course packs when we do not use books. My colleague was telling me that if they did not use books, that administrative function would be overwhelmed.
>
> At that point, I finally made an input. I said, "So what you are telling me is that we are not designing this program for excellence, we are designing it for administrative convenience."
>
> Again I was ignored. But within a few minutes the meeting took an unexpected turn. No one articulated a new strategy. People just began to talk about the program in new ways, asking, "What if we tried this?" and "How would it work if we did that?" My colleagues began to question their own expectations. In a short

period a new design began to emerge on the white board. It was not driven by one person. At various points in the conversation a new person would chime in with insights that were exciting and perfectly timed. People worked together to create a program that they were beginning to believe in.

Influence Through Enactment

This process, in which (1) Bob acted in pursuit of a goal, (2) his colleagues saw his actions and had to make sense of them, and (3) his colleagues responded to and even participated to some extent in his goal, is an example of what Karl Weick calls *enactment*.[11] Enactment is a process of taking actions that create at least part of the situation in which we are acting.

Enactment does not have to be intentional and does not have to compete with other people's views of the world. For example, when an earthquake occurred in southern Italy in 1980, a social scientist named Giovan Lanzara observed that many people's actions created new realities that had not existed before.[12] One man set up a coffee stand on the piazza of a devastated village. On the day after the earthquake he started distributing free coffee to anyone who wanted it. People began to meet, rest, exchange information, and organize activities next to his stand. On the second day, two additional people joined the coffee stand, helping the first man and adding services such as providing milk for children.

The first man on the piazza simply set out to serve coffee to people who were in need. But whether he intended for them to do so or not, other people had to make sense of his actions. Some people made sense of his actions by using his services themselves or by using his stand as a location to organize and help others. Others made sense of his actions by helping him serve coffee or by introducing their own complementary innovations (like serving milk). Some may have even ignored the coffee stand. But no matter how people made sense of them, his purposeful actions influenced other people by requiring those people to make sense of his actions. And because the earthquake left people with limited options for understanding and responding, it was a natural response for people to accept and participate in the world that he was creating—at least until the third day after the earthquake. On the third day, the government agencies arrived, set up formal rescue and aid procedures, and the coffee stand disappeared.

People create new realities all the time, often unintentionally. We are likely to have a particularly significant influence on others when we are purpose-centered, however, because we usually act differently from how people in a comfort-centered state would act in the same situation. People are usually more likely to try to preserve the status quo or to remain inactive than to intentionally seek to create extraordinary realities.[13] Also, we take these unusual actions with more energy, focus, and persistence when we are purpose-centered because our purposes are self-chosen, challenging, positive, and specific. When one person acts in energized ways that persistently disrupt others' expectations, other people are likely to pay attention.

Imagine, for example, that Bob had taken a comfort-centered approach to designing the executive MBA program. If he had, he probably would have accepted his colleagues' first design, suggesting only minor changes. Similarly, if the coffee maker on the Italian piazza had been comfort-centered, he might have chosen to stay home and watch the response to the earthquake on his television. As a result, Bob's colleagues would not have shared their own innovative ideas and the other people in the devastated village would not have offered other services or have rested and planned at a central location. People do not put effort into making sense of others' actions unless the actions that others take are unexpected in some way.

The fact that people feel a need to make sense of another person's unusual actions is documented in research on minority influence. Imagine, for example, that you are sitting in a room with four other people. A sixth person, with a slide projector, is projecting blue slides onto a screen. After each slide the person with the slide projector asks each of the other five people in the room, including you, to tell her what color she is projecting. Three of the other people in the room say that the slide is blue. But one person says the slide is green. What would you say?

Ninety percent of the people who participate in experiments like these see a blue slide, hear three people say that the slide is blue, hear one person say that the slide is green, and then they say that the slide is blue. Ten percent of the participants, however, see a blue slide, hear three people say that the slide is blue, hear one person say that the slide is green, and then they say that the slide is green.[14] In other words, in ten percent of the experiments, the participants actually listen to and agree with the one person who says that the slide is green. If one person can convince others that a blue slide is green 10 percent of the time, what impact would individuals have if they said or did unusual things in situations that are more ambiguous than watching slides on a screen?

To answer this question, Linn Van Dyne and Richard Saavedra conducted a study in which groups were assigned to come up with creative and sophisticated answers to problems that could have many correct answers of varying quality.[15] In half of the groups, they assigned one group member to take a minority viewpoint on issues that the group discussed. After working on these problems for ten weeks, Van Dyne and Saavedra found that the groups that had a member who was assigned to take a minority viewpoint considered more options and ended up with more creative solutions (as rated by independent judges) than the groups that did not have a member assigned to take a minority viewpoint.

This is a common finding in research where people take unexpected actions: those who observe unexpected actions generally end up thinking more, more complexly, and sometimes even more creatively in their efforts to make sense of the actions. The people who take the unusual actions sometimes feel stress over being different, but if they are consistent in expressing their opinions, they not only help others think more complexly, but the people who observe them often come to respect and admire them as being courageous, even when the observers think that the people who do unusual things are wrong.[16] This is also what happened when Bob and his colleagues designed the new EMBA course. As Bob consistently asked them questions that challenged their expectations, their inputs became more thoughtful, more complex, and more creative. They began to enact a new reality.

Consistency is necessary for minority influence to occur. If individuals do unusual things randomly or sporadically rather than consistently, then other people are less likely to truly question their own expectations. Consistency is a characteristic that generally describes people who are purpose-centered.[17] The consistency of people in purpose-centered states is one of the things that make them influential.

The energy and focus of people in purpose-centered states also make them influential. In fact, when Jeffrey Pfeffer, one of the world's leading researchers on the topic of power, listed personal characteristics that have a tendency to make a person influential, the first two characteristics on his list were energy and focus.[18] One reason why energy and focus are so influential, he pointed out, is that when people see that a person is focused and energized, they think that the person's goal must be really important for that person to focus so intently on it and to invest so much energy into it. Thus, when people see an individual take unexpected, energized, focused, and persistent actions, they are likely to question some of their own expectations, think more complexly, adopt some of the ideas of the individual taking unexpected action, and perhaps even offer ideas that build on and contribute to that individual's actions.

Influence Through Contagion

RYAN: One of my colleagues is a woman named Erika James. Whenever I walk into Erika's office, she looks up with the brightest of smiles. Her smile always makes me feel welcome, happier, and more energized, even if I felt concerned, shy, or hesitant before coming to her office.

Erika's influence is an example of what Elaine Hatfield, John Cacioppo, and Richard Rapson call emotional contagion. Emotional contagion is a process in which people begin to feel the same way that the people around them feel. Contagion often happens without people realizing it is happening. We notice each other's facial expressions and other emotional cues, mimic those cues, and then feel the emotions that generally accompany those expressions. This happens to people all over the world.[19] Muscles in the face tend to move to particular positions involuntarily, or automatically, when people feel particular emotions.

Because of the commonality and clarity of facial expressions for conveying emotion, children learn early on to pay attention to facial expressions. In a "visual cliff" experiment, for example, researchers place an infant on a surface that is half solid and half clear Plexiglas.[20] An infant who crawls along the surface and comes to the Plexiglas experiences an ambiguous threat: the Plexiglas feels solid but looks like a cliff. When this happens, the infant's first, instinctive response is to look at her mother's face. If the mother's face is calm, most infants will crawl over the Plexiglas. If the infant detects fear, the infant is likely to shy away from the Plexiglas. Over a lifetime of scanning people's faces to learn about the world, people become very good—at least in normal circumstances—at reading what others are feeling by scanning their faces.

When we scan people's faces, we not only read their feelings, we also tend to mimic their expressions. We wince in pain when we see someone hurt, open our mouths with babies when feeding them, and yawn when we hear other people yawn. This mimicking is instinctive—it happens in milliseconds, without us realizing we are doing it. And when people mimic others' facial expressions they also tend to feel the emotions associated with those expressions. In other words, facial expressions not only express emotions; they also cause them.

Imagine, for example, that someone told you to hold a pen between your teeth without letting your lips touch the pen while you watched a cartoon. Fritz Strack and his colleagues gave these instructions to a number of people participating in an experiment.[21] When people hold pens between their teeth without letting their lips touch the pen, their mouths form a smile. By giving people these instructions, Strack and his colleagues got people to smile without telling them to smile. Then they had the participants in their experiment watch a cartoon. The participants who watched a cartoon with the pens in their teeth found the cartoons to be funnier than the people who watched the cartoon while holding a pen with their lips (a facial position that makes it nearly impossible to smile). This experiment, and others like it, show that our facial expressions have as much effect on our feelings as our feelings have on our facial expressions.

When one person exhibits a facial expression and a second person notices that expression, mimics it, and begins to feel the same way the first person feels, we call that process emotional contagion. This is what Ryan feels, for example, when he walks into Erika's office. People usually feel energized when they are purpose-centered, and their energy tends to be contagious, making other people feel energized as well.

Positive Emotions

As Bob and his colleagues considered the possibility of a more innovative EMBA program, they became energized about what they were doing. The energy that people feel in purpose-centered states influences the energy of the people around them. It also influences the number of thoughts and actions people have available to them, the types of thoughts and actions people have available to them, and the resources that people have to work with. Barbara Fredrickson, a psychologist from the University of North Carolina, has shown this impact in her research on positive emotions.

For example, Fredrickson and her colleague, Christine Branigan, conducted an experiment in which they showed film clips that evoked positive emotions to one group of participants, film clips that evoked negative emotions to a second group of participants, and neutral film clips to a third group of participants.[22] After the participants saw the clips, Fredrickson and Branigan asked them to write a list of all of the things they would like to do right now. Those who viewed clips evoking positive emotions listed more things they would like to do than those viewing the clips eliciting neutral or negative emotions, suggesting that those who felt positive emotions had more thought and action options than those who felt neutral or negative emotions.

Fredrickson and her colleagues have confirmed this finding in multiple studies, showing that people with positive emotions think more broadly about their social world. They include other people when they think of themselves (for example, using "we" to describe themselves instead of "me").[23] They even lose the pervasive and well-documented bias of favoring people from their own race (for example, white people become just as good at recognizing the faces of black people as they are at recognizing the faces of white people).[24] Positive emotions also appear to have a positive effect on how creatively people think.[25]

Bob and his colleagues broadened their thought and action options as they designed the EMBA program, and their ideas led to the creation of new and enduring resources. The effect of positive emotions on resource creation is another finding of Fredrickson's: people who have more options for thought and action are more likely to try more things, develop more skills, learn more principles, gather more information, and so forth. For example, Fredrickson and her colleagues offered a free wellness program to employees in a computer firm. As part of the program, employees practiced daily meditations in which they focused on feelings of love, tenderness, and kindness. Half of the employees were offered the program right away; the other half had to wait. All of the employees filled out surveys, though, examining the mental, psychological, social, and physical resources they had available to them before and after the first group participated in the program. Those who participated in the program experienced an increase in mindfulness, personal growth, relationship quality, social support, sleep quality, the ability to enjoy their present experience, and the initiative to act independently of others, and a decrease in symptoms of illness. Those who did not participate did not experience these changes.

Energy Networks

Positive emotions, then, broaden the thoughts and actions available to people and help them build resources they can use again and again. And because emotions are contagious, one energized person can help other people to think more broadly, act more creatively, and create more resources. With more options and more resources, people can accomplish more than they would otherwise, both through their own efforts and through mobilizing others.

People mobilize others through social networks. Wayne Baker, Rob Cross, and Melissa Wooten, for example, found that the degree to which one person is energizing to other people does more to explain that person's performance at work than factors such as the person's use of information.[26] Erika James, for example, usually energizes people in her social network and is a high performer in the school where she works. In designing the EMBA program, Bob and his colleagues became energized about creating something extraordinary and ended up creating a program that was recognized as a leader in its industry.

Influence Through Results

One of the reasons Bob's colleagues changed the way they approached the program design was the results they began to achieve as they tried out new ideas. People like Bob achieve better results when they have clear and challenging purposes.[27] On the EMBA design team, each time one person shared an idea and other people saw how the idea could work, those other people got excited about the idea. Excitement and agreement are types of positive feedback. It was a moment of success. Each idea that excited the group made the overall purpose seem more feasible. People like to be a part of successful endeavors—especially if their endeavors are creating something extraordinary. As more of Bob's colleagues embraced the purpose, the purpose became more attractive.

Jim Collins discovered a similar pattern in his research on how good companies transformed themselves into great companies.

Collins identified eleven companies in the second half of the twentieth century that had "fifteen-year cumulative stock returns at or below the general stock market, punctuated by a transition point, then cumulative returns at least three times the market over the next fifteen years"—an extraordinary change.[28] When he and his research assistants began the study, they thought that the companies that made these extraordinary changes would have to convince their employees to participate in and get excited about the change efforts. After all, these companies had to do things significantly differently from the way they were doing them in order to achieve these results. Instead, they found the opposite. Leaders in the good-to-great companies did not spend much time thinking about motivation. "Under the right conditions," Collins writes, "the problems of commitment, alignment, motivation, and change just melt away. They largely take care of themselves."[29]

How did these problems take care of themselves? Through little successes that added legitimacy to what the leaders in the company were doing. People in these companies could see these little successes accumulating. They wanted to be part of something that was creating tangible results and that had the potential to create *extraordinary* results. Karl Weick provided a deeper analysis of why the little successes, or "small wins," are influential. Small wins, he explains, attract people's attention, are less likely to be attacked because their size is not threatening, get integrated into other people's agendas because their size makes them easy to include, and

> Once a small win has been accomplished, forces are set in
> motion that favor another small win. When a solution is put in
> place, the next solvable problem often becomes more visible.
> This occurs because new allies bring solutions with them and
> old opponents change their habits. Additional resources also
> flow toward winners, which means that slightly larger wins can
> be attempted.[30]

In the EMBA design meetings, for example, one person would propose an idea that other people saw as both exciting and feasible. Then another person proposed another idea. Each idea made the purpose of creating an extraordinary educational experience a little more legitimate, a little more feasible, and a little more exciting. Soon, no convincing was needed. The whole group was energized about the common purpose.

Actions, Energy, and Results

When people are purpose-centered, they influence others because other people must make sense of the new realities being created. Others must also make sense of how focused, energized, and persistent purpose-centered people are in creating those realities. The energy of purpose-centered people is contagious. Their new actions and positive emotions lead others to think and act more broadly and to build enduring resources. They achieve small wins that accumulate over time and add legitimacy to their purposes. This is what happened in the EMBA design team meetings.

> **BOB:** When we finished designing the program, one of my colleagues leaned back in his chair. He said, "Over the years, I have thought about what it would be like to go back to school. I have always thought, 'I would not want to do that again.' But this program—thIs program has . . ." (he struggled to find the words) ". . . it has commitment."
>
> Our program did have commitment. Our proposal went to the next committee. Some of our design was taken out because it was "too radical." That was fine because other elements remained and the commitment still showed. When the magazines began to rank our EMBA program, *US News and World Report* ranked ours as the best among all U.S. public institutions, *The Wall Street Journal* ranked it among the top three programs every year from 2002 on, and in 2005 (the first year it was included) *BusinessWeek* ranked it the number 4 program in the world.
>
> The rankings were impressive. Yet for me there has always been something even more impressive. For a number of years I had the opportunity to teach in the first week of the program. I would watch some of the finest people I have ever met enter the classroom. They did so with excitement. Part of the excitement

was due to the fact that they were beginning a new program. Another part of that excitement came from associating with faculty and staff who believed in what they were doing. The students could sense that they had become a part of something special. They radiated confidence in the program.

Limits to Possibility and Positivity

A purpose-centered state can lift both the purpose-centered person and the people around that person. People become purpose-centered by asking and answering the question "What result do I want to create?" This question helps us shed inappropriate expectations and set goals that are clear, challenging, positive, and self-chosen. The question can lift us and we can lift others.

There are two questions that should be addressed before we move on. First, can it be dangerous to shed one's assumptions about what is possible and what is not? After all, some things really are impossible, aren't they? And if they are, isn't it foolish to pursue impossible goals? Second, is the setting of extraordinary goals necessarily a positive thing? After all, a person could set goals that are extraordinarily bad. And even if the goals are good, does that necessarily mean that the person with positive goals will have a positive influence?

Impossibility

In his book *The Path of Least Resistance*, Robert Fritz discusses the role of impossibility in determining what result you want to create. He shares the following story:

> Once I was leading a workshop for the Easter Seals foundation. The people with whom I was working were all suffering from lung ailments such as emphysema, lung cancer, and asthma. In one section of the workshop, the objective was for participants to practice separating what they really wanted from what they thought was possible.
>
> One elderly woman was having particular trouble with the exercise.

"Remember, the exercise is to separate what you want from what you think is possible," I said to her. "So, what do you want?"

"I can't say," she replied. "It really isn't possible."

"Well," I said, "for the moment, don't consider whether or not what you want is possible. What do you want?"

"I can't say what I want because I can never have it."

"I can tell you what you want," I said.

"You can?"

"Sure," I replied. "What you want is good health."

"But I can never have it."

"But isn't that what you want?"

"But I can never have it," she repeated.

"Well, if I were a magic genie and could wave a wand and give you perfect health, would you take it?"

She paused for a moment, and quietly said, "Yes."

"If you would take it," I said, "you must want it. Furthermore, even if it doesn't seem at all possible to you—even if it is *not* possible—the real truth is that you want perfect health."

"Yes," she said, "that's so."

"So, now tell yourself the truth about what you want," I said. "It's never wrong to tell yourself the truth about what you want, even though you think it's not possible to have it."

She paused. Then, looking down at the floor, she said quietly, "The truth is I want to be healthy."

"What just happened to you when you said that?" I asked.

"I don't understand this," she replied, looking very different than she had looked up to that point. "I feel physically lighter. As if a weight has been lifted off my shoulders. I feel clearer. It's almost as if there is an energy flowing through me right now."

Whether or not her illness persisted, she no longer had to bear the additional burden of feeling obligated to misrepresent to herself the truth about her desire for health.[31]

The result a person wants may not be possible. But as Fritz points out, one reason to ask ourselves what result we want to create, and to answer honestly, is not only to be free of incorrect expectations, but also to be free of expectations for what we allow ourselves to admit. Sometimes, the healthiest option may be to change our desires. We will not change them, however, if we are not honest about what those desires are. And, if we can put aside questions of possibility just long enough to ask ourselves and honestly answer what result we want to create, then we will often discover that what appears impossible may not be impossible after all.

History is riddled with stories of people who overcame disabilities or disease, who accomplished extraordinary feats that no one else believed possible, or who discovered technologies that enabled others to do things that no one could do before. Some things are impossible. Some things become less desirable or wise as we work on them. But we humans have such a strong tendency to pick up expectations that limit us much more than we need to be limited, that even if we end up discovering that something is impossible, it is hard to imagine a situation in which it is not worth at least asking, "What result do I want to create?"

Negativity

A second question we could raise is whether being purpose-centered is necessarily positive. The answer, of course, is no. People can be as purpose-centered when they try to create extraordinarily negative results as they are when they try to create extraordinarily positive results. Even people who pursue positive purposes can still do negative things or have a negative impact if they are inaccurate or wrong. For example, if the minorities in the minority influence studies can convince others that a blue slide is green, then what effect might we have when the issues have real consequences on people's lives?

Possibilities like these are what make the other characteristics of lift so important. People who are vigilant about the integrity with which they pursue their purposes (internally directed) are likely to detect and correct personal mistakes and errors. People who pursue their purposes with empathy for others (other-focused) are likely to take actions that will help others as well as themselves. And people who desire to learn and grow (externally open) are likely to develop increasingly effective and ethical ways to pursue their purposes.

The other characteristics of lift, then, affect both the content and the process of people's purposes. Consider, for example, how Bob persisted in trying to get his colleagues to adopt a more lofty vision for the EMBA program. When Bob's colleagues ignored him, he could have insisted that they pay attention, called them hypocrites, or demanded answers from them. Responses like these would have been just as "focused," "energetic," and "persistent" as the approach he took, but they would have also been less likely to have had a positive influence or to have enabled him and his colleagues to create a powerful EMBA program.

The reason Bob persisted patiently, quietly, and respectfully toward his goal instead of insisting, blaming, or getting angry is that he was trying to be internally directed, other-focused, and externally open as well as purpose-centered. He was internally directed because he was vigilant about examining and living his core values and would not let himself be shut down. He was other-focused because he empathized with their struggle to give up their expectations. He did not judge or criticize. He just asked questions. He was externally open because he listened deeply to their feelings and their words, considered their feedback, and updated his strategy as he learned from them.

In short, Bob experienced *lift*. His objective was to the get the whole group to experience *lift* as well. In the coming chapters, we will examine each of these other characteristics and how we can experience them.

➤ Practices for Applying the Principles of Lift

When we want to become purpose-centered, we often struggle to come up with exceptional purposes that are not limited by expectations. The following practices can help:

1. **Use zero-based budgeting.** When managers create their budgets they often adjust last year's budget to reflect their plans for this year. In zero-based budgeting, managers start with a blank page. A blank page forces us to think harder about what we want to do and what we need to do it. We can use this process

in many activities: "If I started with a blank page, how would I approach this?"

2. **Recite the mantra "Why not?"** Sometimes, out of habit, we look for obstacles rather than possibilities. When this happens, we can ask ourselves, "Why not?" This question invites us to look for possibilities and not just obstacles.

3. **Expand the scope or the time frame.** Problems tend to focus us on immediate issues. One way to escape this focus is to ask ourselves what the problem will mean months or years from now. Also, thinking of more people, resources, locations, and other ways to widen the scope can also help us put the problem in context and develop new purposes.

4. **Imagine scenarios.** When creating purpose, it can be useful to imagine what those purposes might look like if you achieve them. Visualizing purposes can make them more or less appealing, or can suggest changes in what we want the purposes to be.

chapter 5

Falling Short of Our Values and Not Realizing It

RYAN: When I was nineteen years old, I left home for two years to serve a mission for my church. A mission is both the period that a missionary spends in service and the name of the organization in which missionaries serve, located in a particular place. On my mission I taught, did community service, proselytized, and helped people make life changes such as overcoming addictive habits or developing better patterns of family life. I was excited to serve.

The mission I served in had many leadership positions. It consisted of about two hundred young women and men, but it was led by a couple in their sixties who served as mission presidents. The mission president had two assistants. The assistants supervised twelve zone leaders, the zone leaders supervised about thirty district leaders, and the district leaders supervised the rest of the missionaries. The assistants, zone leaders, and district leaders were all young missionaries. When there were changes in these leadership positions, missionaries often speculated about who the next person to fill a leadership position might be.

I went on my mission to serve other people, not to get promoted into particular leadership positions. Often, in many organizations, there are good and appropriate reasons for people to seek promotions, particularly if they have skills that can benefit their organization or if they can learn from serving in a different position. In my mission, however, the positions were filled with capable and appropriate people and there was plenty for me to learn in any position. If I was truly motivated by love for the people I was serving, then I would not have cared what position I was in—I would have cared only about whether the people I was serving were blessed by my service.

I worked hard. Five months into my mission I was asked to serve as a district leader. Three months later I was asked to serve as a zone leader. One year into my mission, another missionary and I were asked to become partners and tour the mission to help other missionaries improve their teaching skills. When we received this assignment, many missionaries speculated that my partner or I would be asked to be the next assistant to the president. I tried to ignore all of this talk, but it was hard. Two weeks later, the mission president asked my partner to be the new assistant. I was devastated and depressed.

I was devastated that I was not asked to be the next assistant. I was depressed because I had spent the past year telling myself that all I cared about was serving others, but the fact that I felt devastated was undeniable evidence that I wanted more than just to serve. I had been lying to myself, but now I had to admit that I wanted to be the assistant to the president. I wanted to write to my family and friends and tell them that I was the assistant so that they would see how special I was. I wanted to be the assistant because I thought it would validate what a good person I was and prove that others should listen to my opinions. Instead, by realizing that my hard work was motivated by self-promotion as much as it was by love for other people, I had to admit to myself that I was not as good of a person as I had convinced myself I was. That hurt deeply.

Now that I could not deny that I was motivated by self-promotion, I looked back over the past year. I could see how I had, at times, behaved in ways that were more consistent with my desire to be the assistant than with my love for the people I was serving. Sometimes I had worked hard more to show myself and others how hard I was serving and following the rules and less because I cared about the people I was serving. When I did this, my behavior would change in small but real ways. Instead of pooling insights and efforts with the other missionaries to come up with optimal collaborative solutions, I might force my own idea on the other missionaries. I did not consciously decide to do things like this so that I could become the assistant. I really wanted to be a good missionary. But even though my errors were subtle, I was shocked, on reflection, at how often my actions had been inconsistent with the values I wanted to live. When I failed to live my values, I also failed to lift myself and others.

Building Wings That Work

Acting in a way that is contrary to one's values is like building an airplane with poorly designed wings: valueless actions and poor designs both lack integrity. Poorly designed wings were among the Wright Brothers' problems that we described in chapter 2. The glider they built in 1900 did not generate enough lift, so in 1901 they used Otto Lilienthal's lift tables to build larger wings with more curvature. Because of Lilienthal's tables, they thought this would increase lift. Instead, their new wings had almost the opposite effect.

Lilienthal's tables gave the Wright brothers problems for two reasons. The first was that the Wright brothers were using wings that had a different shape from the wings Lilienthal had used. The amount and controllability of the lift that wings generate depends on their shape, their size, the angle at which the wing approaches the oncoming air, the angle of the wings relative to the body of the aircraft, and other factors as well. Lilienthal, however, created his lift tables using gliders that used only one wing shape, so when the Wright brothers made adjustments to their wings—which did not have the same shape as

Lilienthal's—their adjustments generated less lift and less controllability.

Another reason the Wright brothers had problems with Lilienthal's table was that the numbers in Lilienthal's table and equations were not sufficiently accurate. Some could be fixed with more precise measurements. Lilienthal, however, had also measured the forces on the wings relative to the direction the wings were facing, but the Wrights recognized that they should measure pure upward force ("true" lift) and pure backward force ("true" drag) instead. To fix this, the Wright brothers built a wind tunnel, instruments for collecting the data they needed, and as many as two hundred different model wings of varying shapes and sizes. Using these, Orville and Wilbur created new tables using true lift and true drag for about four dozen different wing shapes and other, more accurate numbers for their equations as well. Using these data, they selected a wing design for their glider that generated the lift they needed. This new design had integrity because it was consistent with correct principles for harnessing lift.

The Wright brothers needed wings with designs that were consistent with correct principles to be able to harness lift and make their airplane fly. Before collecting data that were accurate representations of these principles, they could not harness the aerodynamic force of lift. This inability required them to question their beliefs in a critical, thorough, and uncompromising way. Similarly, Ryan was unable to harness the psychological state of lift when his actions were based on a desire for self-promotion rather than on love for the people he was serving. To lift both the people he was serving and his fellow missionaries, Ryan needed to question his motivation in a critical, thorough, and uncompromising way. It was only when he was honest with himself that he could change his motivations and act consistently with his values. As long as he remained convinced that he had pure motives when he did not, he kept slipping into behaviors that were not consistent with his values, no matter how he tried to pretend otherwise.

Ryan is not the only person who has thought he was living his values when he was not. We all do this in more ways than we realize. Sometimes we act in ways that are inconsistent with our values because we have learned inappropriate but automatic reactions to particular life experiences without even realizing we have learned them. Sometimes we simply give in to temptations. But once we do either of these, if we do not have some means to question ourselves, then there is a good chance that those actions will become patterns. We act that way again and again as automatic, unconscious responses to other, similar experiences.

We need to respond automatically in order to keep from being overwhelmed by all of life's experiences. The problem is that many of the responses we learn tend to be inconsistent with values that we claim to hold dear. When people respond automatically to their contexts in ways that are inconsistent with their values, we call that behavior externally directed.

External Direction

Human history is littered with examples of people acting in externally directed ways. On a grand scale, we have examples like the Holocaust, in which government officials, military leaders, and citizens participated in the killing of millions of innocent people. On a less grand scale, we regularly have public figures—many of whom claim to have high standards—caught taking bribes or cheating on their spouses. And, in our everyday lives, average citizens ignore people in need, break their word, speak poorly of others, or fail to exercise self-restraint. When other people act in externally directed ways, we are often surprised or even outraged. Actions like these are surprising because, as researchers who study values have found, most people consider values such as compassion, honesty, self-control, or the preservation of life to be important human values.[1] Why, then, do people fail to live these values?

A more troubling question for each of us may be "Why do I fail to live my own values?" All human beings—each of us—have strong tendencies to be externally directed. The personal values that we fail to live up to may involve courage, wisdom, or friendship, rather than compassion, honesty, and self-restraint, but research suggests that whatever our values may be, we have tendencies to act in ways that are not consistent with those values. And we—like Ryan discovering that he was motivated by self-promotion rather than love—are likely to be just as surprised and disappointed when we discover them. A sampling of this research follows.

Compassion

One of the most famous researchers to examine the question of why people act in ways that are inconsistent with their values was Stanley Milgram.[2] Milgram wanted to understand how the Holocaust could have occurred. He built a machine with a row of switches across the front and an electrode coming out of the back. Each switch was marked with a number, indicating how many volts of electricity would be sent through the electrode if a person flipped the switch. The first switch was labeled "15 volts" and had a verbal description of "SLIGHT SHOCK." The remaining switches increased by 15 volts each ("30 volts," "45 volts," "60 volts," and so on), with the final switch labeled "450 volts" and "DANGER—SEVERE SHOCK."

Milgram used this machine to conduct an experiment in which a person in a gray lab coat brought two people, a "teacher" and a "learner," into the laboratory. The learner was actually one of the research assistants, but the teacher did not know this. The teacher was a volunteer participant from the local community. The person in the lab coat told the teacher and the learner that he was studying the effects of punishment on learning. He led the learner to a chair, strapped his arms to it, and attached the previously described electrode to the learner's wrist. The learner's job was to learn a list of word pairs. The teacher's job was to test the learner. If the learner answered a question correctly, the teacher was to read the next question. If the learner made a mistake, the teacher was to flip the next highest switch on the box, administering higher and higher levels of electric shock to the learner for each wrong answer.

The learner in this experiment did not actually receive an electric shock, but he did act as if he was receiving one. The learner grunted when he received the 75-volt shock, complained when he received the 120-volt shock, demanded to be released from the experiment at 150 volts, grew more emotional as the size of the shocks increased, and screamed in agony at 285 volts. Throughout this process, if the teacher expressed any concern about administering the shocks, the person in the gray lab coat would say, "The experiment requires that you continue."

Milgram conducted this experiment to answer the question "At what point will the teacher refuse to obey the man in the gray lab coat?" He and others conducted this experiment thousands of times. In the basic form of the experiment, 65 percent of the "teachers" obeyed the person in the lab coat until they flipped the very last switch. Every participant flipped at least some of the switches. Many, if not most, of the teachers felt stress over shocking the "learner," but none of them refused to participate and most of them obeyed in spite of believing that they were inflicting significant pain on another human being.[3]

Milgram and his colleagues kept track of the profession, level of education, political affiliation, and many other factors among all of the "teachers." None of the individual factors made much of a difference in the number of switches people flipped, though clearly something was different between the 65 percent of people who flipped all of the switches and the 35 percent who did not. Recently, some scholars have suggested new possible explanations for this difference.[4] We discuss explanations like these in the next chapter. For now, it is sufficient to note that most people learn to obey authority figures early in their lives, and for many of us the automatic tendency to obey people who look and act like authority figures is strong enough to overwhelm other values, even to the point of harming our fellow human beings.

Helpfulness

The trappings of authority are one of many contextual influences that can overwhelm people's values. Another influence is the number of people in a situation. John Darley and Bibb Latane found this out in an experiment.[5] They had students from a university in a large city come to their laboratory to participate in a discussion. Participants took turns speaking through a microphone to students in other rooms. The "students" in the other rooms were actually recorded voices. One of the recorded voices mentioned on its first turn that he found life at a city school difficult and that he sometimes suffered from epileptic seizures. Then, during that recorded voice's second turn to speak, he began to have a seizure. He spoke disjointedly and painfully and expressed worry about having a seizure and dying. The experimenters then measured whether the participants would try to get help for the student having a seizure and how long it took them to seek help.

Darley and Latane hypothesized that participants would be more likely to help the student having an epileptic seizure if there were fewer people involved in the conversation. They argued that when we know that other people are also aware of an emergency, we assume that they are just as responsible for responding to that emergency as we are. This logic diffuses the responsibility among all of the participants. If responsibility is diffused among many people, then one individual does not have much responsibility. Therefore, other concerns like uncertainty, inconvenience, or fear can overwhelm this lessened sense of responsibility.

The experiment confirmed Darley and Latane's hypothesis. They assigned participants to groups of different sizes. Some participants talked only to the recording of the epileptic student. Some participants spoke to the recording of the epileptic student and one other recording of a student. And some participants spoke to the recording of the epileptic student and the recordings of four other students. Those participants who thought they were speaking only to the student with the epileptic seizure came out of the room looking for help faster than those who thought they were talking to more people, and more of these participants came out. The participants who thought that they were speaking to five other students came out the most slowly, and fewer of these participants came out. Gender, speaking order, personality measures, and background characteristics had no effect on how quickly people came out looking for help. The only exception was the size of the community that people came from: people from small communities were slightly more likely to help than people from large communities.

Diffused responsibility is one reason that people fail to help others, but it is not the only reason. Time pressure is another. Darley found this in a study he conducted with Daniel Batson, in which they re-created the Biblical parable of the Good Samaritan, a story in which three people walked past a man who was beaten by robbers. Only one person stopped to help.

Darley and Batson recreated this story by telling theology students to each give a talk in a nearby building. They told some of these students that they were late and others that they had plenty of time. In the path between the building where the students received their assignments and the building where they were to give their talk, Darley and Batson placed an actor lying on the ground and playing the role of an ailing person. Only 10 percent of the seminary students who thought that they were late stopped to help the ailing person, but 63 percent of the students who did not think they were late stopped to help the person. Ironically, Darley and Batson assigned half of the seminary students in each group to give a talk on the parable of the Good Samaritan, and half of the students to speak on an irrelevant topic. Presumably, if a person is giving a talk about stopping to help ailing people on the side of the road, they might be more inclined to stop and help ailing people on the side of the road—and some of them did. The most powerful variable for explaining whether a person would stop to help, though, was whether that person was late. For more participants, being late overwhelmed the value they placed on helping.[6]

Achievement

The trappings of authority in the Milgram studies, additional bystanders in Darley and Latane's study, time pressure in Darley and Batson's study, and cues related to leadership positions on Ryan's mission are all examples of context. A person's context includes the surroundings associated with the situation that the person is in. For example, in the Milgram study the "teacher's" immediate activity was one of instructing the "learner" in memorizing word pairs, but the teacher's context included the laboratory and the person in the gray lab coat. The activity in the bystander study was another person's epileptic seizure, but the context included the number of other people who were also aware of the situation. The activity in the Good Samaritan study was the encounter of an ailing person, but the context was the talk that the students were planning to give and the time at which they were planning to deliver the talk. In each case, people encountered situations that might have elicited compassionate or helpful behaviors, but those potential behaviors were overwhelmed by factors in their contexts.

The potential for context to overwhelm values is not limited to prosocial values like compassion and helpfulness. Context can even overwhelm values that are primarily oriented toward self-advancement, like personal achievement. For example, Margaret Shih and her colleagues recruited a number of Asian women to participate in a study in which they examined how well these women performed on a math test.[7] Before taking the test, however, Shih and her colleagues randomly divided the women into three groups and had each of them take different questionnaires about themselves. One-third of the women filled out a questionnaire that focused on being Asian, one-third filled out a questionnaire that focused on being female, and one-third filled out a generic questionnaire that had nothing to do with race or gender.

After filling out the questionnaire, the women took the test. Those who answered the questionnaire about being Asian performed the best, followed by those who answered the generic questionnaire. The worst scores were obtained by the women who answered the questionnaire about being female. The women in each group had similar average skill levels in math. They all took the same math test. The questionnaires, however, focused each of these groups on different parts of their context—their racial or gender identities.

People in North America, including Asian women, learn stereotypes about Asians, women, and math early and often. According to these stereotypes, Asians are good at math and women are not. The women in this experiment responded largely in the ways that they thought society expected them to respond, even though they had no conscious reason for doing so and no difference in their skill at math. The women who filled out a survey with Asian references performed well on the math test, living up to a value of personal achievement. The women who filled out a survey with female references performed significantly less well, failing to live up to a value of personal achievement.

Automaticity

The experiment with Asian women taking a math test is a useful illustration of both the power of context and how automatically people respond to their contexts. The experimenters did not tell their female participants to "think about being a woman" or "think about being an Asian." There were no explicit connections made between mathematics and gender or race. The women just filled out a questionnaire. Even though the women had no reason to think explicitly about the stereotypical connection between gender, race, and math, the women who answered a questionnaire about their ethnicity still performed relatively well and the women who answered a questionnaire about their gender still performed relatively poorly.

The study with the epileptic student was similar. When it was over, Darley and Latane asked the participants if the size of the group affected their decision to help. The participants said "no"—even though the size of the group was the most powerful predictor of whether and how quickly the participants looked for help. In other words, participants made sense of and responded to the cues in their context automatically and without explicit thought.

This kind of automatic response is not unique to Asian women in North America or students in a city university. It is fundamental to human behavior. We all react automatically to cues in our environment every day and we do not realize what we are doing. Questionnaires are just one of many techniques that psychologists use to get people to respond automatically. John Bargh and his colleagues provide an example of another technique.[8] They gave participants the set of five-word lists below. For each list, they asked the participants to select four words and write a grammatically correct four-word sentence.

1. him was worried she always

2. from are Florida oranges temperature

3. ball the throw toss silently

4. shoes give replace old the

5. he observes occasionally people watches

6. be will sweat lonely they

7. sky the seamless gray is

8. should now withdraw forgetful we

9. us bingo sing play let

10. sunlight makes temperature wrinkle raisins

After writing sentences, participants were told to take a short walk. They walk much more slowly than normal. This is because the purpose of this activity was not to test their ability to create grammatically correct sentences, but to get their unconscious minds to think about what it is like to be old. If you look closely at the lists, you will see that they contain words such as "worried," "Florida," "silently," "old," "lonely," "gray," "forgetful," "bingo," and "wrinkle." The effect of including these words is that even though our conscious minds focus on creating sentences, our unconscious minds pick up on the pattern they see in the words and respond to that pattern without noticing it.

Simple experiences like this word activity are sufficient to change the speed that people walk with, increase or decrease a person's performance, lead people to act more or less compassionately and helpfully, and even get New Yorkers to act rudely or politely.[9] If our context primes us to perform well; to act more politely, compassionately, or helpfully; or to act in other ways that are consistent with our core values, then we are like well-designed wings, lifting ourselves and others. However, if our context primes us to perform less well; to act less politely, compassionately, or helpfully; or to act in other ways that are inconsistent with our values, then we are like poorly designed wings, unable to generate lift for ourselves or for others.

Bargh, one of the world's leading researchers on the automatic processes that our brains use to think, suggests that about 95 percent of our thoughts and actions are caused by automatic, unconscious thought processes.[10] If automatic processing is so important to our daily functioning, though, and if our values are so important to us, why do we not learn thought and action responses that are consistent with our core values? The answer to this question is similar to the reason we often fail to approach situations from a purpose-centered state.

How We Learn to Act Contrary to Our Values

By the time Ryan's mission president had asked Ryan's partner to be the next assistant to the president, Ryan's subtle ways of vying for the position were automatic to him. As with most automatic reactions, Ryan was largely unaware that he was vying for the position and acting in ways that were contrary to his values. People become unaware of the inconsistency between their values and their actions through at least two processes: self-justification and learning others' justifications. An excellent illustration of this process is the "Pyramid of Choice."

Self-Justification

Carol Tavris and Elliot Aronson describe the pyramid of choice as follows:

> Imagine two young men who are identical in terms of attitudes, abilities, and psychological health. They are reasonably honest

and have the same middling opinion of, say, cheating: they think it is not a good thing to do, but there are worse crimes in the world. Now they are both in the midst of taking an exam that will determine whether they get into graduate school. They each draw a blank on a crucial essay question. Failure looms . . . at which point each one gets an easy opportunity to cheat by reading another student's answers. The two young men struggle with the temptation. After a long moment of anguish, one yields and the other resists. Their decisions are a hair's breadth apart; it could easily have gone the other way for each of them. Each gains something important, but at a cost: one gives up integrity for a good grade, the other gives up a good grade to preserve his integrity.

Now the question is: how do they feel about cheating a week later? Each student has had ample time to justify the course of action he took. The one who yielded to temptation will decide that cheating is not so great a crime. He will say to himself: "Hey, everyone cheats. It's no big deal. And I really need to do this for my future career." But the one who resisted the temptation will decide that cheating is far more immoral than he originally thought: "In fact, people who cheat are disgraceful. In fact, people who cheat should be permanently expelled from school. We have to make an example of them."[11]

The process by which these two young men come to view cheating as "no big deal" versus "disgraceful" is called self-justification. People tend to engage in self-justification when they have two inconsistent thoughts or beliefs, such as "Cheating is an immoral thing to do" and "I just cheated on a test," because the inconsistency makes them feel uncomfortable. Leon Festinger, one of the most influential cognitive psychologists of the twentieth century, called this uncomfortable feeling "cognitive dissonance."[12] Because dissonance is uncomfortable, people tend to justify, or rationalize, their thoughts and actions by telling themselves (and sometimes others) a consistent and worthwhile story about these conflicting thoughts, such as "Hey, everyone cheats. It's no big deal. I really need to do this for my career." What people do less often when confronted by inconsistent thoughts is admit they were wrong and try to make amends. In fact, not only is it less common for people to admit that they are wrong, but as the research on the confirming evidence bias that we reviewed in chapter 3 suggests, even when people are confronted with evidence suggesting they are wrong, they actually tend to defend their actions more tenaciously, finding even more reasons to justify their position.

When professors teach their students about self-justification, the students are usually surprised by the fact that people believe their justifications. Self-justification, though, is not the same as lying. When people lie, they say things with the intention to deceive others. They know that what they are saying is not true. When people justify their thoughts or actions, they either believe, or come to believe, that their justifications are true. On Ryan's mission, for example, before his partner was asked to be the new assistant, Ryan justified his actions by convincing himself that his efforts to work harder than others or to approach other missionaries aggressively were evidence of how much he was willing to do for the people he was serving. In the occasional moments in which he became aware that his actions were not consistent with his values, his justifications would quickly drown out these moments of realization.

We believe our self-justifications in part because of how convincing they are, but also in part because human memory is imperfect. As time passes, our minds forget or distort the evidence or experiences that might contradict our justifications. Research shows, for example, that people often remember their teenage squabbles with their parents or eyewitness accounts in courtroom trials differently than the actual events occurred.[13] As a result, the fictional young man who cheated in Tavris and Aronson's pyramid of choice developed a worldview that identifies conditions that make cheating okay. The strength of his justifications and the weakness of his memory made it easy to believe in these conditions. He could then cheat a little more; this required a little more justification, and this justification provided more circumstances in which cheating was justified. Soon, cheating was normal. At that point, everyone can see the young man's dishonesty except for the young man himself. It is much easier to see hypocrisy in others than in ourselves.

Learning Others' Justifications

People also come to act in ways that are inconsistent with their values by learning justifications from other people, such as when a person takes a new job and learns "how things are done around here." When this happens, we learn both behaviors and justifications for those behaviors, often without thinking about whether those behaviors are consistent with our values. It is in our early childhood, from our parents or primary caregivers, that we learn some of the most powerful beliefs that keep us from living consistently with our values. Sometimes, these beliefs are justifications for choices that have been passed down for generations, affecting our professional lives as much as our personal lives.

An example of inheriting beliefs that keep people from living their values comes from a colleague of ours named Julie, a manager in a large European company. One day Julie was participating in a team-building session with the members of her leadership team. They were discussing what it felt like to be part of their team. Julie decided to be honest. She told her team that she felt she was the weakest member, that she was not getting much out of her experience, and that she did not believe she was adding much value.

Julie's teammates were shocked by her statements. Each person told her that they saw her as a valuable and important member of the team. This, in turn, shocked Julie. Instead of returning after the next break, she went upstairs to her hotel and cried for the rest of the day. It was clear that her experience in the morning had touched her deeply, but she was not sure why.

Over the next few weeks, Julie pondered her experience and learned some principles about how she was preventing herself from living her values. She realized, for example, that she valued being a person of voice, influence, and contribution, but that she had instead been silencing herself. She had learned to do this in her early childhood without even realizing it.

Julie first learned to silence herself because of the influence of her father. He was very critical of her from the beginning, and that criticism continued into adulthood. For example, one day when Julie was promoted to be the vice president of talent in her organization, she called to tell her father. He replied, "What kind of a title is that? Sounds like nonsense to me. And what right do you have to be a vice president, you're just a little pischer."

Julie's father was not the only voice teaching her to silence herself. Julie grew up as an American in London. Peers in her schools teased her regularly for her "ugly" American accent. As a result, she learned to speak with an English accent and did whatever she could to hide her "American-ness" from other people. Criticisms like the ones she learned from her father and from the children who teased her taught Julie that it was safer to hide her voice rather than to contribute what she had to offer. She carried this belief with her into adulthood. As an adult, her friends and co-workers wanted and needed her contributions and opinions, but she withheld them. No one was teasing her about her accent now. She seldom saw her father. In fact, she never encountered her father at work, where she was silencing herself the most.

What Julie did encounter at work was her boss. Julie's boss was an austere British man in a powerful role. As a result, he was also the embodiment of the forces that had silenced her in her childhood. As a child she had learned categories such as "male," "authority," and "British"—cues that she would pick up on occasionally from her context that suggested the potential of criticism. These cues, as a result, would spark in her an automatic response to hide anything that might be criticized, and as a result, to avoid voicing her potential contributions.

When people react to cues like "male," "authority," and "British" in the same way that they reacted to them as children, they are engaging in a process called transference.[14] The problem with transference is that the same reactions that were appropriate in childhood are often no longer appropriate. Julie's boss, for example, was not her father. Even so, Julie reacted to him as if he were her father. She failed to share her opinions because she was afraid of being criticized. When people transfer what they learn in childhood to adult contexts, they seldom consider acting differently until they have experiences like Julie's conversation with her team. Sometimes people need dramatic experiences to see that they can be more internally directed.

From External Direction to Internal Direction

It is useful to understand how we become externally directed because an understanding of our external direction helps us see how we can become internally directed. We are externally directed when our automatic reactions to cues in our context are not consistent with the values we normally espouse when we consider those values consciously.[15] We respond in automatic and inconsistent ways to these contextual cues because we either learn other people's justifications or justify our own actions. These justifications define how we see the world and which cues we notice and respond to. Over time, as we engage in these responses, justify them, and our memories fade, these responses become automatic or largely automatic, and we lose our ability to see that we are acting in ways that are inconsistent with our values. Because of their justifications, participants in the electric shock experiments, the experiment with the epileptic student, the Good Samaritan experiment, and the experiment with the Asian women failed to act in ways that were consistent with their values. Because of his justifications, Ryan began seeking attention and acting aggressively as a missionary. And because of her justifications, Julie silenced herself at work.

Once we know that we are being externally directed or have a tendency to be externally directed, we can do something about it. For example, when Julie realized that she was not voicing her thoughts to her boss, she also recognized that she needed to share this realization with her boss. She invited him to have a cup of coffee with her. She told him her story, and to her surprise, he then shared a personal story with her. Julie's relationship with her boss changed completely. The two of them began to work together as equals, supporting each other in their work instead of simply giving, receiving, and reporting on assignments.

Julie's personal change did more than just change her boss. As she worked to contribute more, Julie became more willing—even eager—

to express her ideas and opinions and to share her knowledge. Now, she even talks about things like "gut feel" instead of worrying that people will think that expressing her intuitions will make her seem "soft." She helps other executives see how their decisions affect employees. All around her, she lifts people to higher motivation, trust, and opportunity. Julie even made peace with her father before he passed away.

> **RYAN:** Like Julie, I have also tried to be more internally directed. Unlike Julie, my changes are less dramatic. Once I realized that I had a tendency to seek positions and personal advancement even though I wanted to be driven by a concern for others, I started paying more attention to how I felt in public situations. Now if I am in a public situation and I feel the desire to act in ways that I think will make me look good to other people, I try to stop and question my motivations. I apply the principles that we will discuss in chapter 6. I have learned, and am continuing to learn, that I tend to act with the most integrity when I question my integrity.

chapter 6

Becoming
Internally Directed

S tephen, a friend of ours, told us about an experience he had when he was a teenager. Stephen loved basketball. He was good at it, too. He won awards, dominated the leagues he participated in, and had some college coaches paying attention to him. When he joined the high school Varsity team, however, his coach almost never let him play. Stephen gave his best effort in every practice, followed the rules, outplayed his teammates, and worked constantly to improve, but no matter what he did his coach would not give him any more playing time.

Eventually Stephen and his parents found out that all of the players struggled with the coach—even the kids who had the most playing time. Apparently, this coach demoralized his teams every year. He had some of the most talented players in the state, yet his teams would lose early in the state tournament and his players would say things like "I cannot wait for the season to end so I can start enjoying basketball again." The coach hardly ever spoke to the players, and when he did, he was usually angry, bordering on abusive.

A quiet kid, Stephen was a little intimidated by the idea of confronting his coach. In his senior year, however, it began to be clear that Stephen would probably go through his entire high school experience without a chance to have any significant playing time on a team where he was unquestionably the best player at his position. Stephen's parents could tell how much this hurt him, so they offered to talk to the coach for him. Stephen did not want his parents to talk to the coach, but he eventually agreed to talk to the coach himself. His parents guided him on how to talk to the coach effectively in hopes of improving the relationship and improving the situation for everyone involved.

The next day, Stephen asked his coach if he could talk to him. The coach looked unhappy and asked Stephen what he wanted. Stephen said that he would like to earn more playing time and asked the coach if there was anything he could do to improve his skills and earn more playing time. The coach swore under his breath and walked away. Stephen realized that the coach had no reason for not letting him play more. The next day the coach put Stephen on the third team, where he was unlikely to ever get any playing time at all.

Stephen could not stop thinking about how poorly the coach treated him. One night he sat in his bedroom crying. Before going to sleep, he prayed. When he did, he felt an intuition: even though his coach was not a good coach, he was a good man, and he needed to forgive his coach. When Stephen felt this intuition, he realized that he had grown to hate his coach. Stephen was failing to live his values of loving and forgiving others.

Many of us might be surprised or offended by the claim that we are failing to live our values if we had been treated like Stephen. After all, if a young person like Stephen feels hate toward an adult in a powerful position who treats him in ways that are nearly abusive, that hate seems justified. This, however, is the point. Even in a case like this, where Stephen has done nothing wrong to the coach, Stephen must justify his feelings of hate because they are not consistent with his values. The research on cognitive dissonance and the confirming evidence bias, in fact, would suggest that most of us would do what Stephen did: engage in self-justification. After all, most of the other players on the team blamed the team's problems on the coach.

After his prayer, however, Stephen saw that even though his justifications were correct, they did not help him or his coach. He became internally directed by deciding to forgive his coach. Stephen looked for ways in which his coach was a good man in spite of being a bad coach. He saw how his coach helped other students in the high school through counseling and administrative work. He complimented his coach for what he saw. Gradually, he felt better about his coach. He began to be excited about playing basketball again. He practiced hard because he loved playing the game. He quit trying to impress the coach or anyone else. He became internally directed. Practice became fun, and Stephen was lifted by his experience.

Changing Our Stories

How did Stephen become internally directed? He saw that he was living a story of hate toward his coach and that this story was inconsistent with his values of forgiveness and love. Then he created and acted out a new, forgiving story. This word, "story," is important.

We use the word "story" to describe what Stephen did because justifications are stories—stories we tell to explain why we did what we did and that guide the automatic reactions that keep us from acting in ways that are consistent with our values (as we discussed in the last chapter). One of the most powerful things we can do to help us act in ways that are consistent with our values, then, is to change our stories. Researchers have identified at least two types of stories that we can use instead of justifications: implementation intentions and reasons.

Implementation Intentions

To understand how implementation intentions work, imagine that you are in a room with another person who is quizzing you with flash cards. Each card has the name of a color written on it, but the color in which these names are written is not the same color as the name that is written. For example, a card that has "red" written on it may be written in green ink, or a card that has "blue" written on it may be written in yellow ink. Your job is to name the color of the ink as quickly as you can each time you are shown a card. How much effort would it take for you to name the color of ink on each card correctly each time?

Thomas Webb and Paschal Sheeran posed this challenge to a number of people in an experiment they conducted.[1] Naming the color of the ink actually required a fair amount of effort because the participants had to fight the tendency to read the words. Some of the participants slogged through the task. Others, however, got help. Webb and Sheeran asked them to state specific intentions for what they would do with each card, such as "As soon as I see the card I will ignore the word and say the color of the second letter." Simply saying a sentence like this made a significant difference in how much energy it took for participants to perform the task.

Webb and Sheeran used a creative way to measure the amount of energy it took for participants to name the color of ink on the cards. They asked the participants to solve unsolvable puzzles as a second task. The participants did not know that the puzzles could not be solved. By measuring the amount of time the participants persisted in trying to solve the puzzles, though, Webb and Sheeran could compare how much energy the participants used on the color-naming task. They found that participants who stated their specific intentions persisted longer and made more attempts to solve the unsolvable puzzles than the people who did not.

Psychologists have performed other, similar experiments, sometimes in the same order, sometimes in reverse, using different activities or ways of measuring.[2] The results are similar. People expend less energy on tasks that require mental effort when they state specific intentions for how they plan to implement their task. This is because implementation intentions help people override their tendencies to react automatically to a situation (for example, by reading a color name) and begin creating new, automatic tendencies (such as stating the color of the ink).

Implementation intentions are stories. They are small stories that describe what a person will do in a particular situation. They take the form "If X occurs, I will do Y." And if we want to use implementation intentions to be internally directed, then "Y" needs to be an action that is consistent with the values by which we are trying to live. For example, we might say, "When I see someone who needs help, I will stop to help them." Or, "If I feel uncomfortable when someone in authority tells me to do something, I will say, 'I'm not sure why, but I have an uncomfortable feeling about that request. I need to think about it and get back to you.'" Or, "If someone accuses me of a fault, I will pause, examine the validity of that person's claim, and refrain from reacting angrily."

The more specific an implementation intention is, the more help it will be in changing behavior. For example, "If my mother accuses me of a fault . . ." will be more effective than "If someone accuses me of a fault . . ." Specific implementation intentions become automatic more quickly because we do not have to expend as much energy trying to figure out if a situation matches a specific description. Thus, to use implementation intentions to become more internally directed, people must identify (1) the specific contexts in which the behavior they want to regulate is likely to happen and (2) a new and specific response to that context that would be more consistent with one's values. A specific description of the context helps people pause rather than react automatically. A specific description of the new behavior, if implemented over time, can become a new automatic response.

Reasons

A second type of story we can use to become internally directed is a reason. Reasons are stories we tell to explain why we should do something. We can see the power of reasons in an experiment conducted by Gregory Maio and his colleagues,[3] who asked participants to (1) write a paper explaining their reasons for supporting or opposing the importance of treating other people equally, (2) perform a word puzzle with words like "equality," "even," "same," "balance," and "fair" in it, or (3) do nothing. Thus, one group thought of reasons to treat people equally, one group thought of the word "equality" but did not think of reasons for treating people equally, and one group had no reason at all to think about equality.

After completing the first activity, Maio and his colleagues divided the participants into red and blue teams and told them that they would play a game of twenty questions—with a twist. The twist was that the participants' teams would get to start the game with some extra points. The way to determine how many points they would get was by assigning points to the next group of participants to play the game. They could give the future red and blue teams sixteen points each. Or they could give the future team that was the same color as their own team more points than the other team (for example, if the participant was on the blue team, then the participant could choose to give twenty points to a blue player and twelve points to a red player). The participants would get as many points to start with as they gave the future team that was the same color as their own team. Thus, the current participants would have an advantage if they favored the future team that was the same color as their own team.

When Maio and his colleagues examined the choices of the people in each group, they found that more of the participants who came up with reasons for treating people equally distributed the future team's points equally than the participants who unscrambled words or the participants who did not engage in the first activity. In other words, participants were more likely to treat people equally when they had reasons for treating people equally.

The research of Maio and his colleagues is important because, on the one hand, a great deal of research suggests that people rely heavily on values to make sense of the world and act within it,[4] and yet on the other hand (as discussed in the last chapter), people often act in ways that are inconsistent with their own values. The research that Maio and his colleagues conducted suggests that this may be because most values, for most of us, are truisms. We learn from early childhood that these values are important, but we never spend much time thinking critically about why they are important. As a result, when we encounter cues that make us feel like reacting in ways that are not consistent with our values, we have no reason to resist that impulse, other than the existence of the value itself. In contrast, there are clear and even automatic reasons for acting on that impulse. If participants who have more and better reasons for treating others equally actually treat other people more equally, then all of us might be more likely to live our values if we have more and better reasons for doing so.

Additional research supports this claim. Maio and his colleagues conducted a similar experiment, focusing on helpfulness. They found that participants who had reasons for being helpful spent more time helping another person than those who did not come up with reasons.[5]

Stories

Implementation intentions are stories about what we plan to do in particular situations. Reasons are the stories we tell to explain why we do things. These stories have profound impact on whether and to what extent we live our values.

We can see the impact of implementation intentions in Stephen's experience with his coach. He may not have realized it, but when he decided that he would try to forgive his coach he was using implementation intentions. His implementation intention took the form of the thought "When I interact with my coach, I will look for positive things to focus on."

Stephen also used reasons to help him forgive his coach. He believed that forgiveness would bring him peace, that this peace would prevent him from disturbing others with his anger, that his anger and hate could consume him if he let it, that his anger was pointless (it had no obvious impact on his coach), and that he also had faults and needed forgiveness. These reasons were important, because Stephen had many justifications for not forgiving his coach: his coach had treated him unfairly, was not coaching well, was destroying the team, was wasting the talent of the boys on the team, and he may have even been damaging some boys' chances to play basketball in college. Stephen needed strong reasons to forgive his coach in order to overcome the justifications that supported the impulse to hate the coach.

The impact of stories like implementation intentions and reasons is one of the reasons we propose the question, "What would my story be if I were living the values I expect of others?" as a way of becoming internally directed. As the research on implementation intentions and reasons suggest, stories have at least two features that can help us live our values: implementation intentions and reasons. Implementation intentions are story plots, which describe how particular people take particular actions in particular situations. Reasons (and justifications) are morals for stories, telling us why we should behave in particular ways.

Stories can motivate and direct our actions. Jim Loehr—a psychologist who wrote the book *The Power of Story*—argues that in addition to plots (or what he calls "action,") and morals (or "purpose"), stories also need truth to motivate the action.[6] The truth of the stories we tell about our own actions and lives lies in the integrity of our storytelling. Is the story a justification to make up for the fact that we are not living our values, or does the story represent an effort to live consistently with our values in spite of pressures to behave otherwise? Is the story honest about the events that are occurring around us, or are we including only information that confirms what we already believe?

Loehr once told a story that illustrates these principles well. Loehr and his colleagues at the Human Performance Institute (HPI) train people on how to improve their performance in work and in life by managing their energy physically, mentally, socially, and spiritually. This was not happening for one of Loehr's clients, who was smoking multiple packs of cigarettes a day when he arrived at HPI. To improve this man's performance in work and in life, they asked him to examine his life, write his story so far, and write the story that his life could be. During this process, they learned that this man adored his young daughter. She was the most important thing in life to him. As they worked with him, he eventually wrote the following story:

It is a beautiful day, and your daughter is radiant. She is eighteen years old. She is at her high school graduation. She looks gorgeous in her robes, and she is smiling at everyone. As the ceremony ends, she runs up to your wife to give her a hug. She thanks your wife for everything your wife did to make this day special for her, saying, "Thank you, Mom. This day was perfect. The only thing that could have made it better was if Daddy hadn't died."

Loehr's client went home from the program and never smoked again.

Loehr's client's story has a clear moral: "If you don't stop smoking you could die young." It tells the truth. It is uncompromising about the impact that smoking is likely to have on this client's health. Even more important, though, this story connects to a truth that is even more central to this man's life than whether he lives or dies: if he keeps smoking, he could very well deprive his daughter and himself of opportunities to share the most precious moments of her life. Depriving her (and himself) of those opportunities is a more painful thought for him to bear than the thought of his own death. Finally, this story has—or at least implies—a plot. It is a hypothetical story about the future consequences of today's actions. It suggests that if he continues to smoke multiple packs a day, he could miss out on the most important moments of his daughter's life. On the other hand, if he quits smoking, he will probably be there for those moments. The action he wanted to take became perfectly clear.

What We Expect of Others

BOB: The top management team of a large company once sent all their senior managers to a famous seminar on quality. They hoped this would improve the company's performance in the marketplace. After the seminar, I sat with these people in a strategic planning meeting. I noticed they were assuming that their company's quality, productivity, and overall performance would improve as a result of having sent their senior managers to the seminar. I was concerned by this assumption, so I told them about another company that I was acquainted with. The senior managers in this other company went to the same seminar. Three years later, the seminar had not created any observable improvements in the company.

The management team was riveted by my story. They had spent a lot of money sending their people to the seminar. One of them blurted out, "Why did it fail?"

I replied, "You tell me."

The room was silent. Then one of the more senior members of the group spoke quietly. "The leaders of the company didn't change."

I nodded. I told the executives that they were making many assumptions about how other people would change. Then I challenged them. "Identify one time when one of you said that you were going to change your behavior."

The room was silent again. After a few moments, another person asked me for suggestions. I made a few suggestions of simple but significant changes that I had seen executives in other companies make. The group quietly considered these options. They decided to adjourn to think about what they should do.

It is easy to judge these executives for expecting their employees to live up to standards to which they themselves were not living up. Before we judge them, though, we would do well to remember that we all have a tendency to be victims of our own self justification. Hypocrisy is easier to see in other people than in ourselves. Fortunately, the fact that we can see hypocrisy in others suggests a way for us to see it in ourselves as well. If we think that others' actions are hypocritical, it means we do not think they are living certain values that we expect of them. And if we think that it is important for others to live those values, then it is important for us to live them as well if we do not want to be hypocrites. This is why the phrase "if I were living the values I expect of others" is such an important part of the question we recommend for becoming internally directed. We need more than stories. We—like the executives who sent their employees to the quality seminar or like Stephen with his coach—need to create stories about living the values we expect others to enact.

The question "What would my story be if I were living the values I expect of others?" does three things for us if we answer it honestly. First, it helps us identify what values are important to us by helping us notice what we expect of others. Second, it helps us critique ourselves on how well we are living those values. And third, it helps us create a story with a plot, a moral, and a truth that will help us become more internally directed.

Internal Direction: Moments of Dignity

Before Stephen chose to forgive his coach, his story was about being mistreated by his coach and having the joy of basketball robbed from him. Stephen was the object rather than the subject in most of the sentences of this story, and most of the verbs in the story were passive. Those are characteristics of an externally directed story.

After Stephen chose to forgive his coach, his story changed. Stephen appreciated the good he saw in his coach, he practiced hard, he improved his skills, and he enjoyed the game. He was the subject rather than the object of most of the sentences in this story, the verbs were action verbs, and the moral of the story was value driven. Stephen was internally directed. He was energized by basketball and by life, he quit trying to impress the coach, and he focused on interacting positively with his coach and on playing hard, fun basketball.

Energy, focus, and clear direction are characteristics that an internally directed state often shares with a purpose-centered state. These states are similar because a value is a type of goal—a principle that we strongly feel we should strive to live[7]—and stories are composed of plots that enable characters to achieve goals.[8] Values are more than just ends we strive to achieve, though, and stories are not just descriptions of what people do. Values are also personal and societal ideals, and stories are illustrations of characters who live (or fail to live) those ideals. When we live our highest ideals and the highest ideals of the societies we live in, we experience what Joshua Margolis, a business ethicist, calls a "moment of dignity."[9]

To help us understand what a moment of dignity is, Margolis draws on an observation from Stanley Milgram, the psychologist who ran the experiments in which participants were asked to shock another person if the other person did not answer his word-pair questions correctly. These experiments have occupied the minds of ethicists for many years because they raise the issue of whether people are actually responsible for their actions. After all, if humans are hardwired to react automatically to cues in their contexts, how can they be responsible? And if they are not responsible, then how can we claim that their actions are ethical or not?

Milgram began to answer these questions himself. After he published findings from his early research on the topic, many people criticized Milgram's experiments, saying that they should have been discontinued at the first sign of stress or discomfort in the participants. Diana Baumrind (whom he calls "the critic") was one of these.[10] She used language to suggest that Milgram *made* the participants shock the victims. In response, Milgram wrote:

> The critic feels that the experimenter *made* the subject shock the victim. This conception is alien to my view. The experimenter tells the subject to do something. But between the command and the outcome there is a paramount force, the acting person who may obey or disobey. I started with the belief that every person who came to the laboratory was free to accept or to reject the dictates of authority. This view sustains a conception of human dignity insofar as it sees in each man a capacity for choosing his own behavior. And as it turned out, many subjects did, indeed, choose to reject the experimenter's commands, providing powerful affirmation of human ideals.[11]

The last two sentences of this paragraph help us understand what Margolis means by dignity. Dignity is the "capacity for choosing [one's] own behavior." The 35 percent of participants who thought for themselves and chose to do what they believed was right in spite of the demands of an authority figure (some sooner and some later) affirmed human ideals by acting with dignity.

People do not, however, always act consistently with their potential dignity. We presume that this is why Margolis uses the phrase "moments of dignity": that is, because moments of dignity are times in which people choose to act consistently with what they take "to be of value, and thus worthy of respect, about human beings," sometimes in contrast to the impulses they feel in the context they are in.[12] Dignity occurs in moments when people exercise their distinctively human capacity to live their highest values. This is the distinctive feature of an internally directed state. People feel the dignity within them when they exercise their strength to act for themselves and when they are free from the constraints of self-justification.

Strength

> **RYAN:** During my sophomore year of college, I had an experience that surprised me. It was a Saturday afternoon in the fall. There was a football game. Most of my friends and roommates were going to the game and then to a dance afterward. I wanted to go, but my paper on Shakespeare's play *The Tragedy of King Lear* was due on Monday. I knew that if I did not get it done on Saturday night, it would not get done. I could think of all kinds of justifications for putting the paper off. I imagined ways to try to get the work done anyway if I put it off. Eventually, I went to the library to write the paper. Going to the library felt a lot like getting out of a warm bed on a cold morning to exercise. I did not want to do it, but I knew it was the right thing to do. I set my mind to it and got to work.

Ryan's analogy between physical exercise and doing the right thing when it is difficult suggests that the ability to live one's values is a strength. Christopher Peterson and Martin Seligman, two leaders of the positive psychology movement, made a similar argument in their book *Character Strengths and Virtues: A Handbook and Classification*.[13] Peterson, Seligman, and their colleagues compiled this book as an alternative to books like the American Psychiatric Association's *Diagnostic and Statistical Manual of Mental Disorders*, which focuses exclusively on disease, disorder, and pathology as the primary means for diagnosing the human condition.[14] Peterson and Seligman argue that strengths—which include values such as wisdom, knowledge, courage, humanity, justice, and temperance—are just as diagnostic of the human condition as disease, disorder, and pathology, and that these strengths have not received sufficient attention in psychology. They compiled this classification as a step toward fixing this imbalance.

Character strengths like wisdom, courage, and temperance are enduring traits that people can develop over time. Moments of dignity, in contrast, occur when people use these strengths—especially when their automatic impulse is to act in ways that are not consistent with their values. When Ryan was surrounded by friends going to a football game and a dance, his automatic impulse was to go with them. By making himself go to the library instead, he exercised character strength. He engaged in an act of self-regulation.

Self-regulation is the process of using one's conscious mind to inhibit one's automatic response to the situation and to replace it with a controlled response. Ryan had to use self-regulation to make himself go to the library, Stephen had to use self-regulation to look for the good in his coach, and the participants in Webb and Sheeran's experiment had to use self-regulation to state the color of the ink instead of reading the names of the colors on the cards. In fact, Webb and Sheeran's experiment was inspired by another set of experiments on self-regulation that showed how using self-regulation is like a exercising a muscle: when we exercise a muscle, that muscle gets tired and is weaker when the exercise is complete. If we exercise our muscles regularly, though, those muscles get stronger and can do more work before getting tired.

Roy Baumeister and his colleagues provided evidence that self-regulation exercises our brains in the same way that physical activity exercises our muscles.[15] They did this by asking people to eat radishes while sitting in front of a pile of freshly baked chocolate chip cookies, give speeches on topics that were not consistent with their beliefs, suppress emotions, cross out the letter *e* from words in a text, solve anagrams, and watch dull movies. Like Webb and Sheeran, they examined how strong people felt afterward by measuring how long participants persisted in their next activity. Every time the participants used self-regulation, they persisted less than those who did not use self-regulation and reported feeling more tired—just as they would have felt after exercising a muscle. Baumeister and colleagues also conducted experiments in which participants spent two weeks exercising self-regulation by monitoring and improving their posture, regulating their moods, and monitoring and recording their eating. Those who did these exercises performed better in self-regulation activities at the end of the two weeks than they had before the two weeks began. Again, exercising self-regulation was just like exercising a muscle.

Some of the effort required to exercise self-regulation can be mitigated, as Webb and Sheeran's color-naming experiment suggests, by using implementation intentions to retrain our automatic reactions. Even so, the research on implementation intentions suggests that implementations have only a "medium-size" effect on people's behaviors.[16] This means that when the automatic reactions we are trying to replace are weak or only moderately strong, then implementation intentions are usually strong enough to change those reactions with relatively little effort. If we have engaged in the same, strong, automatic reactions for a long time, however, then even if we use implementation intentions we will still need to exercise self-regulation, and probably for quite a while, before our new reactions become automatic.

Self-regulation requires effort, but like physical exercise, it feels good when we are successful. Carl Rogers, one of the most influential clinical psychologists of the twentieth century, recognized this experience in the people he worked with. Rogers spent his career helping patients live lives that were more consistent with their deeply held values and with the emotions they experienced, whether those emotions were positive or negative. He wanted to help people be honest with themselves so that they could experience an authentic life. When people achieved consistency among their emotions, values, and actions, he called it "congruence." He studied congruence (or the lack thereof) in people's everyday experiences as well as in his patients. He said that when people achieved congruence, they felt a "sense of strength which is experienced in being a unique person, responsible for oneself." When we recognize that "I am the one who chooses," it is an invigorating experience.[17]

Freedom

Rogers also observed that when we achieve congruence, we experience freedom from the justifications that keep us from living our values. If we could live with such integrity, he said,

> We would be much more comfortable, because we would have nothing to hide.
> We could focus on the problem at hand, rather than spending our energies to prove we are moral or consistent.
> We could use all of our creative imagination in solving the problem, rather than in defending ourselves.
> We could openly advance both our selfish interests, and our sympathetic concerns for others, and let these conflicting desires find the balance which is acceptable to us as a people.
> We could freely change and grow in our leadership position, because we would not be bound by rigid concepts of what we have been, must be, or ought to be.[18]

This is the freedom that comes when we identify the values that are important to us, critique ourselves on how well we are living those values, and act out a new, value-driven story with a plot, a moral, and truth.

An example of the kind of freedom Rogers describes can be seen in Oprah Winfrey's decision to apologize for a call she made to Larry King on *Larry King Live*.[19] Oprah called King to defend the endorsement she gave to James Frey's book *A Million Little Pieces*. After Oprah publicly endorsed the book, a Web site named *The Smoking Gun* published evidence that much of Frey's book, which he had published as a memoir of his life, was actually fictional. King hosted Frey on his show after *The Smoking Gun* published its exposé, and while he was interviewing Frey, Oprah called in. Instead of admitting that her endorsement was a mistake, she justified it, saying that the publisher should have done more to check the facts and that the message of the book still resonated with her, even if the story was not true.

What happened next was remarkable and unusual. Oprah devoted an entire show to apologizing for her telephone call to Larry King. Some people have expressed skepticism about Oprah's motives for doing this. We probably cannot ever find conclusive evidence to say that she was not at least partially pressured into it. But even if she received some pressure to apologize, very few people have ever said the words "I was wrong" and "I am deeply sorry" on national television. Research on cognitive dissonance suggests that once people start justifying their actions, they are more likely to continue justifying their actions than to apologize and to change. Erika James, our energizing colleague mentioned in chapter 4, studies how leaders handle crises. She has told us that when leaders find themselves in crises of their own making, experts tell them over and over that if they want to recover they must admit their mistakes, but few of them ever do. At least some of Oprah's decision to apologize had to have been her own, and she is relatively unique among public figures—if not among all of us—for doing it.

Two other comments that Oprah made on this show are also important to see how free people feel when they experience an internally directed state. First, when she confronted Frey, she said, "It is difficult for me to talk to you, because I really feel duped." Then, toward the end of the show, when a visitor on the show told her that "the hardest thing to do is to admit a mistake," Oprah replied, "It really wasn't that hard." This is an interesting change, and one that anyone who has had to apologize can recognize. When we first apologize, it often seems daunting. We feel embarrassed and foolish, and admitting our mistakes seems hard. Then, after we do it, we are surprised at how easy it was. The difficulty of apologizing disappears because we experience the freedom that Rogers described: we have nothing more to hide and no need to defend ourselves. We are free to live in a more complex, nuanced, and richer way.

The Influence of an Internally Directed State

Stephen was like Oprah in her decision to apologize on television and like Ryan in his decision to go to the library. By looking for the good in his coach, Stephen exercised self-regulation rather than giving in to the temptation to focus on what was wrong with his coach, thereby increasing his strength of character. By acknowledging that his hate was inconsistent with his values, Stephen freed himself from the justifications that were holding him captive to destructive feelings and actions. As a result, he experienced the strength and freedom that come in moments of dignity. He lifted himself, in Rogers' words, with the "sense of strength which is experienced in being a unique person." He was more comfortable. He was more focused on, and creative with, the issue at hand. He was growing. And he was beginning to advance his interests.

Stephen also lifted his team, advancing their interests as well. He made the decision to forgive his coach as his basketball team was winding down its regular season. At this point, his team was following the same pattern it had in all of its previous years under Stephen's coach: even though the team had won eleven of its first twelve games, negativity and frustration eventually took over. The team won only two of its last eight games. Players were going through the motions, exerting little effort for the team, and waiting for the season to end. But this year, something different happened.

One of the assistant coaches called a "players only" meeting. He asked if any of the players wanted to express their feelings. The room was quiet. Then, to the surprise of everyone—including himself—Stephen stood up. His was internally directed because of his decision to forgive his coach: he was free from worry about what people would think, he had the strength to challenge his teammates, and he spoke with dignity. He talked about the potential of the team and what it could do in the state tournament. He talked about how hard he worked, even though he got hardly any playing time. And then he told them, "I could live with that if the people who get playing time were also working hard." He expressed his honest feelings about how he struggled with the people who were not working hard for the team, and asked them to start playing hard.

Stephen's teammates were riveted to his words. They all committed to work. Their team won the first game of the district tournament. The second game was tight. In the second quarter, the coach put Stephen in. He had five steals, four points, and a few assists in only a few minutes. The team won the game handily and went on to win the district and regional championships. In the first game of the state tournament, Stephen's team lost a close game to a team that was ranked thirteenth in the country. Stephen's influence on his team illustrates how an internally directed state influences others by elevating them, calming them, and increasing their effectiveness.

Elevation

Stephen's story of telling his teammates to work harder is similar in many ways to a story that Kurt, an engineer, wrote in a study conducted by Monica Worline and her colleagues.[20] Kurt and his team were developing a new product for their company. Other employees kept asking Kurt's team to add features to the product. Eventually, Kurt's manager took a stand. He said that he would not let any new features creep into the product. Many employees, including the "war team" and the manager's boss, were unhappy with the manager and tried to force him to add features. Kurt's manager knew, however, that the product would not ship on time if they added more features, and that this was more important to the company than the features themselves, so he held his ground. Kurt thought his manager was courageous. He respected his manager and said that since seeing this, he has tried to take a stronger stand whenever he believed it was the right thing to do.

After collecting and analyzing dozens of stories like Kurt's, Worline and her colleagues found that when people observe courageous action it affects their beliefs about what they can do, their relationships, and their understanding of their groups. Kurt saw himself as more capable of taking action that he might have been scared to take previously. He had more respect for his manager. And he was more committed to doing what was right for his organization.

The kind of impact that Kurt's test manager had on Kurt occurs when people observe any action that they think is virtuous. When we see virtuous action, we tend to experience an emotion that Jonathan Haidt, a psychologist from the University of Virginia, calls "elevation."[21] Elevation involves a warm, open feeling in the chest and a desire to live one's values more fully. Haidt's research suggests that people feel elevated when they see virtuous action (in person or in videos), when they remember it, and when they read about it in books. His interviews with people from other countries suggest that this is true in countries around the world.

One reason, then, why people in an internally directed state tend to lift others is that they tend to act in ways that are consistent with their highest values. When they do, and other people see those actions, it inspires the others to want to do the same.

Calmness

Our actions can inspire others when we are internally directed, and our emotions can calm them. Consider the story of Oprah Winfrey, for example. After apologizing, she became internally directed. What seemed hard before ("It is difficult for me to talk to you") became easy ("It really wasn't that hard"). She was stronger and freer. The tension she felt went away and she became calm. In Carl Rogers's words, she felt comfortable because she had nothing to hide or defend. The comfort and calm we feel in an internally directed state can be contagious. Also, if we are calm and comfortable in a situation in which people expect us to be tense, they need to make sense of our emotions. If we are serene in such situations, we are often, in Rogers's words, "less feared, because others [are] less inclined to suspect what lies behind the façade."[22] They are comfortable around us because we are comfortable and because we have nothing to hide from them.

Effectiveness

We also tend to be more effective when we are internally directed. For example, Kennon Sheldon and Andrew Elliott found that college students who set goals that were consistent with their personal interests and core values performed better on those goals than on goals that were not consistent.[23] Walter Mischel and his colleagues gave marshmallows to preschool children and told them that if they did not eat them for a few minutes they would get more marshmallows. The preschoolers who regulated their marshmallow-eating performed better in academics, had better social skills, and coped better with problems years later.[24] There is even some evidence to suggest that businesses that employ virtuous practices might outperform businesses that do not.[25] Again, Carl Rogers provides us with an explanation for this: if people do not feel that they have to hide or defend their actions, they can devote their creative energies to the activities at hand.

The effectiveness of people in an internally directed state has an impact similar to that of people in purpose-centered states. When a person performs effectively, other people notice. The actions of the effective person are seen as more legitimate, and people want to participate in and learn from the effectiveness they see.

We can see the influence of effectiveness, calmness, and elevation in Stephen's interactions with his teammates. After Stephen forgave his coach, he focused his creative energies on improving his basketball skills. His teammates could see his skills at work, and this increased effectiveness gave him greater legitimacy. When Stephen confronted his teammates about their own lack of effort, they knew that Stephen had more reason to be angry with the coach than almost any of them, and yet Stephen was not using the coach as an excuse. His words were consistent with his actions and they were elevated by his integrity. They could sense that Stephen had no agenda to hide and nothing to be defensive about. His calmness helped them be calm. They stopped reacting to their coach and began to be internally directed themselves. They elevated their own effectiveness and performed exceptionally in the state tournament.

When Internal Direction Is Unappealing

An internally directed state is a moment of dignity in which people experience the freedom and strength to act in ways that are consistent with their values. People are likely to experience a moment of dignity if they ask and answer the question "What would my story be if I were living the values I expect of others?" This question helps people become internally directed because it helps them identify values that matter to them, critique the degree to which they are living those values, and act out an honest story that lives the values. In a moment of dignity people feel calm, unconflicted, and eager to invest their creative energies in the issues at hand. Their calm emotions and virtuous and effective actions elevate others, help others feel comfortable, and inspire others to participate in their efforts.

Our description of how people lift others when they are in an internally directed state paints a positive picture of the process, and the process *is* usually a positive one. There are exceptions, however, and even if the decision to become internally directed has many benefits, it can be difficult or painful at the outset. When people are in an externally directed state, the idea of saying "I was wrong and I am sorry" seldom looks appealing.

The longer we have been externally directed, the more we have justified our beliefs and the more difficult and undesirable it will be for us to admit we are wrong. If Julie (the businesswoman in chapter 5 who was afraid to speak up) cried for an entire afternoon when she realized that people thought her contribution was valuable, then imagine how hard it is for people who have to admit that they caused pain to others, or who are likely to get punished, expelled, fired, or sued if they admit they are wrong. The consequences for most admissions of error will seldom be as daunting as getting fired or sued, but even so, admissions of error can still be quite difficult for people to make. Fortunately, admitting our mistakes strengthens us, frees us, and increases our dignity as well.

Becoming internally directed can be just as hard for others as it is for us. This is why some people are not lifted when we are internally directed. Although most people feel elevated when they see others live their values, there are plenty of examples throughout history of people who demean, ostracize, hurt, or even kill others who are striving to live their values (such as Mahatma Gandhi or Abraham Lincoln). This does not mean that the influence of the person who is living his or her values is not positive. More likely, it means that the people who respond negatively to such a person are so steeped in their justifications for their own behavior, and so afraid of admitting that they are justifications, that they would rather demean, ostracize, hurt, or kill a person who is living his or her values than admit that their actions have been wrong and that they are sorry.

The fact that people might harm us for trying to live our values could dissuade us from trying. This is another reason we need a compelling story for living our values. In addition to helping us see how we should live our values and giving us reasons for living those values, stories also take on a life of their own. People who change the world in small or large ways are willing to risk harm for the sake of their story. They care more about creating and sustaining their story of a moral world than they are about their own comfort, prosperity, or life. If the story they are trying to tell lives on, they will have given a greater gift to the world than they would have if they had chosen to live below their highest values.

Other problems could also arise if we focus only on being internally directed. For example, what if a person values hurtful or destructive things? What if people do not know how to live their values in constructive ways? Or what if people focus on only one value and exclude other values? It is because of possibilities like these that people also need to be other-focused, externally directed, and purpose-centered to experience *lift*. For example, if people are other-focused, they feel empathy toward the people they influence and do not want to hurt them. If people are externally open, they want to learn how to live their values in more effective ways. And if people are purpose-centered, they have a clear view of what the situation is and are better able to judge which values are relevant to managing the situation well. Internal direction lifts us to higher levels of integrity, but integrity alone is not enough. Well-designed wings would not make an airplane fly without air, an engine, and a control system as well.

➤ Practices for Applying the Principles of Lift

When people want to become internally directed, they often struggle to recognize their automatic tendencies, have trouble coming up with concrete stories to tell, and give up their self-justifications. The following practices can help:

1. **Ask.** Other people often have less trouble recognizing habits that prevent you from living your values than you do. Choose someone who spends time with you regularly, and ask this person for honest feedback. You could let this person write the answers to you if they have trouble giving feedback directly. You can also use the assessment at http://apps.leadingwithlift.com/assess to collect systematic data on your tendencies.

2. **Find people who model the values you want to live and spend time with them.** This can provide learning opportunities and inspiration to help with your effort.

3. **Recite the mantra "No excuses."** Self-justification is so common and so habitual that it can be useful just to tell yourself "No excuses!" any time you make a decision. Signs with these words on the desk, the bathroom mirror, the refrigerator, the computer, the car dashboard, and other places can also help.

4. **Future perfect storytelling.** If it is hard to create a story about living your values, try starting at the end of the story. Imagine a title for a newspaper article or an entry in a diary (your own or someone else's) that describes the goal you have accomplished. Imagine what the article or entry has to say about what you did to live your values as you pursued this purpose.

Seeing Others as Objects

BOB: One day during my childhood, my stepfather sent me to the corner store to buy milk. I moved slowly along the sidewalk, basking in the sun and using the curb as an imaginary tightrope. Just before I reached the store, I heard a blast in the sky. I saw a thick, white trail of smoke, and followed it to find the lowest-flying jet I had ever seen. I watched for several seconds as the plane moved toward the horizon. The wings fell off and the airplane disintegrated into nothingness. I stood, frozen, then turned toward home. I raced up the porch steps, burst through the front door, and blurted out my story. My stepfather scoffed at me and asked, "Where's the milk?" Most of my early memories of my stepfather are like the memory of my failure to get the milk from the corner store. He criticized me often and, over time, I hardened.

Years later, when I was a father and Ryan was a baby, I was playing with Ryan on the floor. Suddenly I felt a wave of jealousy. I was surprised, and stopped to reflect. I realized that I was jealous of Ryan because he had what I did not have—a father who loved him for who he was, who cared about his feelings, needs, and desires. Ryan was not an object to me, but a human being that I treasured for his own sake. I wished that I had experienced the same thing.

The contrast between seeing other people as objects—as Bob's stepfather saw him—and seeing others as unique and valued human beings—as Bob saw Ryan—was captured by a philosopher named Martin Buber.[1] Buber wrote that human beings experience two psychological states with regard to other people. On one hand, other people can be objects to us, fitting or not fitting into our agendas and keeping us from or helping us get what we want. Buber suggests that if we feel this way about a person, that person becomes an "It" to us. We call this psychological state "self-focused." On the other hand, if we experience another person as a human being, whom we value and empathize with, then that person is not an "It" to us but a "You" or a "Thou." We say this psychological state is "other-focused." Self-focused and other-focused states are temporary experiences, but as we will explain, temporary experiences can have powerful consequences.

Empathy

Psychologists have studied self-focused and other-focused states. For example, Daniel Batson conducted a number of experiments to examine whether human beings are capable of caring for others for no other reason than just to care, or if humans care for others only as a means to achieve their own ends.[2] This is an important question because almost all research in the social sciences—psychology, economics, political science, sociology, and anthropology—is grounded in some way in the assumption that human beings are motivated by self-interest.

Batson argued that if people help others for self-interested reasons—for example, if they help people who are in pain because they want to stop the pain that they feel when they see others' pain, or if they help people because they enjoy the satisfaction they get from having helped someone—then they would avoid helping other people if they can get those same benefits in a way that is easier than helping. If people care for the sake of caring, however, then they would help others even if there are easier options for getting satisfaction or reducing pain.

To test this hypothesis, Batson conducted experiments in which he presented participants with other people who were in distressing situations. When participants in the experiments encountered the distressed people, they could either help them or choose a second option, such as escaping the situation easily, gaining benefits through other methods besides helping, and so forth. Through all his experiments, Batson kept trying to find alternative motivations for people to help, rather than empathic caring alone. In each situation, though, people continued to help. The accumulating evidence from these experiments led Batson to conclude that when people feel empathy, they feel for the other person and care for the sake of caring alone. Empathy, then, is more than just "enlightened self-interest." It is an experience of feeling others' emotions that makes us capable of caring for others. This capacity, however, is fragile and can be quickly lost, which is one reason why social scientists' predictions of human behavior based on self-interest are accurate so much of the time.

Empathy is a characteristic of an other-focused psychological state, but it is also more. When Buber described the self-focused and the other-focused states, he did so using the terms "I-It" and "I-Thou." He placed the hyphen between the two words to illustrate the fact that who we are is tangled up with, and cannot be separated from, who others are. If we see others as human beings, so that we share their feelings, need their needs to be fulfilled, and want to understand their perspectives, then we not only mourn with their losses, help when they need help, and celebrate their victories with them, but we also become secure, calm, trusting, engaged, selfless, considerate, kind, or helpful. Similarly, if we see others as objects, then we not only treat them as objects, but we also tend to become insecure, tense, controlling, aloof, selfish, reactive, lonely, suspicious, or defensive. The way we are toward others lifts others up or weighs them down as much as it lifts us up or weighs us down.

Fluid Dynamics

The ideas that other people lift us up or weigh us down because of our own psychological states, and that our psychological states lift up or weigh down the people around us, are similar to the relationship between an airplane wing and the air it flies through. The Wright brothers learned about this relationship by reading about the work of scientists who studied fluids. Fluids are liquids and gases, like water and air.

The scientist whose discovery was most important to understanding how fluids make lift possible was Daniel Bernoulli.[3] Bernoulli studied fluids 177 years before the Wright brothers flew their first powered airplane. He was working as a professor of mathematics at the Imperial Academy in St. Petersburg. He was interested in William Harvey's research on how the heart moves blood through the body, so he began to use mathematics to study the movement of fluids.

Fluids are made up of molecules that are only weakly attracted to each other. Because this attraction is weak, fluid molecules move relatively freely within space. This means that fluids take the same shape as the containers that hold them. In contrast, the attraction between molecules in solid objects is strong, so solid objects usually retain the same shape no matter what container they may be in.

Bernoulli used mathematics to study the relationship between the speed and the pressure of blood flowing in the body. To do this, he poked a hole in a horizontal pipe and put a straw, pointing upward, in the hole. When a liquid, like water, passed through the pipe, some of the water would go up the straw. Bernoulli measured how far the water went up the straw. He discovered that he could use this measurement to calculate the pressure of the water in the pipe. In fact, because of this discovery, physicians all over Europe began to measure blood pressure by sticking pointed glass tubes into people's arteries to see how far the blood would rise. (It was many decades later before scientists found a less painful way to measure blood pressure.)

Bernoulli was less interested in measuring blood pressure than he was in understanding the laws of fluid motion. He knew that the energy in his pipe-and-straw system did not change. Water molecules need energy to exert pressure and to flow quickly through a pipe. Thus, when Bernoulli compared the speed and the pressure of the water, he realized that the pressure must go up for the speed to go down and the pressure must go down for the speed to go up.

This relationship between pressure and speed helps us understand how fluid molecules can lift a solid object up. When a solid object (like the wing of an airplane) encounters a fluid (like air) flowing in the opposite direction, the solid object turns the fluid molecules: some of the molecules flow over the wing, and some of the molecules flow under the wing. Whichever way the molecules go, however, they remain in contact with the wing's surface. If the shape and angle of the wing turns the air in the right way, then the air molecules that go under the wing will go slower than the molecules that go under the wing. As a result, the slower molecules underneath the wing will exert more pressure on the wing than the molecules on top. The pressure on the bottom will push the wing up. This upward pressure is called lift.

With Bernoulli's discovery, the Wright brothers knew that their wings needed to turn the air molecules to generate more pressure below the wings than above them. Similarly, Buber's work suggests that if people "turn" their psychological states to empathize with people, they can lift themselves and others. Like a wing moving through the air, we constantly influence others and are influenced by them in return. We cannot stop influencing or being influenced. We can, however, choose what kind of influence we want to be. If we are in an other-focused state, we are like wings that turn the air to create more pressure on the bottom than on the top. We generate *lift*. This is what Bob did as he played with Ryan. If we are in a self-focused state, we are like wings that turn the air to create more pressure on top than on bottom. We generate no *lift*. This is what Bob's stepfather did when he scoffed at Bob for not getting the milk. To learn how to become other-focused, it is useful to first understand how we become self-focused.

Self-Focus

RYAN: One day at work, I was in a rush to get to my next appointment. As I walked down the hallway, I passed a woman who looked dejected. For a moment I felt I should stop and ask how she was doing. As soon as that feeling emerged, I had a slew of thoughts such as "I'm in a hurry. She can be pretty negative. And talkative too. If I stop to listen I'll get bogged down and depressed. I really need to get a lot done today." I wavered for a moment, but when we passed each other in the hallway I only said "Hello." I felt guilty for a moment, but I kept walking to my appointment.

This interaction, which lasted only a few moments and may seem inconsequential, is actually a rich description of how Ryan chose (and how most of us choose) to be self-focused rather than other-focused. It illustrates how we regularly send and receive emotional messages to and from each other without realizing we are doing it. It also illustrates how our emotions and actions invite others to act empathically in small or large ways.

Emotional Invitations

When Ryan passed the woman in the hallway, her facial expression, gait, and other emotional cues acted like an invitation: Ryan felt an impulse to show her empathy. We can see why Ryan felt this way when we learn about research that William Hutchinson and his colleagues conducted.[4] Hutchinson and his colleagues are neuroscientists. They used microelectrodes and an fMRI machine to study how neurons in their participants' brains registered pain.[5] During the procedure, the scientists provided the participants with sensations such as hot, cold, a pinprick, or a basic touch. One of the neurons they observed responded only to mechanical stimulation, like a pinprick. The scientists also observed, however, that when they pricked themselves, and their participants watched the pinprick, the same neuron fired, as if the patient had been pricked instead of the scientist.

Neuroscientists have observed similar neurons and effects in other studies. For example, some neuroscientists flashed pictures of angry faces on a television screen for people who were participating in their experiments. The angry faces were replaced so quickly by faces with no emotional expression that the participants' conscious minds did not realize that the angry faces had appeared. Meanwhile, the neuroscientists observed what happened in the participants' brains.[6] Even though the participants did not know that they had seen angry faces, a part of their brain that processes emotion mimicked the emotion that participants saw in the angry faces. Scientists have also conducted similar studies focusing on emotions like fear and happiness.[7]

Research like this suggests that emotional expressions (like anger) and emotional experiences (like pinpricks) do more than just communicate a person's emotions to an observer. Because we tend to mimic each other's emotions, emotions and emotional experiences can also be seen as invitations for observers to empathize with, or even to participate in, another person's inner life and experience. We seldom intend to send others emotional invitations. At least initially, emotions are usually unconscious reactions.[8] But even though emotions usually emerge unintentionally, they nevertheless act like invitations—invitations to participate in the emotional bonds that human beings share with each other to greater or lesser extents. In other words, when Ryan passed the dejected woman in the hallway at work, her emotions sent him an invitation that empathic neurons in his brain were inclined to respond to, but that he chose to ignore.

Adding Nuance to Empathy

When Ryan passed the woman in the hallway, he felt an impulse to ask her how she was feeling. He does not, however, feel that way every time he sees this woman, every time he sees a dejected person, or every time he sees this particular woman looking dejected. Sometimes he does, and sometimes he does not. What makes the difference?

Many neurons in our brain incline us to mimic the emotions we see in others. If all our brains ever did was reflect the feelings of others, though, then all we would do when we see sadness is get sad. All we would do when we see anger is get angry. And all we would do when we see happiness is feel happy. Human empathy is actually much more complex.

When we see sadness, we may feel sad, but depending on the situation, we may also feel curious or even bemused. When we see anger we may get angry, but we may also feel fear (if we think the person might try to hurt us in some way), surprise (if we did not expect that person to get angry), or even pleasure (if we were trying to anger him or her). If we see someone who is happy, we may feel happy, but we may also feel sad (if we wanted something else to happen), grateful (if we were uncertain how the situation would unfold), or indifferent (if the person is happy about something that we do not care about). Our responses to others' emotions will not always be empathic, and even when they are, that empathy can take different forms.

Humans develop more complex empathic responses over time because we use our experience to develop mental models of how the world works. We are often unaware of our mental models, but as we act, observe, and receive instruction, we develop models that enable us to notice more cues and to respond in more nuanced ways.[9] Thus, if we see people frowning (like the woman Ryan saw at work) we may experience different emotions or feel inclined to take different actions. Depending on our mental models, our reactions may take into account our history, the location, the time of day, the type of frowns on their faces, other nonverbal expressions, any words they may happen to say, the direction in which they are walking, or countless other cues in our context. As a result, we may feel inclined to talk to some people, to give other people their space, to offer a sympathetic smile, to give a hug, to inquire further, or to engage in any number of other responses.

When humans communicate effectively, we do so because we do not rely only on the focal message that is being sent in any given moment. We also read the other cues that are relevant to the situation, like history, location, expressions, actions, and so forth.[10] Our brains use mental models automatically to label and react to these cues, adding nuance to our empathy.[11] Mental models can even enable us to feel empathy for people who are not present. Brain imaging studies show, for example, that when we imagine how others might be feeling, our brains activate the same circuits they activate when we reflect on our own feelings.[12]

When Ryan passed the woman in the hallway, the feeling he had was unique, specific to that situation in that moment. He worried that it would be time consuming if he had to ask her how she was doing and listen to her problems, but the truth was that it would not take that long, she does not always need people to stop and listen, and Ryan does not feel an empathic need to talk to her every time he sees her. Most of the time, it is sufficient to wave, say hello, or smile.

The unconscious invitations for empathy that we receive from others throughout each day are seldom very demanding. When they are demanding—if there has been personal tragedy or a major struggle—we may need to put more time and effort into our empathy, or we may need to use the other lift questions to help us temper our response in a way that is manageable, but still empathic. The unconscious invitations Ryan perceived as he passed the woman in the hallway were not demanding, though. His justifications were only excuses. His choice to ignore the impulse he felt to empathize with her was exactly that—a choice.

Self-Betrayal

The choice to ignore our impulses to act empathically is more than a lost opportunity. According to Terry Warner, a philosopher, it is also an act of self-betrayal.[13] Warner calls it this because we hurt ourselves when we make that choice. We hurt ourselves because our inaction requires justification, as discussed in chapter 5, and our justifications turn us into insecure, tense, aloof, selfish, suspicious, defensive people.

To see how our justifications for ignoring the impulses we feel to empathize with others makes us insecure, selfish, defensive, and so forth, consider the justifications that Ryan used with the woman in the hallway. Ryan justified ignoring this woman's feelings by labeling her as negative, talkative, and depressing. In other words, Ryan blamed her for his lack of empathy. And by blaming her for his lack of empathy, he also made himself into a victim—her victim. He was a victim of her negativity, her long-winded descriptions, and her depressing stories. Ryan chose to ignore her feelings, and justified it by blaming her for victimizing him.

By blaming his co-worker, Ryan made himself insecure (a victim who can be taken advantage of), tense (touchy about his justifications), aloof (giving this woman only the slightest acknowledgement), selfish (caring only about his own wants and needs), suspicious (of what she might do to take advantage of him), and defensive (of his justifications). His co-worker invited him to be empathic, helpful, secure, calm, selfless, open, and kind, but Ryan, without realizing it, decided to become insecure, tense, aloof, selfish, suspicious, and defensive. He betrayed himself.

This is a frightening idea. It suggests that if someone else has a bad day and needs someone to listen for a few moments, we can use that person's needs as an impetus to turn ourselves into victims and him or her into our oppressor. More frightening still is the fact that Ryan's interaction with the woman in the hallway is a relatively minor incident within the realm of possible ways in which people can betray themselves.

Self-betrayal can have major as well as minor consequences on both the lives of people who betray themselves and others. One reason why it can have major consequences is that justifications, like the ones we use to betray ourselves, tend to escalate our commitment to act in particular ways. Barry Staw and his colleagues found this, for example, in a study of loan officers, who have to justify why they give loans to some people and not to others.[14] Loan officers, they found, have to justify why they should trust their clients. When new evidence suggests that a client will not be able to pay off the loan, loan officers often rely on their old justifications rather than on the new evidence. Each time officers fail to write off a loan, they have to justify it further, which makes it harder for them to be convinced by new disconfirming evidence and more likely to fail to write off the loan the next time. Their commitment to keep acting the same way escalates further and further.

Self-betrayal works in this same way. The longer it takes for us to recognize and put an end to our self-betrayal, the more committed we become to our self-betrayal and the harder it becomes for us to stop. When Bob came running in the house to tell his family about the airplane that exploded in the sky, for example, it was a wonderful opportunity for empathy. Here was a child who was excited and would have flourished if a parent had joined in the excitement by listening to the story with rapt attention or by coming outside to see. Instead, Bob's stepfather ignored any impulse he may have felt to empathize. All he could see was Bob's failure to get the milk—a justification that blamed Bob and made his stepfather a victim of Bob's incompetence and negligence. It justified his stepfather's self-betrayal and gave him more reasons to continue acting that way in the future. As a result, he was defensive, aloof, angry, and insecure in his relationship with Bob, causing rifts in the family that took years to heal. Blame and victimization go on and on whenever commitment to self-betrayal escalates, making families dysfunctional, damaging careers, dividing communities, and poisoning organizations.

Anguished Relationships

Imagine that you work in an organization's product-development unit. You keep in touch with your customers, and you have shown throughout your career that you have a pretty good feel for the kind of products your customers want. One day, you come up with an exciting new idea that you present to your boss. You think this idea has the potential to make millions of dollars for the organization. Your boss shows no discernable emotions as he listens to you. When you finish, he hesitates for a fraction of a second, and then, in a flat tone of voice, says, "That sounds like it could be a good idea. Why don't you look into it and see what kind of investment you can come up with." How do you feel after hearing your boss respond?

Our Inability to Hide Our Self-Betrayal

Most people would feel rather deflated after getting a response like this from their boss. As discussed in chapter 4, we tend to feel energized when the people we interact with express the same emotions we feel and de-energized when they express different emotions.[15] This is particularly true when we are excited or want to celebrate something. Shelly Gable and her colleagues, for example, studied people in committed relationships and found that when participants failed to share the excitement that their partners felt over positive events, it did more damage to their relationships than the failure to empathize with their partners over negative events.[16] Human beings need to connect with each other on an emotional level.

In the previous example where you approach your boss with an exciting idea, there may, however, be more going on than a lack of emotion. For instance, what if your boss actually thinks that your idea might be a good one? Perhaps he feels an impulse to share your excitement with you, but he also feels fear because your idea is somewhat radical. Pursuing your idea would require the product-development unit to take significant risks and to develop new capabilities, and he is afraid to tell you that he is afraid. So instead of getting excited, and instead of confiding his fears to you, he betrays himself. In his mind, he blames you for taking up his time and wanting to do crazy things. He does not want to say this out loud, though. Instead, he tries to hide his feelings. He suppresses his emotion and suggests that you could look for investment, but does not offer to invest in your idea himself.

In this scenario, you would probably feel more than just deflated. Your boss is not just lacking emotion, he is actually suppressing emotion. Emotional reactions, like the anger, fear, resentment, or worry that come with blame and victimization, are automatic and unconscious reactions. It takes effort to suppress them. In fact, the attempt to suppress emotion spurs repetitive thoughts about the emotion, making slips in our effort likely.[17] And when we slip, showing what we really feel, even if it is only for a fraction of a second, other people pick up on those emotions. They may not pick up on them consciously. As we saw earlier, when scientists showed angry faces to their participants for only a few milliseconds, the participants' unconscious minds detected and mimicked that anger, even though they did not realize it.[18] We may not be aware of it, but we feel and react to other people's emotions as we interact with them. As a result, when we blame people in our minds, our accusations often come through, consciously or unconsciously. Blame can damage our relationships even when we try to suppress it. In fact, research shows that suppressed negative feelings can inhibit the development of new relationships as well as strain our ongoing ones.[19]

Self-betrayal, then, can harm our relationships with others even when we try to hide our emotions—even when we try to "make" ourselves do the "right" thing. If we do and say what we think the right things are, but we do them in a self-focused way, our self-focused, blaming feelings seep out nonetheless, and our relationships suffer.

How Self-Betrayal Becomes Appealing

If self-betrayal hurts others and us, then why do we engage in it? In answering this question, it is important to remember that self-betrayal is a choice. If we feel an invitation to empathize, we have an option to respond to that invitation or to ignore it. We do not have to betray ourselves (or others). And if we do betray ourselves, we are responsible for that choice. If we do not acknowledge that we are capable of choice and responsible for our actions, then we are likely to continue to think of ourselves as victims and to remain in our self-focused state.

Although it is important to remember that self-betrayal is a choice, there are also some circumstances that make it harder to respond to the unconscious invitations that others send us to show them empathy. In particular, the degree to which others have empathized with us has a strong influence on how easy or hard it is for us to respond to the invitations to show the empathy we feel. If people failed to provide us with the empathy we needed in the past, or fail to provide us with the empathy we need in a current situation, it becomes harder to provide empathy to others. Accumulating research suggests that the need to feel that we belong—which is a feeling that comes when others empathize with us—is a fundamental human need.[20] When people do not show us the empathy we need, we usually feel hurt or offended.

> **RYAN:** Early in our marriage as my wife, Amy, and I tried to make ends meet, Amy would often figure out clever ways to rearrange our budget so that we could afford to buy things, like a new piece of furniture. In many of these cases, she found clever solutions. If I were empathizing with her, I would have listened closely to her explanation and celebrated her idea with her. Unfortunately, I often failed to do this. I was uptight about our finances and distracted by other things. In those moments, Amy usually withdrew, feeling less inclined to show empathy to me or the children until she recovered from my lack of empathy.

Amy (like the rest of us) has a tendency to be offended or to hurt when people do not show empathy in appropriate moments. Naomi Eisenberger and her colleagues, for example, studied the brain activity of people who were excluded from participating in social activities.[21] Excluding the study participants from social activities, where they could engage in empathic interaction with others, activated the same part of their brains that gets activated when we experience physical pain. Our self-focus can inflict pain on others.

When we feel pain, we tend to focus on ourselves: negative emotions demand our attention so that we will try to relieve our pain.[22] And, if we are focused on ourselves, it is hard to feel empathy for other people. When Ryan's self-betrayal hurt Amy, Amy felt a need to focus on her pain rather than on others. In other words, when we betray ourselves, we invite others to betray themselves as well. Mark Leary and his colleagues found this in their research on hurt feelings: when our feelings are hurt, our most common reactions are, in order, (1) anger, (2) arguing and defending ourselves, (3) telling the offenders that they have hurt our feelings, and (4) countering with a nasty remark. We often use more than one of these responses. In the long run, our relationships are often weakened temporarily or permanently and we worry that they will be hurt again. We also worry about what others think of us, experience a decrease in our self-esteem, and sometimes even experience recurring hurt feelings.[23]

The long-term impacts of self-betrayal and self-focus can be more powerful than the short-term impacts. Research on childhood relationships, for example, suggests that children need empathic interactions with their caregivers to develop a secure base from which they can venture forth to explore life's possibilities and develop constructive relationships.[24] When people do not develop secure bases, or have weaknesses in their secure bases, those weaknesses surface later in life as insecurities, preoccupations, or dysfunctions that make it harder for them to respond well to the invitations for empathy that others unconsciously send them. As a result, self-focus becomes a habitual response for them in certain types of situations.

Collusion

If one person's self-betrayal invites another person to self-betrayal, then self-focus has the potential to spread like a disease. The social impact of self-betrayal can be devastating. We can see this in our previous example of the interaction between a boss and an employee in a product-development unit. This example was inspired by a true story.

The product-development story is a story about two colleagues of ours, Joe and Micah. One day, Joe came up with a new idea for a product that could possibly have made the organization millions of dollars. Joe proposed this idea to Micah. We do not know exactly how the original conversation went, but we know that Micah suggested that Joe's idea was not worth investing in. Joe felt blame in Micah's response: instead of empathy or consideration, Joe had the impression that Micah thought he was being a bother.

Joe was hurt, and responded by betraying himself. He told his friends and co-workers that Micah was an idiot with no foresight and a poor manager. Joe may have been at least partially right, but by doing this, he was blaming Micah, making himself into a victim, damaging the relationship further, and spreading his self-betrayal to others in the organization.

Although Micah was not willing to invest in Joe's idea himself, he left open the possibility that Joe could try to get other people to invest in the idea, so Joe talked to people in other organizations about his ideas. Some people were interested, and Joe told Micah about it.

When Micah found out that Joe was getting investment from other organizations, he accused Joe of acting against the interests of their own organization. He told others that Joe was seeking investment outside the organization. Joe and Micah made more and more accusations against each other. Some people in the organization took sides. Others avoided these discussions. The cycle goes on today. Joe and Micah have a miserable relationship. The workplace has been poisoned. The organization lost the opportunity to make millions of dollars from Joe's idea (other organizations have since come up with similar ideas and begun implementing them), and the poisoning of the workplace continues to undermine other opportunities as well.

The story of Joe and Micah illustrates how self-betrayal can damage organizations, communities, and even financial opportunities in addition to making individuals miserable and corroding relationships. What is particularly scary, though, is how people in these relationships need their partners to continue betraying themselves without realizing it. If we were to ask Joe, for example, if he wanted Micah to accuse him of disloyalty to the company, Joe would say, "Absolutely not!" Joe, however, has made himself into Micah's victim by accusing Micah of being an idiot, of lacking foresight, and of being a bad manager. If Micah were to actually give Joe's idea a chance for internal investment, Joe would either have to admit that Micah is not so bad, or he would have to find another way to maintain his victimhood. Joe, however, has been so public and explicit about his victimhood that he, like the loan officers who could not write off bad loans, is highly committed to it and to his blame. He needs Micah to continue being a bad manager in order to maintain his identity as a victim.

Micah's situation is similar to Joe's. If we asked Micah, he might claim that he wants Joe to focus on the organization's existing products. If Joe stopped pursuing his idea and focused on other products, though, Micah would no longer have a reason to blame Joe and to be a victim. He needs Joe to be "disloyal" so that he can justify his self-betrayal. Our self-betrayal, then, as this story illustrates, does more than invite others to betray themselves. It also provides them with ongoing excuses for betraying themselves. Their self-betrayal, in turn, provides us with ongoing excuses to betray ourselves. It is like we are unconsciously colluding to provide each other with excuses to betray ourselves. This is why Warner—the philosopher who introduced us to the idea of self-betrayal—calls relationships like these "collusions." They are not intentional collusions, like groups of business executives conspiring to fix prices. They are unconscious collusions, where people, without realizing what they are doing, conspire against themselves.

When people participate in collusive relationships, it is often surprising how easily they can say or do just the right thing to get other people to take offense and react with blaming actions of their own. They can do this so easily because people who have betrayed themselves are usually anxious to take offense (even if they do not admit this to themselves). Self-betrayal makes us insecure (waiting for the next attack), defensive (trying to protect ourselves from getting hurt by blaming other people, and, ironically, feeling hurt as a result), and selfish (focusing on our own pain and needs rather than on others'). This is how Bob was in his interactions with his stepfather. His stepfather felt insecure about measuring up to Bob's deceased biological father. To protect himself, he learned to find fault in Bob. Bob, in turn, protected himself by avoiding, undermining, rebelling, and ridiculing. These actions provided more excuses for Bob's stepfather to see himself as a victim and to find fault in Bob. The cycle of collusion went on. If we do not break a cycle like this, it can go on and on, hurting the people involved and the people around them.

The End of Self-Betrayal

Joe and Micah have not yet broken their cycle of collusion. Bob and his stepfather ended their collusion, but only after many years. Bob's stepfather ended his self-betrayal first.

BOB: In my early teenage years, my mother, stepfather, and stepsister went through a religious conversion, joined a new church, and changed their lives in dramatic ways. They attended church actively, served others, quit working on Sundays, and began to live a healthier lifestyle. It was a wonderful decision that magnified the meaningfulness and joy in their lives. Over time, my stepfather even began to make overtures of peace and kindness toward me.

In spite of the wonderful changes that were occurring in their lives, I distrusted their decision and felt embarrassed about those changes. I had spent almost my entire life being treated like an object by my stepfather and treating him as an object in return. He was not a human being to me; he was a threat to my happiness and social survival. I had years of justification to prove it. Now he was treating me like a unique person with intrinsic value. I could not comprehend treating him that way in return. I was committed to seeing him as a bully who was responsible for my problems. I was so bound by my justifications that they had become part of my identity. When he stopped giving me the excuses I needed to be a victim and to blame him for my victimhood, I did not know who I was or how else to act. I needed him to treat me badly so that I could feel good about acting and feeling negatively toward him.

When my stepfather changed, he stopped betraying himself and started trying to empathize with me. I could no longer justify treating him badly because of the way he was treating me. I needed new excuses for blaming him for my troubles. I found one almost immediately. This church my family had joined was an unusual one. Almost no one in our neighborhood belonged to this church, and it was embarrassing that they would join such a weird church. Now I was not only my stepfather's victim—I was a victim of my whole family.

It took a long time for me to begin to see my self-betrayal. It began as I watched my family change. Their lives became increasingly purposeful. I lived with them and saw this every day, so I could not deny it. Also, many of the people who belonged to my family's new church visited our home. I met them, whether I wanted to or not. They were not weird. They were normal people who were trying to live extraordinary lives of love, service, and purpose. Their lives, and the lives of my family, eroded my claim that this church was embarrassing.

As my embarrassment over my family's decision melted away, I stopped blaming them. But I was still not ready to stop betraying myself in my relationship with my stepfather. I was less antagonistic toward him than I had been in the past, but I did not want to trust him or develop a constructive relationship with him. He was hurt, I think, by my unwillingness to forgive him, but he gave me space to work through my feelings. I got married, had children, and he became a good grandfather to my children.

One day I was listening to a speaker who told a story about forgiving his abusive father. I felt as though I were the only person in the room and the speaker was speaking directly to me. He said that the relationship changed when he had an intuition that he should ask his father for help and advice. He did not want to do that, because it would suggest that he respected a man who had hurt him deeply. Eventually, he swallowed his pride and asked his father for help and advice. By doing so, he began to forgive his father and built a loving relationship with him.

As soon as I heard this story, I knew I needed to do the same thing. It was just as hard for me as it was for the man I heard it from. My stepfather was shocked when he received my telephone call, but when I asked him if I could get his help and advice the next time he visited, he treated my request with respect. He even dressed in his best suit when he came. His help and advice was a blessing to me, and I finally reached a point where I could love my stepfather and let him love me. I became other-focused, and being other-focused was a joy. Learning how to become other-focused is what we turn our attention to next.

chapter 8

Becoming Other-Focused

Hugh is a friend of ours who worked as a manager in a research facility at a Fortune 500 company. The company faced a serious recession and threats to its profitability, so the executive team downsized the company from 244,000 employees to 51,000 in only a few years. Hugh and the other remaining employees were shocked, fearful, and uncertain about their future. Most of them became self-focused—a common reaction when people feel threatened. These employees would have benefited from empathizing with each other, but instead some of the employees began saying bad things about each other, sabotaging each other's work, and taking credit for others' successes. Presumably, they did this to make themselves look better than their co-workers. Then, if there was another downsizing, their co-workers would be more likely to lose their jobs than they would.

Once some people began to undermine their co-workers, others did the same things. Some did it to retaliate. Others did it as a preemptive effort to protect themselves. People justified their actions, self-betrayal flourished, trust eroded, performance dropped, and work was not enjoyable. Hugh agonized over the situation. He did not want to undermine his fellow employees, but he also knew that if he did not protect himself, people could undermine him and he might lose his job. Even Damon, a young man he had once helped get promoted, had undermined him. He began to think that being kind would only make him vulnerable.

During this time, Hugh had a conversation with his wife. She empathized with him, offering love and support. She listened to his explanations about the new direction his company was going in. They examined his career prospects. They reviewed their finances, both in terms of daily living expenses and long-term savings. They decided that if Hugh had to leave his job and they had to get by on a lower income, even though it would be difficult, they could do it.

Knowing that he was loved and supported by his wife, Hugh returned to work and began doing things differently. He refused to see people as objects or as enemies. He saw them as people with struggles, fears, hopes, feelings, and needs. This included Damon. Even though Damon continued to act aggressively and Hugh was tempted to see him as an enemy, Hugh kept looking for the best in him. Hugh told Damon about the good things he saw in him. Damon was suspicious, but Hugh persisted. Eventually Damon was promoted to vice president, with Hugh reporting to him, and he treated Hugh as a colleague and friend.

Hugh also called meetings with small groups in his facility. In these meetings, he asked people provocative questions such as "What do you want this company to look like in ten years?" Initially, Hugh's co-workers were skeptical of him. He was a middle manager. Who was he to be asking about the company's long-term goals and strategies? Hugh persisted, though, and eventually people began to seriously consider and openly discuss their answers to the questions.

Eventually, many of Hugh's co-workers acknowledged the need to make themselves and their company more competitive. They needed to manage their careers more competitively for their own sake and for the sake of the company. They also realized that managing their careers competitively did not mean that they needed to undermine each other. Many of these employees began to come up with ideas for helping each other develop the skills they would need to help their company and their careers. They created a constructive work environment and improved the performance of their facility along the way.

Seeing the Humanity in Others

Hugh lifted himself, Damon, and many others in his organization by becoming other-focused. He changed his behavior, but this change was less important than the change in his psychological state. When Hugh was self-focused, the thought of doing kind things such as speaking well of others and helping them advance their careers looked as though it would only make him vulnerable. As a result, he felt stuck between two bad options: he could undermine his co-workers (which seemed unavoidable if he wanted to protect his career) or he could be kind (and get taken advantage of by his untrustworthy co-workers). Hugh felt this way because he was self-focused. He did not feel like being kind. Therefore, even if he decided to be kind, his lack of kind feelings would have leaked out in his emotions or actions, and his co workers could have easily labeled his kind actions as insincere or manipulative. Insincerity would have given them excuses to be manipulative or insincere themselves, and one self-betrayal would have inspired more self-betrayals, as described in chapter 7.

Hugh did not perform kind actions while he felt self-focused. Instead, with the help of his wife, he became other-focused. And, since he was not focused on himself, he was not worried about people taking advantage of him. Without his self-focused worry, he could empathize with others' needs more clearly. He felt the fear that his co-workers felt about their careers. He could sense that they needed the same kind of empathy that he received from his wife. He also knew that they would benefit from being challenged to think about the company and their role in the company differently. Because of the empathy he felt for his co-workers, his desire to help them was no longer an obligation: it was spontaneous. Gathering employees and asking them to envision the future was a natural thing to do.

Empathy is natural—as long as we do not impede our empathy with self-betrayal. We can empathize with others by simply imagining how they might feel. Kevin Ochsner and his colleagues showed this by using an fMRI machine to scan the brains of the participants in their experiment while the participants looked at photos.[1] As their participants did this, Ochsner and his colleagues asked them to focus on their own feelings or to judge the feelings of the people in the photos. Ochsner and his colleagues found that whether people were judging their own emotions or others' emotions, the same three regions of their brains were activated.[2]

Self-judgments and other-judgments also activated other, separate regions of the brain in Ochsner's experiment. The other activated regions of the brain presumably help people distinguish between different sources of emotion. Three of the regions of their brains that people use to judge emotions, however, do not differentiate between different sources of emotion: When we imagine others' emotions, we simulate those emotions in the same regions of our brains that we would activate if they were our own emotions. Thus, empathizing with a person can be as simple as imagining how they feel or mimicking their expressions. We often do that automatically.[3]

How Do Others Feel?

The idea that we can become other-focused by imagining how others feel is the basis for the question that we recommend to help people become other-focused: "How do others feel about this situation?" As with the other questions we have introduced, we chose the words in this question carefully.[4] For example, one of the critical words in this question is the word, "feel." By asking how people feel—as opposed to how they think—we open ourselves up to the possibility of receiving invitations for empathy, as discussed in chapter 7. If we respond to these invitations by empathizing with others, we enter—or remain in—an other-focused state.

The power of feeling the world from other people's points of view can be seen in a story told by Miguel, an anthropologist who was studying Laotian immigrants in Chicago. Most of these immigrants were poor, few of them spoke English, and very few people cared about them. They appreciated the interest that Miguel took in them and often asked him for help.

One of the most common requests that Miguel encountered was from Laotians who had received eviction notices from their landlords. They struggled to earn enough money to pay the rent, eat, and maintain a living. They wanted to ask their landlords for more time to pay the rent, but they could not speak English. They would ask Miguel to plead with their landlords to not evict them. Miguel pleaded with landlords many times, but he never succeeded.

One day, after reluctantly agreeing to plead with yet another landlord, and knowing that he had very little chance of success, Miguel had an idea. It was a crazy idea, but nothing else had ever worked, so he decided that he might as well give it a try. Standing next to his Laotian friend, he knocked on the landlord's door. A gruff man opened the door, looked at the Laotian, and looked at Miguel. He knew what Miguel was going to ask. He asked harshly, "Whaddya want?"

Miguel put the palms of his hands together in a praying position. He bowed slowly and low. Rising from his bow, he said, "My name is Lithmouthay. I come from the valley of the rising sun. I lived there happily with my wife and children. Then one day the wheeled dragons roared over the hill spitting fire. We tried to run, but my wife and children caught fire and burned to ashes. I came here because I had nowhere else to go." He put his palms back together, bowed low and slowly again, and then stood silently next to his Lithmouthay. The landlord looked at Miguel, looked at Lithmouthay, and then said to Miguel, "Okay. He can stay."

Why did the landlord allow Lithmouthay to stay? Like Ochsner and his colleagues asking the participants in their experiments to imagine people's emotions, Miguel asked the landlord to feel the situation from Lithmouthay's point of view. Then the landlord felt empathy for

Lithmouthay's pain, fear, and loneliness, even though he did not understand Lithmouthay's language or customs. When we feel another person's loneliness, pain, or fear, as the landlord did for Lithmouthay, one of the most common impulses we feel is a desire to help.[5] This is how Hugh's wife felt when she imagined how Hugh felt. She wanted to help him, went through their finances, and offered support. Then, when Hugh imagined how his co-workers might feel, he also empathized with their fear about their careers and wanted to help them.

When Empathy Is Difficult

Empathy is a natural response to others' emotions, but it is not always easy to experience, even when we imagine how others might feel. Sometimes we do not want to be other-focused—or at least we do not want to be other-focused toward a particular person. Hugh, for example, had been hurt and had even had his work undermined by someone he had helped. Why would he want to be other-focused toward a man like that? Similarly, Lithmouthay owed money to his landlord. Why would his landlord want to feel empathy for him?

Questions like "Why would I want to be other-focused toward a man like that?" and "Why would I want to feel empathy for him?" are questions that imply blame. They imply that people who betray us or who do not pay their rent do not deserve our empathy. They suggest that we have not let go of the justifications that make us victims by blaming others. It can be nearly impossible to feel empathy while we cling to justifications like these.

What if justifications like these are accurate, though? Is it possible that some people really are undeserving of our empathy? We would argue that the question of whether someone is deserving of our empathy is not useful. More useful, we believe, is the question "Will my lack of empathy lift me or lift others?" The answer is no. Even if the blame that we place on others is accurate, the act of blaming makes us insecure, selfish, and defensive and invites others to be insecure, selfish, and defensive as well.

When we blame others, we make ourselves into victims. We justify it by inflating their vices and our virtues, and this gives us a distorted view of the world.[6] This is one more reason why all four of the questions for *lift* are important: to feel how others feel in a situation, we often need to deflate our virtue and others' vices. We can do this by asking what our story would be if we were living the values we expect of others. This helps us question the justifications we use to convince ourselves that we are virtuous. Once we realize that we are not as virtuous as we have convinced ourselves we are, we see our virtues and vices more accurately, we see others' virtues and vices more accurately, we have a harder time seeing ourselves as victims, we have an easier time seeing how we might have some responsibility in the situation, and we find it much easier to empathize with others.[7]

Another tool that can help us let go of justifications that we are afraid to let go of is our association with people who feel empathy for us. When we enjoy the company of people who are other-focused, our justifications often melt away on their own. The empathy that we feel from these people often makes our self-focused justifications seem less appealing and makes other-focused feelings seem more attractive. Hugh felt this way when he received empathy from his wife. It showed in the concern she expressed and in her willingness to live on a lower income if that was necessary. Her empathy was much more pleasant than the suspicion, defensiveness, and tension he felt at work. This idea was the basis of Carl Rogers' research and therapy: empathizing with his clients, he found, had a tendency to melt away justification.[8]

Empathy may melt away self-justifications, but the melting away of self-justifications cannot be forced. Lithmouthay's landlord's justifications may have melted quickly, but it took Hugh days and weeks of first talking to his wife and then struggling at work before he was able to feel empathy for his co-workers. If we learn our justifications in early childhood, they may take years to slowly melt away. Each justification is different from every other justification. We all carry justifications with us that become our assumptions about how life works. We often do not even know what justifications we are carrying with us, and thus we cannot tell when and how those justifications will melt away.

We may not be able to predict when justifications will melt away and we will become other-focused, but we can do things to make

ourselves more likely to experience an other-focused state. If we regularly ask ourselves, "What would my story be if I were living the values
that I expect of others?" we are likely, over time, to identify and eliminate
many of the justifications that prevent us from being other-focused.
And if we regularly ask, "How do others feel about this situation?" we
are more likely to receive the invitations for empathy that others regularly and unconsciously send to us.

Stakeholders

Our discussion of the question "How do others feel about this situation?" has focused so far on the word "feel." When we crafted this question, however, we deliberately used the plural word "others" rather than
a singular phrase like "the other person." We did this because there
may be any number of people who could be influenced in any situation. The people who may be influenced are stakeholders; each of them
has a stake, or an interest, in the situation.

The word "stakeholder" is used most commonly with business au-
diences. For example, Ed Freeman, a business ethicist, writes and teaches
extensively about stakeholders. He focuses on stakeholders like employees, stockholders, customers, suppliers, local communities, and the
natural environment. Freeman and his colleagues help business leaders make more ethical decisions by encouraging them to take a stakeholder perspective: to consider the situation they are facing from the
points of view of the employees, stockholders, customers, suppliers,
local communities, and the natural environment when they make decisions.[9] This is what we do when we ask ourselves the question "How
do others feel about this situation?"

People often worry that empathizing with all of their stakeholders
will require them to sacrifice their own benefits or the benefits of
some of their more common stakeholders. This is often the case. We
have also found, however, that empathizing with all of the stakeholders in a situation often increases everyone's benefits in the long
run. For example, in 1990 BankBoston faced regulatory pressures
from the government (one of its stakeholders) to increase investment in underserved urban neighborhoods (another of BankBos-

ton's stakeholders).[10] Initially, this kind of investment probably looked like it would lower profits, which would be a sacrifice for the stockholders (another of BankBoston's stakeholders).

BankBoston increased its investment in urban neighborhoods by creating a new bank, called First Community Bank. As managers in this new bank began to build the business, they sought the perspectives of their stakeholders in the urban communities, in nonprofit organizations, and from their own stockholders. They did this so that First Community Bank would be constructive for the communities in which they operated, beneficial for the employees and urban clients, and profitable for shareholders. They hired managers from local communities. They required managers to attend community events. Their community development officers acted as liaisons with particular ethnic groups. They translated documents into relevant languages for members of these groups. These efforts helped rejuvenate declining communities.

It took five years of investment before First Community Bank made a profit, but it eventually achieved the highest sales out of all of Bank-Boston's retail operations. It also generated innovations like venture capital for inner-city investment, multilingual ATMs, and special products designed for newcomers to banking. These innovations were so successful that they are now used throughout BankBoston as well as in First Community Bank. By caring about their stakeholders' needs, BankBoston lifted itself as well as its community stakeholders.

The concept of stakeholders can be useful in everyday situations as well as in business. For example, in the story of Lithmouthay, Lithmouthay, Miguel, and the landlord all had an interest in the situation. In Hugh's story, each of the employees, their families, the customers and shareholders of the company, and perhaps other people each had an interest in the situation. Each stakeholder's interest in and perspective on the situation is unique. As a result, each stakeholder can provide unique opportunities for learning, insight, and action.

BOB: I first learned about the opportunities that stakeholders provide for learning, insight, and action by playing basketball.

When I began playing basketball, I was self-focused: I just wanted to impress the sixth-grade cheerleaders. It was not long, however, before I learned to focus on others.

One reason why I learned to focus on others was that I was the point guard: it was my job to make everyone else on the team better. The way to win the cheerleaders' attention would have been to score as many points as possible, but I was supposed to set up the plays, draw defenders to me so that other people could get an open shot, and make good passes so that other people could score.

To play my position well, I had to try to understand how my teammates felt and what they needed to succeed. As I began to empathize with their needs and feelings, I found that there was more joy and success in lifting my teammates than there was in focusing on me. My teammates, my coach, the fans, and I were all stakeholders in our team, and I began to feel joy in their success as well as in mine as I empathized with them. There is much more joy to be felt when we enjoy the success of others as well as our own.

I also learned from empathizing with my teammates. By focusing on their feelings and needs rather than on my own, I began to learn how to pass, penetrate, set picks, and run plays in ways that complemented their strengths and helped them to play their best. The more I tried to do this with the different people I played with, the more I learned about how to improve my skills as well. My teammates also felt this way, and over time we could hardly stand to play with people in self-focused states: they destroyed what was most precious about playing basketball.

Experiences like these can occur in even the most combative relationships. For example, Troy, a colleague of ours, is a professional mediator. He specializes in disputes between environmentalists, the logging industry, and other groups that have an interest in how natural resources are used. Once, Troy described a conflict between two of these groups. There was no resolution in sight, until one day when one person from each of the groups happened to bring their children to the same park on the same day.

These two opponents at the park talked about their children and their personal lives. As they did, they began to see each other as human beings with legitimate needs, perspectives, and feelings. They quit characterizing each other negatively and instead began to explore things they had in common. They returned to the negotiating table with different and more open-minded perspectives about the other group and shared this perspective with people from their own groups. Other members of their groups began to empathize with their opponents' needs, wants, feelings, and perspectives. As they did, they came up with new ways to integrate their interests.

High-Quality Connection

Hugh's meetings with his co-workers, Miguel's petition for Lithmouthay, Bob's basketball team, and Troy's clients meeting in a park can each give us insight into what it is like to experience an other-focused state. Empathy, of course, is the most fundamental characteristic of an other-focused state. And closely related to empathy are impulses to act and mutual rapport.

Impulses to Act

Empathy is an emotional experience, and emotions tend to prompt action responses.[11] For example, when people are afraid, they feel a desire to fight or flee. When people are curious, they want to explore. When people are disgusted, they want to recoil. When people feel love, they want to touch. When people feel empathy, they participate compassionately in other people's emotions. This means that the action response most commonly associated with empathy is the impulse to help, whether our help is intended to relieve suffering (as in Miguel's story) or to contribute to others' success (as it did on Bob's basketball team).[12] These impulses to help can be particularly complex when we empathize with people who are in a self-focused state. Like Hugh with his co-workers, we want to help alleviate the pain, fear, or hurt feelings that lie beneath their selfishness, defensiveness, or standoffishness.

Other action impulses are also possible. When Troy's clients met in the park, for example, their empathy led them to relinquish their negative characterizations of each other and to cooperate with each other. When we empathize with people who are happy, we usually feel a desire to celebrate with them. And when we empathize with people who are in an other-focused state, we appreciate their empathy and even revere their dignity. We lift them and are lifted by them in an experience of mutual rapport.

Rapport

If we had observed Hugh's meetings with his co-workers or the negotiations between Troy's clients, we might have noticed the clothes people were wearing, the places they sat in the room, the items they brought with them, and the topics they discussed. We might have noticed patterns in their conversation, or which people were likely to tell jokes and which ones were likely to get distracted. We might also have noticed how people's facial expressions and tone of voice changed, suggesting distrust, worry, or antagonism in the early stages of the conversations and comfort, interest, and excitement in the later stages. If we had recorded these meetings on video and then watched them in extreme slow motion, however, we might have seen even more.

Almost thirty years ago, a scientist named William Condon analyzed extreme-slow-motion videos of people engaging in conversation.[13] He began by watching four-and-a-half seconds of a dinner conversation over and over again, in frames of one-forty-fifth of a second. After hours and hours of examining this clip, Condon finally picked up on what his intuition had been telling him all along: the man lifted his hands at the same time that the woman turned her head. Once he saw those movements, he saw other synchronized movements as well, in this video clip and in others. People did not make the same movements, but their movements would begin and end at the same time. One person's shoulder might hunch while another person leaned forward; one person's cheek might rise while another person lifted her eyebrows. These people were moving together in time, and they were moving to the rhythm of their speech, like a dance. Even the volume and pitch of their speech fell into rhythm.

People move together in time when they feel empathy for each other. When people do not empathize with each other, their conversations, expressions, and movements are out of synch and often feel awkward.[14] When people empathize with each other, their minds and bodies join together in rhythmic patterns that reinforce their relationship and feel uplifting.[15] This does not happen when we try to mimic others intentionally.[16] It occurs when our movements synchronize spontaneously because of the empathy we share with each other. It is an experience that Hugh and his co-workers and Troy's clients had mostly because of the mutual empathy they felt when they worked through their differences, shared ideas, and got excited about new possibilities.

Jane Dutton and Emily Heaphy, organizational scholars, call the rapport that people achieve through mutual empathy a "high-quality connection."[17] This kind of rapport is a high-quality connection because it allows people to express a wide range of emotions, it can withstand the strain of difficult circumstances, it is open to new ideas and influences, and it releases oxytocin and endorphins in the brains of people who participate.[18] Oxytocin and endorphins are chemicals that give people a sensation of relaxed pleasure, or calm energy. Daniel Goleman argues that the ability to establish connections like these is the foundation of social intelligence,[19] and Randall Collins, a sociologist, explains how the energy that people feel in interactions like these are the motivating force behind the social structures we develop in our societies.[20]

As Hugh and his co-workers envisioned ways to work together to make themselves and their company more competitive, and as Troy's clients came up with ways to collaborate in spite of their contradictory interests, they experienced many, if not all, of the characteristics of high-quality connections. They felt empathy and concern for each other and were inclined to act on each other's behalf. They remained committed to their relationships in spite of facing difficult situations and expressing a wide range of emotion. They listened to each other's ideas, came up with new ideas, created new ways of working together, and got excited about their ideas. They lifted themselves and, in the process, lifted each other.

The Influence of an Other-Focused State

People who experience other-focused states can lift others in many ways. We have seen some of these in our discussion so far. For example, when we feel empathy for others, we can help them overcome suffering and increase their performance; melt away their justifications; increase the energy they feel; and help them feel secure enough to consider new ideas, take risks, and explore new possibilities. We can benefit from considering a few forms of influence further, including energizing others, integrity, resilience, trust, and learning.

Energizing Others

The energy that people experience when we empathize with them does more than make them feel good. As we discussed in chapter 4, those who energize others also tend to perform better than those who do not. When we energize others, they usually exert more effort on our behalf, are more open to learning, are more likely to share innovative ideas, and are more likely to share their resources with us.[21] In other words, when we focus on others, we often improve our own performance. Wayne Baker illustrates this point with a story about a loan officer named Janet.[22]

> [Janet's] job was to make loans, and she was evaluated on the volume of loans she produced. One day she experienced a shift of perspective. She stopped trying to make loans and started trying to help. Instead of looking at the person across the desk from her as a loan to be made, Janet saw the person as someone with needs that she might be able to help satisfy. If she thought they didn't need a loan, she would tell them so, even if they qualified for one according to her bank's rules. If she thought her potential customers could do better by getting a loan at a competitor's bank, she would give them the name of a loan

officer at the bank. Eventually she engaged potential customers in a broad conversation about their lives, families, and needs, and then worked hard to help them, no matter what kind of help they needed. She even began the practice of sharing cab rides with strangers, just so she could strike up a conversation and see if there was some way she could assist them. What happened? All she helped were so grateful that they did everything they could to help her. Even if they didn't get a loan at her bank, they would recommend Janet to all of their friends, family, neighbors, business associates, colleagues, and just about anyone else. The result was an explosion in Janet's loan productivity. She made more loans—and made more money—than ever before. She had become *extraordinarily* successful by taking herself out of the equation and helping others without regard to how it might help her.

Janet experienced what sociologists like Baker call generalized reciprocity. Reciprocity occurs when one person gives a gift or a favor in return for receiving a gift or a favor from someone else. We saw some of this in Janet's story: some of the people for whom she did kind things did kind things for her in return. This is specific reciprocity.

Reciprocity can also be general. As Janet did things for people with no expectation of return, people began to think of her as a person who cared about them, rather than about whether she could sell them a loan. As a result, they referred people to her regularly and spontaneously, without keeping track of what she had done for them. Because she gave freely and without expectation, she also received freely and without expectation, and not necessarily from the people that she had done things for. This is general, rather than specific, reciprocity.

Integrity and Resilience

Empathy can also help people be more resilient and act with more integrity, because it helps people feel secure. Hugh, for example, was not able to organize his group until he and his co-workers felt secure. His wife helped him feel secure by empathizing with him and helping him, and Hugh's empathy did the same for his co-workers.[23] Empathy is particularly important when people face adversity or other forms of pressure, because people become more resilient when they have people who can empathize with them and help them feel secure. When people feel secure, it lowers their anxiety, enables them to make sense of the situation, and helps them find the courage to go on.[24]

The safety and security that other-focused people provide can also help people act with more integrity. Integrity can seem like a risk when there are pressures to compromise one's integrity. If people feel secure in their relationships with other people, though, then they are less likely to give in to these pressures.[25] A good example of this can be found in teenagers who stand up against their peers and refuse to engage in illicit drug use, smoking, alcohol, or early sex. Research indicates that teenagers are much more likely to do this when they enjoy secure and loving relationships with their parents. Saying no to peers can feel risky to socially conscious teenagers who worry about losing friends. If teenagers are secure in their relationship with their parents, the potential of losing friends is a risk that they are much more willing to take.[26]

Trust

Safety and security can also be a foundation for trust.[27] Sameer, for example, is a colleague of ours who managed the business books division of Adkar Robbins. Adkar Robbins was acquired by Saline Books. The people in Sameer's company were worried about what would happen to them, the products they managed, and their company. Waiting to find out, they felt threatened and performed only their most basic job requirements. Sameer had little control over what would happen, but he made an effort to be other-focused, empathizing with the feelings of his employees, his customers, his peers, and the stockholders.

While attending a conference, Sameer heard from a colleague that the Saline Books executives were thinking about closing down many of his product lines and firing many of his employees. He thought that this would be a tragedy. He believed that the people and the products in his unit had the potential to create significant value for his customers and his company. Sameer wondered if the managers in Saline

Books would alter their plan if they knew the strategy behind the products that he and his employees had developed. He decided to talk to Peter, his counterpart in Saline Books. This was risky, because if Sameer shared strategic information with Peter, Peter could use the information to improve his own product line, making Sameer's division redundant.

Sameer decided to take the risk. He arranged a meeting and flew to Peter's office. He began by telling Peter part, but not all, of his division's strategy. Peter understood the sensitivity of the information that Sameer was sharing with him and understood that Sameer was taking a risk by trusting Peter. He respected Sameer for taking that risk and shared a little bit of strategic information about his own division in return. Sameer also saw Peter's respect and willingness to share, and opened up further. In other words, both of these men saw the other as human beings with legitimate feelings that they could empathize with. They developed a rapport for each other, which helped them feel secure in their relationship.

As the two men shared more information with each other, they began to come up with ideas that they could not have come up with before they shared their information. For example, they realized that some of their redundant product lines would no longer be redundant if they were sold internationally. Soon, the two men developed and began to implement a joint strategy, growing their business in new ways. When the executives at Saline Books released their plan for integrating the two companies, the business books divisions were the only divisions that did not have to eliminate lots of people and product lines.

Learning, Experimentation, and Innovation

The story of Peter and Sameer illustrates how empathy and rapport can help people feel secure enough to trust each other, how trust helps people share information freely, and how people can learn and innovate more easily when they share information. Amy Edmondson, Richard Bohmer, and Gary Pisano found similar patterns in their study of hospitals that tried to implement a new technology called minimally invasive cardiac surgery (MICS).[28] Before the invention of

MICS, heart surgery involved breaking a person's rib cage in two in order for the surgeon to be able to work on a person's heart. The invention of MICS allowed surgeons to operate with only a minor incision in the person's chest. To conduct MICS, however, surgeons could not control all information and decision making as they had previously. The whole team had to share information, coordinate, and solve problems together.

Some of the teams that Edmondson and her colleagues studied were successful at implementing MICS and some were not. The teams that were successful did more than share information, coordinate, and solve problems during surgeries. They also spent significant amounts of time talking through procedures after they were over in an effort to learn from them. Teams could do this, though, only if their members felt safe doing so. Many of the team members did not feel safe because they did not feel they could disagree with the surgeon.

Innovation is similar to learning. Andrew Hargadon, one of the world's leading innovation researchers, has found that innovation occurs when people share knowledge across social domains where knowledge has not been shared before.[29] People are often reluctant to share knowledge with people that they do not normally associate with, though. If they are like Sameer and Peter, it may be because they are afraid that the knowledge may be used against them. Or it may simply be that they feel uncertain working across differences, such as positions, opinions, political parties, demographics, geography, and so forth. If people can develop the trust to work across social domains, though, they can come up with new ideas that benefit themselves and others, the way Sameer and Peter and Hugh and his co-workers did.

Questions and Concerns About Being Other-Focused

An other-focused state can lift the person in that state and the people around that person. People become purpose-centered by asking and answering the question "How do others feel in this situation?" This question can help us see others as human beings with legitimate feelings and needs, and feel empathy for them. When we are in an other-focused state, we energize people, inspire them to share resources and to invest effort into our projects and theirs, and help them feel secure. The security they feel can help them be resilient, find the strength to act with integrity in the face of pressure, trust, learn, experiment, and innovate.

There are a few issues that should be addressed before we move on. One is the concern people have that being other-focused will interfere with their own legitimate agenda. We all have work that we need to get done and activities that we want to enjoy. If we are empathic toward others, will we get overwhelmed by all that we feel we need to do?

In our experience, people seldom become overwhelmed by being more empathic. Most of the time, the impulses we feel to empathize with others require little more than to just be civil—to treat people with respect, to say hello, to smile, or to offer a kind word. This is hardly overbearing. Occasionally, however, invitations to empathy ask more of us. In many cases, we will not regret putting in extra effort to respond to these invitations. Other times, however, we will need to temper the impulses to action we feel as part of our empathy: we cannot solve all of the world's ills individually, even though we may want to. In these cases, we can use the lift questions to temper our impulses, remembering other worthy purposes we also want to pursue; values such as wisdom, patience, and caution that prevent us from biting off more than we can chew; other stakeholders who also need our empathy and attention and among whom we need to divide our attention and effort; and feedback from which we can learn about what we are capable of doing at this point in time.

Another issue is the concern that we might lose our identity if we focus on the needs and feelings of others. Again, we find that this is not the case when people experience true empathy. Most people find that when they become other-focused, they do not lose themselves, they become their best selves. They like who they become when they care about others. This makes sense when we realize that our identities are actually tangled up in our relationships with others.[30] We are social creatures, biologically wired to empathize with each other. Becoming other-focused does not eliminate our unique characteristics; it draws on them to help us make the most of our interactions.

Sometimes people are also concerned that an other-focused state is unprofessional. A reporter may need to record a scene of human distress or a doctor may need to perform surgery without becoming involved emotionally. It is appropriate to be careful not to let our emotions impair our decision making. Keeping our emotions from impairing our decision making is not the same thing, however, as betraying ourselves. A more appropriate way to manage our emotions is to temper them by being purpose-centered, internally directed, and externally open. Reporters are likely to write better stories by funneling their empathy with clear values and purposes than they are if they view the people they write about as objects that can advance or impede their careers. Similarly, patients are more likely to be satisfied with their treatment and medical teams are more likely to contribute meaningfully to surgical tasks when doctors feel empathy for them, guided by clear goals and feedback. There may even be situations when reporters, doctors, or other professionals should not temper their empathy at all, perhaps even violating the typical code of conduct in favor of deeper empathic values.

Finally, it is possible that someone who is in an other-focused state might be easier to take advantage of than someone who is not. It is more common for people in an other-focused state to help others feel secure and to inspire them to reciprocate, to invest effort, to trust, to show integrity, to learn or to innovate. Even so, it is possible that people will take advantage of an other-focused person from time to time. We can, however, do things to reduce the chances that others will take advantage of us by becoming purpose-centered and internally directed as well as other-focused. We are more likely to insist on arrangements that are suitable to us as well as to others, for example, if we have clear purposes and values. Hugh did this by challenging his co-workers as well as supporting them, and Troy's clients did this by coming up with solutions that met the interests of both groups, not by capitulating to the demands of the other group. In both cases, people were lifted by ideas that met the needs of everyone involved, not by giving up or getting their own way.

➤ Practices for Applying the Principles of Lift

Empathy can be hard to feel if the people toward whom we are trying to feel empathy act in unkind or unproductive ways. It can also be difficult to feel if our empathy is impeded by justifications. The following practices can help:

1. **Try to understand others' unfulfilled needs.** People can be particularly hard to empathize with if their actions are unkind, manipulative, arrogant, or selfish. People who act like this often do so because they received no empathy during critical moments in their lives. If we ask ourselves what could have happened to this person to lead them to act this way, recently or in their early life, it often becomes easier to empathize with them. Asking this does not mean that we should condone their actions. We can empathize with people and still not condone their actions.

2. **Ask "Might I be in the wrong?"** Sometimes we are in the middle of a situation and we want to empathize with someone but we cannot. Our self-justifications are too strong, and we cannot stop the situation to address what our story would be if we were living the values we expect of others. Warner offers another question that can be helpful in situations like these: "Might I be in the wrong?"[31] When we have used this question ourselves, we have always found the answer to be "Yes" in at least some way. Acknowledging this makes it much easier to empathize.

3. **Spend time with people who are in an other-focused state.**
   Being around people who are in an other-focused state tends to
   melt away our justifications and make us more empathic ourselves. Remember, though, that empathy is not the same as self-
   pity. People who reinforce your self-pity will not make you more
   empathic.

chapter 9

Fearing Feedback

RYAN: After studying Japanese for two years in college, I had an opportunity to spend a year studying corporate strategy and international business at Hitotsubashi University in Japan. I was thrilled and scared about the opportunity. Even though I studied Japanese for two years, my skills were limited. My ability to read and write Japanese improved regularly as I studied and practiced, but I did not speak or understand Japanese very well.

Upon arriving in Japan, I was embarrassed at how poor my ability to speak and understand Japanese was. I would try to speak to people, but I usually had to ask them to repeat themselves many times. I felt like I was stupid and I was a burden to the people I was speaking to. For example, if I was in a train station and I did not know which train to take, I would ask for directions. People would give me the directions, but I would not understand. Sometimes I would ask them to repeat themselves, but after they had repeated themselves two or three times I would just pretend that I understood

163

and say thank you because I was too embarrassed to ask again. I tried asking other people, but that was embarrassing as well. Sometimes I would spend fifteen or twenty minutes standing by a map with my dictionary trying to figure out what train to get on, rather than have to bother more people and humiliate myself further by asking anyone for directions.

I also struggled in school and felt like I bothered my classmates. I would often retreat to my apartment where I would be alone so that I could practice reading and writing Japanese. I deceived myself, thinking that if I improved my reading and writing, my speaking and listening might improve as well.

Not long after arriving in Japan, I made two friends who taught me an important lesson about my approach to learning. The first of these two friends was a Japanese man who spoke near-perfect English. Although Japanese children studied English in high school, and almost all Japanese children became relatively fluent in reading and writing English, at the time when I lived in Japan very few Japanese people were fluent at speaking and understanding English. I was impressed, so I asked him if he had ever lived in the United States. He said he had not. Great Britain? No. Australia? Canada? No. No. How then, I asked him, did he develop such impressive English skills? He told me that he developed his English skills by practicing with audio tapes, and more impressively, by standing on street corners giving speeches in English with his friends. When I heard his answer, I was embarrassed. Before coming to Japan, I was supposed to practice with audio tapes for my Japanese classes. I often felt stupid because of how poorly I did at these audio exercises, so instead I found ways to get the answers I needed for my homework without really working through the audio activities.

The second friend who helped me see why my approach to learning was not working was another exchange student from the United States. He was nearly fluent in speaking and understanding Japanese. He developed his speaking skills, he said, by going to restaurants, public baths, newsstands, and other public places, starting up conversations in Japanese with anyone he could. When I compared his approach with my tendency to get embarrassed and quit when I could not understand people, it was obvious why he was nearly fluent and I was not. Learning Japanese—or any skill—is a process of taking action, receiving feedback, reflecting on and deriving insights from the feedback, and then applying the insights gained from feedback by acting again in a different way. Seeking and using feedback is critical for learning, but no learning happens at all if people are afraid to act and to receive feedback.

Flying Gliders Without Control Systems

The Wright brothers understood the importance of acting, getting feedback, and acting again in designing and flying airplanes. Before the Wright brothers, the people who attempted to build flying machines did not have sophisticated methods (if they had any methods at all) of using feedback to adapt to flight conditions while they were airborne. As mentioned in chapter 2, even Otto Lillienthal (who built and flew so many gliders that people called him "the flying man") came up with no better method for adapting his gliders to flight conditions than to shift his body weight around on the glider. Lillienthal's limited ability to adapt to feedback not only prevented his learning, it also led to his death.

In contrast to Lilienthal, the Wright brothers realized that in order to develop a flying machine that could adapt to changing flight conditions in real time, they would need controls that could help an airplane adjust its flight along three dimensions: raising one wing up while lowering the other (roll), turning the nose of the aircraft right or left (yaw), and raising or lowering the front and rear of the aircraft (pitch). Before the Wright brothers, no one had explicitly recognized the need for controls that accounted for all three dimensions.

The Wright brothers developed controls that would help them maneuver their glider in all three dimensions. They developed controls for roll when Wilbur twisted the cardboard box and came up with his wing-warping idea. To adapt to pitching movements, they used an elevator: a moveable, horizontal surface that they mounted in front of the wings. And to adapt to yaw movement they attached movable, vertical rudders to the back of their wings. They developed different versions of these controls, tested them, and used the feedback that their testing generated to improve their controls. Eventually, they had controls that worked well and they were proficient at using these controls.

The Wright brothers designed and became skilled at using aircraft controls because they were not afraid to do what Ryan was afraid to do: practice, get feedback, and practice more. In our *lift* framework, when people are afraid of feedback we say that they are internally closed. In other words, they close themselves off to feedback. People are afraid of feedback, according to psychologist Carol Dweck, when they have a fixed mindset, a belief that their abilities are relatively unchangeable attributes.[1] If people believe that their abilities cannot change, then feedback does not help them learn, and it is considered a judgment of their personal worth. If feedback is a description of their personal worth, and there is a possibility that the feedback might be negative, then the prospect of receiving feedback is frightening. Ryan did not understand it at the time, but this was a problem he struggled with in Japan. He was afraid that his inability to speak and understand Japanese implied that he was not smart, talented, or worthy.

The Belief That We Cannot Change

The idea that people fear feedback because of a belief that their abilities are fixed occurred to Dweck as she studied how children learn.[2] In one experiment Dweck conducted with Dick Reppucci, two adults asked the children to solve puzzles.[3] One adult gave the children solvable puzzles, and the other one gave them unsolvable puzzles. After a while, the adults tested the children's puzzle-solving ability with two solvable puzzles. The adult that had given the children solvable puzzles gave the children the test puzzles first. Then, a while later, the other adult gave the children the same two test puzzles.

After the children completed the tests, Dweck and Reppucci compared how well each child performed when tested by the adult who had been giving solvable puzzles with how well each performed when tested by the adult that had been giving the unsolvable puzzles. When the children received the test puzzles from the adult who had given them unsolvable puzzles, they responded in one of two ways. Some of the children solved the puzzles more quickly. After all, they had seen these puzzles before. The rest of the children took longer to solve these puzzles or did not solve them at all—even though they had solved the same puzzles before. After receiving so many unsolvable puzzles from this person, they assumed that they could not solve puzzles given by this person.

Why did these two groups of children respond so differently to puzzles that they had already solved? The children who quickly solved the second round of test puzzles believed that their abilities could improve with persistent effort. They also believed that success depended more on factors that were in their control than on factors that were out of their control. In contrast, the children who took longer or failed to solve the second round of test puzzles believed that persistent effort could not do much to improve their abilities and that success depended more on factors that were out of their control than on factors that were within their control.

Dweck, her colleagues, and others who have also become interested in this topic found similar results in research with adults, in activities such as taking pre-med chemistry classes, giving performance appraisals, and managing simulated organizations. When people believe that their ability is fixed, they tend to blame failure on lack of ability, see failure as insurmountable, underestimate their performance, expect success to be temporary, set lower goals, develop less efficient strategies, perform well in repeated activities but poorly when confronted with challenges, and fail to acknowledge change in other people when their performance improves—to name only a few of the findings from this research.[4]

Ryan faced many of these problems as he struggled to learn how to speak and understand Japanese. For example, he set lower goals and used less efficient strategies by practicing reading and writing in his apartment instead of going out and practicing speaking and listening.

When he ran into challenges—such as when he did not understand the directions people gave him in train stations—he would feel stupid, worry about his ability, and struggle more to understand the next person he would ask. Sometimes he would just give up and read maps or train schedules instead. He was afraid that his ability might be fixed and that he might not be able to learn Japanese after all.

In spite of his fears, Ryan never gave up completely and never considered the challenge of learning how to speak Japanese to be insurmountable. His ability to speak and understand Japanese was not improving as quickly as he wanted it to, but it was improving, and he knew plenty of people—like his two friends—who had succeeded in developing their speaking and listening skills. Although much of Dweck's research focuses on people's general tendencies to be internally closed or externally open over time, Dweck also points out that "People can have different mindsets in different areas. We might think that our artistic skills are fixed but that our intelligence can be developed. Or that our personality is fixed but that our creativity can be developed."[5] In other words, a person can be externally open in one domain or activity and internally closed in another. The psychological state that people bring to a particular type of activity guides their approach toward that activity. Further, even when people tend to approach an activity in an externally open state, certain situations or cues can still drive people into an internally closed state without them realizing it.

I Can Change—Just Not While Doing This

RYAN: I had an experience with becoming internally closed and not realizing it while I was writing this book. When we began writing we decided who would write each part, how to share ideas, and how to give each other feedback. When I began my first large chunk of writing, I was externally open. I wanted to write a great book, but I had no idea how to do that. I had a few ideas to start with and I was sure that I could figure it out along the way. Some of my ideas worked, and some did not. When my ideas did not work, I appreciated the feedback because it helped me figure out how to write well. I had fun watching this book unfold and loved the feeling of "figuring it out."

While I was working on the book, I was evaluated for a contract renewal at the business school where I teach. The school's tenured faculty members reviewed my accomplishments and decided whether they thought I would earn tenure in three years if they renewed my contract. They decided to renew my contract.

After my contract was renewed, many people congratulated me. They told me how smart I was or how I was an example of the kind of person that we needed at the school. I was moved by their kindness. A few weeks later, though, I noticed a change in my experience with writing this book. It wasn't fun anymore.

I noticed other changes in the way I was writing the book as well. I was annoyed by negative feedback. I was worried about how long it was taking to write. Because I was worried about how long it was taking to write, I tried to work harder. But even when I worked harder, I was surprised at how often I was tempted to find other things to do. Somehow, I had become internally closed.

Praise for Ability

To understand how Ryan became internally closed, consider another experiment. This time, Dweck and another psychologist, Claudia Mueller, gave a group of children some problems to solve and then studied the impact that compliments had on the children's beliefs.[6] They focused on two kinds of compliments: praise for effort (such as "Wow! You really worked hard at that!") and praise for ability (such as, "Wow! You are so smart!"). When they complimented children on their effort, the children wanted to work on additional hard problems, persisted on those problems, enjoyed their work, and performed well. When they complimented the children on their ability, the children wanted easier problems, quit sooner, did not enjoy their work, performed worse, and almost 40 percent of them lied about their performance to others. The only difference between the two groups was that one group was praised for effort and the other for ability.

Why did praising children's abilities make them less likely to take on challenges, persist, enjoy their work, perform well, or report their performance honestly? Because praising people's abilities teaches them that their success is dependent on their personal characteristics: you succeeded at this because you were smart, so if you fail you must be dumb. Why would anyone want to take on or persist in challenging tasks if they might fail and find out that they are dumb? How can people enjoy their work if there is a chance that they might find out that they are lacking in the essential characteristics they need for success? And why tell people the truth about how poorly they performed? That just means that other people will know how deficient they are.

Adults are not that different from children when it comes to praise.[7] Related research and personal experience both suggest that praise for ability can get adults thinking that their ability is fixed. Look, for example, at how many of our leaders in government, business, or other professional domains surround themselves with "yes men" and "yes women," avoiding the possibility of receiving negative feedback. And leaders are not the only ones who avoid feedback. Entire organizations—employees as well as bosses, according to the research of Danny Miller[8]—have strong tendencies to get caught up in their successes, until it leads them to failure.

When members of organizations focus on their success so much that they fail, Miller calls it "The Icarus Paradox." This name comes from the Greek myth about a father and son who made wings out of feathers and wax. Icarus, the son, died when he flew too close to the sun, melting the wax in his wings. Organizations and their members often do the same thing. They develop competencies that help them succeed. People in the organization see the success and take it as evidence that their competencies (the organization's "fixed" abilities) are the keys to success. They overemphasize these competencies as critical to their success.

Organizational members are right when they assume that their competencies made their success possible. But when they focus on applying their competencies over and over again instead of on continually learning and improving, those competencies can take on a life of their own. Members ignore feedback in favor of revering these cherished competencies. If they ignore feedback long enough, they plunge their organizations into failure. If people in organizations like the ones Miller describes revered the efforts they put into learning from feedback to create their competencies more than they revered the competencies themselves, they might have avoided the major failures that came later.

Praise for ability was also one of the reasons Ryan became internally directed. Ryan's colleagues meant only the best when they complimented him on his contract renewal, and Ryan felt wonderful while he was receiving those compliments. Like one of the children in Mueller and Dweck's experiments, though, the idea that he was the kind of person that his colleagues wanted to keep led Ryan to focus on his ability rather than on the effort, learning, and feedback that made his contract renewal possible. Soon, he was afraid of feedback that might tell him that he was not the kind of person his colleagues would want to have around, he was avoiding work, the writing was no longer fun, and he sometimes even avoided writing.

Performance Goals

Ryan's third-year review had one other effect that he did not recognize until later: it changed the kind of goals he was setting.

> **RYAN:** Before I went through my third-year review, my broad goal was an outcome goal: to write a great book that would help each person who read it become a positive force in any situation. My daily goals were learning goals: to figure out how to write the section of the book that I was working on in a way that was accessible, enjoyable, useful, and grounded in scientific research. As a result, each day presented a fun challenge to figure out how to write that section. Feedback was welcome: it would help me do a better job.
>
> As I went through the contract renewal process, however, my goals changed without me realizing it. My contract renewal was one step on the way toward earning tenure. When the faculty and administrators at a university decide whether to give tenure to a professor, they judge that professor's work and also ask professors at other universities to judge the professor's work. On the basis of these judgments, they decide to offer you permanent

employment or to kick you out of the university. There are only two outcomes. Your entire academic career is put on the line for people to decide if what you have done is worthy to merit your remaining one of their colleagues. Thinking about my contract renewal got me wondering if I would be worthy of tenure, and that worry changed my goals.

My primary concern as I worried about tenure was not about tenure itself, but about how I would look if I did not get tenure. The first three years of my contract had gone well, but my current projects were not progressing as quickly as I wanted them to. I set more aggressive deadlines for completing the book. As a result, as I thought more and more about tenure, my outcome goal (writing a book that would help the people who read it) slowly changed into a performance goal: getting the book done quickly and moving on to my other projects so that I would get tenure and avoid feeling foolish in front of all the people who would know that I had failed. Each day became an effort to get as much done as I could, rather than an opportunity to learn how to write the book as well as possible.

In everyday language, the terms "outcome goal" and "performance goal" could mean the same thing. We use these terms differently, however, to make a point. Outcome goals and performance goals are both goals that focus people on an outcome, like writing a book. When we set performance goals, however, we pursue these outcomes in order to "perform," or to put on an act. We act like we are on stage. We want to look good, or at least avoid looking bad. The reason we are pursuing the outcome is egocentric; it focuses us on what other people think about us.

This difference between outcome and performance goals suggests that deadlines, like the deadlines that Ryan set for himself, are not necessarily bad things. Deadlines can help us get work done. In Ryan's case, however, his deadlines were driven by a desire to not look stupid by failing to get tenure. As a result, his deadlines did not focus him on figuring out how to write a book that could help other people in a reasonable amount of time. Instead they focused him, unintentionally, on the goal of writing a book quickly so as to not look foolish.

When people's goals are oriented toward performing well for the sake of looking good (or for not looking bad), they experience an internally closed state.[9] In fact, even if people tend to be internally closed or externally open most of the time, the type of goals they set can override that tendency. Gerard Seijts and his colleagues found this in an experiment with MBA students.[10] The students participated in an exercise in which they ran a mobile phone company. Seijts and his colleagues told one group of students that they had to triple the company's market share (the percentage of customers who signed up for their company's services). They told them that this was a difficult goal but that other students had achieved it. They told another group of students that their goal was to try out six different strategies for increasing market share. The students who were told to triple market share performed significantly worse than those who tried out six different strategies. In fact, after accounting for the type of goals these students were given, the degree to which the students tended to be internally closed or externally open had no effect on their performance. The goals overwhelmed their general tendencies in this activity.

> **RYAN:** Just like the students in this study, my goal to finish the book quickly so that I would be more likely to get tenure overrode my desire to learn how to write each section of the book as well as possible. I struggled with this for a couple of months before I realized that my goals had changed. Once I realized that my goals had changed, I reset my outcome goal of trying to write an engaging, helpful book. I also reset my daily learning goals. Feedback was welcome again, the work became fun, and I could tell that both the quality and the speed of my writing had improved.

From Internally Closed to Externally Open

The fear of feedback can prevent parents from learning how to rear their children well, children from learning from the wisdom their parents have to offer, leaders from learning what is really going on with their organizations, employees from learning when their careers are derailing, all of us from learning how to deal well with life's challenges, and much, much more. We cannot learn and grow without feedback. A desire to learn from feedback is one of the most important orientations to life that we can adopt, but it is not always an easy one to adopt.

People tend to be afraid of feedback (and are thus internally closed) if they believe that their abilities cannot be changed. If their abilities cannot change, then feedback is not information about how to improve, it is a reflection of their unchanging and unchangeable abilities. When people are afraid to learn how to improve their abilities, they are reluctant to take on challenges (fearing how it will reflect on them), quit easily, expect failure, lower their aspirations, use less efficient strategies, think others are also unable to change and grow, lose interest in learning, perform worse on complex, changing activities, and sometimes even lie about their performance.

There are at least two reasons why people might become internally closed, even if they have a general tendency to be externally open. First, when people receive criticism or praise for their ability, they tend to believe that if they fail, it must be because they lack the inherent ability that is necessary. In an internally closed state, then, people either have or do not have the necessary ability, and there is not much that anyone can do about it.

The second reason why a person might become internally closed is that they have goals that focus them on how well they perform in relation to others. Performance goals focus people on relative outcomes— on how brilliant or foolish they look in comparison to others, not on what they can learn from experience.

RYAN: When I lived in Japan, I did not know what internally closed and externally open states were, or what to do about them. I struggled with my fear of looking foolish for most of the time that I lived there. I was fortunate, though, to have evidence—such as my own gradual improvement and the speaking ability of my friends—that Japanese skills could actually improve. Because of this I would, from time to time, overcome my fear and force myself to engage in conversations with people. With much practice and some embarrassment, I improved enough by the end of my time in Japan to pass the second-highest level of the national examination for Japanese language proficiency.

Even though he was embarrassed, Ryan's Japanese improved because he forced himself to practice speaking and listening in conversations. In other words, his efforts were driven as much by discipline and determination as by an interest in learning and a desire for feedback. Since his time in Japan, he has learned how to become excited about learning and interested in feedback, which is the topic of the next chapter.

chapter 10

Becoming Externally Open

RYAN: My wife, Amy, teaches piano. On January 1, 2007, she set a new year's resolution for our oldest children, Mason and Katie, to learn how to play the piano. Amy knew that this would not be easy: they would probably resist her efforts. As she wondered how to handle this resistance, she decided that the children needed a role model. If they could see that learning to play the piano was a good thing, that it was hard work for other people too, and that their parents were investing as much into the effort as they were, then they would probably not resist as much. Therefore, Amy decided, their father should learn how to play the piano too. Having come to this conclusion, she announced it triumphantly to Mason and Katie's father, who knew very well the dangers of saying no.

Amy sat down at the piano to give me my first lesson on January 1. I was a childhood dropout from piano lessons. I knew a few of the basics, but I really had no skill. I listened to her instructions and did the best I could. She assigned me a song named "Cuckoo," and told me to practice it for a week.

On January 2, I sat down to practice playing "Cuckoo" for the first time. I was alone; there was not a single person in the house. Even so, as I held my fingers over the keys to begin practicing the song, I felt a wave of fear course through my body from my head to my feet. The feeling was palpable. I was in shock. I thought to myself, "This is crazy! There is no one else in this house for me to be embarrassed in front of. Why on earth should I be so scared to practice playing this song?" I understood then that my fear of receiving negative feedback ran deeper than I realized. I had an unconscious belief that my piano-playing ability was fixed and that there wasn't anything I could do about it.

This may have been my unconscious belief, but my conscious belief was different. I knew that I could improve my piano-playing skills by practicing. I reminded myself of that, and I tried to play the first line. I failed miserably, but at least I was pushing the keys. I tried playing only the upper hand, and then the lower hand. I tried playing both hands at the same time. I tried practicing holding one note on one hand for two or three beats while moving my fingers on the other hand after each beat. Then I tried mastering a single measure. By the end of my first practice, I was able to play one measure. By the end of the week I was playing one or two lines. I was starting to feel good about my progress and even found practicing to be fun. After about a month of practicing, I was playing the song pretty well. I told Amy how well I was doing. She told me I needed to play it for her before I could start practicing a new song.

The next day, I sat down to pass off the song. With relatively high confidence, I began playing, but before I got through two lines I was making mistakes I had not made for weeks. I could not believe it! I had this song down. Why was I making such basic mistakes? Amy laughed and said, "That's why you have to play it for me." After five or six attempts, I was finally able to play the song well. Amy told me that I had "passed" and assigned me my next song—one that was a little harder. This time there was almost no fear as I began practicing.

Opening Up to Feedback

As Ryan practiced playing "Cuckoo," he began to experience an externally open state. Because he saw that his skills were improving, he changed his assumption that his piano-playing abilities were fixed to an assumption that his piano-playing abilities could be improved. As a result, he became more eager to take on the challenge of playing the piano and more open to receiving feedback about how well he was playing. He even began having fun when he practiced. The belief that abilities can be learned, a desire to take on challenges, an interest in acquiring and learning from feedback, and the simple enjoyment or fun that is found in an activity are all characteristics of an externally open state, characteristics that tend to lift the people who experience them. However, this brings up the question "What can people who are inclined to be internally closed toward a particular activity do to lift themselves from an internally closed to an externally open state?"

Learning Goals

To see how people who tend to be internally closed can experience an externally open state, it is useful to consider what Seijts and his colleagues did in the mobile phone company exercise (see chapter 9): They assigned a learning goal to the MBA students by telling them to try six different strategies for increasing market share.[1] Asking the students to try six different strategies got even those students who tend to be internally closed to be externally open.

Like these MBA students, people become externally open when they have to come up with multiple strategies because they realize that there is more than one way to do the activity. If there is more than one way to do an activity, some ways are probably better than others. The only way to find out which ways are better is by getting feedback. Now, however, the feedback is about strategies, not about a person. Feedback about strategies is not threatening. In fact, it is appealing, because it helps people figure out which strategies to use. Then, as people learn which strategies work best in which situations, they improve their ability to perform that activity. As their ability increases, they see that it is not fixed; it can be improved. Coming up with multiple strategies, then, helps us see that our abilities are not fixed. This means that we can begin to be externally open when we ask and answer the question "What are three (or four or five) strategies I could use to accomplish my purpose for this situation?"

Ryan came up with and tried multiple strategies as he attempted to play "Cuckoo." He tried playing with just his upper hand or his lower hand. He tried playing with two hands, but only two or three notes at a time. Each time he tried a different strategy, he could see how well that strategy was working. In other words, he got feedback on how well it was working. As he began to play more than a few notes at a time, he came up with new strategies for learning to play multiple measures. Slowly, his skills improved and he quit worrying about whether he was capable of playing. Instead, he was convinced that he could learn to play. He became interested in learning, and was excited about the progress he was making.

Learning and Performance

One of the ironies of the contrast between learning goals and performance goals is that when people engage in complex, changing activities, they often perform better with learning goals than they do with performance goals. Ryan, for example, had trouble playing "Cuckoo" well when he was focused on performing. There are a number of reasons for this. One reason is that humans have a limited amount of attention to spend on any given activity. If we use up part of our limited attention worrying what other people will think of us, we have less attention to spend on actually performing the activity. Also, if we are not focused on learning, but the requirements of an activity change over time, then we will be less able to see how these changes affect us and less able to adapt. And, as we mentioned previously, people who are externally open invest more effort, persist longer, look for and use feedback, believe in themselves, and have higher aspirations.[2]

Another reason why learning goals can improve performance is that learning goals require people to break up an activity into smaller components. When Ryan came up with strategies for learning how to play "Cuckoo," for example, he broke both his learning process and the song he was learning into smaller pieces. This is how people create strategies: by breaking a goal into smaller steps and identifying ways to accomplish each step.[3] People achieve learning goals by coming up with and trying out multiple strategies or different ways of breaking up and completing the activity. When people focus on components of an activity, the activity seems more manageable, people can draw specific feedback from the activity more easily (updating their strategies along the way), and they stay more committed to their goals.

Research supports the idea that people tend to perform better when they have small, short-term goals as well as larger, long-term goals when they face complex tasks. For example, in another experiment, Gary Latham and Gerard Seijts challenged students to earn money in a toy-making business where the cost of supplies and the prices that customers would pay changed regularly.[4] They gave some students a difficult goal, some students a difficult goal and a number of interim goals, and some students a vague goal. The students who had interim goals as well as a difficult goal made almost twice as much as the students with a vague goal and almost six times as much as the students who had only difficult goals. As discussed in chapter 4, small goals enable people to achieve small wins that increase people's confidence, make future solutions more visible, and generate resources that can be used in achieving the next win.[5]

Coming Up with Strategies in Real Time

So far, we have discussed the question "What are three (or four, or five) strategies I could use to accomplish my purpose for this situation?" as something we should ask before we start an activity. Sometimes, however, the characteristics and constraints of a situation are much more uncertain than playing a piano or participating in an experiment—too uncertain to even begin to guess what kinds of strategies could be employed without actually trying to do the activity. And sometimes, even if we think we understand the characteristics and constraints of a situation, we may not understand them as well as we think we do. In cases like these, it may be better to wait and ask ourselves to come up with three or four or five strategies as we perform the activity, rather than before we start. Consider a professional example:

BOB: A few years ago some of my colleagues and I were working with the executives of a Fortune 500 company that was trying to change its culture. We conducted many interviews. We analyzed the company and its industry. Using our analyses, we worked with the company's top management team to design a workshop that we would run four times, each time with one hundred of the top managers in the company in an effort to begin the process of cultural change. The first two sessions of the workshop went well.

In the third workshop we faced a unique challenge: the head of the human resources (HR) department attended. The HR department acted like the secret police. If someone made a politically incorrect statement in front of an HR person, it could destroy that person's career. People in the company dreaded having meetings with representatives from HR. The executives told us that the third workshop would fail. They said that the attendees would not be candid.

This was true. People were much less forthcoming with their opinions. We had trouble making the same progress that we had made in the two previous sessions of the workshop. We began to worry that we were going to fail.

On Thursday morning, it was my turn to present. On previous Thursdays this session had been a turning point: the groups had experienced collective breakthroughs. Yet in week three the attendees were not even approaching a breakthrough. My colleagues and I were tense. Failure was staring us in the face.

Three minutes before I was to walk on stage, one of my colleagues told me that we were in big trouble. I knew that. He then said that I needed to throw my presentation away. Instead of presenting anything I had ever presented before, I needed to stand in front of the group and do whatever they needed.

My first reaction was anger. He was asking me to do an impossible thing! What if I stood there and looked like an idiot?

Who was he to ask me to do this? Would he do it? I was internally closed. I was worried about my ability and how I would look. I was afraid of negative feedback and of failure.

The anger lasted only seconds. I knew he was right. I teach and write about putting the common good first and learning in real time. I often teach about times when we must "walk naked through the land of uncertainty."

I nodded. I have been on a number of these kinds of journeys. I walked toward the stage and focused on being attentive enough to get feedback and learn from it in real time. I would start talking, trying different strategies, until they were hearing my most authentic voice.

I began by telling them I just left my presentation back on the chair. I was standing before them with no organized content. I told them I was full of fear but I was putting myself in this situation not for money, but for the good of the company. I described the success of the two previous workshops and how this one was looking like a failure. I told them that many people had privately predicted this outcome but I could not believe it. I could not believe that mature adults would allow their company to go down the drain because they were afraid of one man in the audience. The private advice, however, had proved correct. They were afraid and were willing to watch the company fail rather than confront reality.

The room was in a deep and sacred silence. I asked a few questions and they responded frankly. As I stood there, I came up with an idea for an activity that would help them assess their true situation and decide if they wanted to confront it. They went to breakout rooms to do the activity. After they left, I collapsed into a chair while my colleague congratulated me. The group was going to make it. There were some big issues ahead, but they would act.

Improvisation and Flow

When Bob's colleague challenged him to throw away his presentation, he had no time to come up with a list of strategies. He could, however, start speaking, try strategies as they occurred to him, and trust that he would find the best strategy in real time.

Christine Moorman and Anne Miner, two organizational scholars, point out that although we usually think of creating strategies and executing strategies as two different activities, done at two different times, people can also bring the creation and execution of strategies together in time.[6] When they do, they are engaging in improvisation. This is what Bob did when he approached the executives in an externally open state: he engaged in improvisation and invited them, implicitly, to join him in improvising.

Initially, Bob improvised by taking actions, observing the executives' emotional expressions, and then updating his strategies. For example, as he tried the strategy of comparing their workshop to the workshops in the previous weeks, he could tell by their facial expressions and the way they leaned in their chairs that what he was saying meant something to them. He tried other strategies as he spoke to them, and received other emotional reactions. Each reaction led him to update and try out even more strategies. Eventually, he started asking them questions, enabling them to join even more fully in the improvisational exercise, and this gave him even more data and enabled him to invent a new collaborative activity for moving the group forward.

Improvisation can lift the people who improvise successfully by giving them a "flow" experience. Flow is a word that psychologist Mihaly Csikszentmihalyi came up with to describe the psychological state that people experience when they perform their best and feel their best.[7] Csikszentmihalyi studied this topic for decades and found that no matter what activity people were doing—whether the activity was done as work or as leisure—when people were engaged in optimal life experiences, they reported similar characteristics that made the activity feel engaging, exhilarating, and in many cases, fun.

The study described in chapter 4, in which Ryan studied nuclear scientists and engineers, sorted out these characteristics to see how they relate to each other.[8] Ryan found, for example, that the central feature of the flow experience is the merging of one's awareness of a situation with automatic and appropriate responses to that situation. In other words, flow is the experience of successful improvisation, creating and acting out effective strategies in real time.

Flow requires clear goals and standards to guide people's concentration, as we described in chapter four. It also requires taking on challenges that push the limits of people's abilities, as well as actively seeking feedback. These are characteristics of an externally open state. As people embrace challenge, gather feedback, and develop an awareness of the unfolding situation, they come up with strategies for acting in the situation. Then, as they apply those strategies automatically and update their strategies, they begin to experience engagement and even exhilaration, they feel an increase in their sense of competence, and they lose track of time.

This is how Bob felt as he improvised with the executives in the culture-change class. After a few minutes, he could tell that he understood the situation well and that his strategies for handling the situation were working. He felt capable of handling the situation, he lost track of time, and as he collapsed into the chair he felt a quiet exhilaration over the experience.

People do not always have to do their strategy making and their strategy implementation at the same time in order to learn, perform well, and enjoy what they are doing. Sometimes people come up with strategies, then implement them, then update their strategies and implement those over longer periods. Donald Schön studied architects, engineers, managers, and psychotherapists who approached their work this way.[9] Their approach was just as externally open, and they still learned, performed well, and enjoyed their activities. The simultaneous creation and execution of strategy that people do in improvisation and flow may be an "optimal" way to experience activities, but it is not the only way.

Flow, like lift, is a psychological experience. They share many characteristics. Both of them involve goals (centering on a purpose), standards (internal direction), learning from feedback (external openness), and positive emotions. The difference between flow and lift, however, is that lift is also other-focused. A person may experience flow, for example, while robbing a house, but people who steal are unlikely to be other-focused. Csikszentmihalyi, in the final chapter of his bestselling book on flow, acknowledged this. He described how people can experience flow in activities like art, science, tennis, or chess, but can be miserable people when they stop engaging in those activities. Csikszentmihalyi argued that people should develop an integrated goal for their lives that would bring meaning to all of their activities: a goal that is "generalized to other people, or to mankind as a whole."[10] In other words, a goal that is other-focused.

We agree that a unifying, other-focused goal for a person's life is a worthwhile thing. But as we explained in chapter 8, focusing on others can also be part of a person's psychological state. Empathizing with others in one's immediate psychological state is important (as discussed in chapters 7 and 8) because people who do things for others without actually feeling empathy for them can often weigh them down rather than lift them up. We can usually tell when other people do not feel empathy for us, even if they are doing things for us. Also, even if people have broad life goals that are "generalized to other people, or to mankind as a whole," they can lose track of those goals in their day-to-day lives. Flow is a wonderful experience, but if we are to lift others as well as ourselves, we would do well to be other-focused as well as purpose-centered, internally directed, and externally open.

The Influence of an Other-Focused State

An externally open state—like the other-focused, internally directed, and purpose-centered states—also has the potential to lift others as well as to lift oneself. People in externally open states lift others by liberating other people from labels that might otherwise constrain them, inviting others to be externally open as well performing artfully and adaptively (both alone and with others), generating knowledge that can be shared with others, and freeing people to celebrate others' successes as well as their own.

Freedom from Labels

BOB: I was once invited to a six-day retreat with twenty-two spiritual leaders from many different religious backgrounds. I felt a little fear when I thought about going to this retreat because I suspected that there might be some people in the group who felt negatively toward my religious tradition. If I went to this retreat, I might be judged and criticized. I was fearful of getting intense negative feedback.

My administrative assistant noticed what was going on. With an impish grin she asked me if I was afraid. She knew she had me. I groaned and told her to order the plane ticket. I may have been afraid, but at least I recognized it and began making the effort to become externally open.

In the first hour of the retreat I was on edge. I was tempted to judge and label other people—the very thing I was afraid they would do to me. I knew I had to get out of that state but I was still fearful. I made a choice to change.

The retreat was full of intimate conversation. We listened to each other's stories of personal trial, failure, and triumph. One man spoke of developmental rituals in the wilderness and accounts of his personal transformation. Another man told of enduring brutality while participating in demonstrations in the sixties. He saw his efforts change the racism of people he thought would never change. A woman spoke of her service in the midst of violent gangs and of occasional sacred moments when anger was turned to love. As we listened to each other, our need to label each other and to differentiate ourselves began to fade. We began to see at least as much of what we had in common between us as we saw of what was different.

The temptation to impose judgmental labels on others (and on oneself) arises when people are internally closed, not when people are externally open; it comes from the belief that people's fundamental character, abilities, and intelligence cannot change. We can see this in research conducted by Peter Heslin, Gary Latham, and Don VandeWalle,[11] who asked people to take on the role of managers evaluating their subordinates. After measuring the people's beliefs about how fixed or changeable personalities and abilities are, Heslin and colleagues showed them two video clips of "one of their employees" at work. They asked them to evaluate that employee's performance. Then they showed two more video clips of the same employee and asked the participants to rate the employee again. In one experiment, they showed two clips of the employee performing poorly and then two clips of the employee performing well. In another experiment, they showed the clips in reverse order.

When the participants saw the videos, those who believed that people can change their abilities adjusted their performance ratings much more than those who believed that people cannot change. In other words, when participants who thought that people cannot change saw a person perform poorly, they labeled that person as a poor performer, and they were reluctant to change that label. If they saw a person perform well, they labeled that person as a good performer and were reluctant to change. The participants who believed that people can change their abilities, in contrast, did not label the employees as "good" or "bad," but rated the employees according to how they performed.

Parents, teachers, spouses, coaches, and the rest of us often behave similarly to the "managers" in Heslin and colleagues' study. When we label people, they have to deal with the weight of being labeled, and also with the fact that many labels become self-fulfilling prophecies. Without realizing or intending to, people often constrain us to act out the stereotypes they place upon us. For instance, managers who believe that people have fixed abilities provide less coaching to improve employees' performance.[12] This makes sense because if you think that people cannot change, why would you bother investing time and energy to help them improve? By neglecting to coach their employees, though, these managers can contribute to the employees' poor performance and are then likely to blame it on the employees' lack of ability.

Even positive labels can be damaging if positive labels praise people for their ability rather than their efforts. This makes it more likely that people will avoid future challenges and feedback.[13] For example, employees with managers who saw their abilities as changeable were free to act without the constraints of their managers' labels, learn from feedback, and improve their performance. Similarly, when Bob attended the religious retreat, he built relationships with the people he met at the retreat and they were able to learn from each other because they were not constrained by the labels that they might otherwise have placed on each other. They were all lifted as a result.

Modeling Openness to Challenge and Feedback

RYAN: On January 2, 2007 I was so struck by the fear I felt when I tried to play "Cuckoo" that I kept thinking about it. Before experiencing that fear coursing through my body, I had no idea how afraid I was of receiving feedback that might suggest that I was stupid. The next day at dinner, I told the story to my family. When I finished describing the fear that I had felt, I asked our children why they thought I had felt it. Mason knew the answer instantly: I was afraid of feeling stupid because I was not any good at playing the piano. He could relate to my fear.

When I saw how quickly and easily Mason was able to answer my question, I felt grateful that Amy had decided that I would learn how to play the piano with the children. I realized that by learning how to play the piano with them, I was showing them that I was willing to do the same thing that was being asked of them and I was also showing them that it was okay to do something that might make you feel stupid for the sake of learning and growing. By doing something that I was not good at, I was also implicitly giving them permission to do something that they were not good at. Perhaps, if their father—a person who provides for their needs, helps them learn the answers to life's questions, and lays down many of the rules of the household— is willing to fail, take negative feedback, and perhaps even feel foolish for the sake of learning, then it is okay for them to take on challenges for the sake of learning as well.

This is the same thing that Bob did for the executives in the culture change workshop. As they saw his efforts to be externally open for their sakes, despite the risk of failing and looking foolish, it gave them the courage to say things that they had avoided saying all week.

People notice and respond to cues that prompt them to become more or less externally open. In chapter 9, for example, we discussed how people who hear praise for their abilities or receive goals that focus on performance tend to become internally closed. Similarly, when we praise others for their effort, set goals that focus on learning, or engage in other actions that suggest we value learning and feedback, other people notice those cues and begin to feel that it is okay to seek and receive feedback and to learn from that feedback. Stuart Bunderson and Kathie Sutcliffe saw this in a study they conducted with teams that manage the business units of large companies.[14] The people in these teams became more open to learning by noticing their teammates' behavior and following the behaviors their teammates were engaging in.

Four things need to happen for people to learn from the behaviors that other people model: (1) people have to notice the behavior being modeled, (2) they have to have a label for the behavior that will help them remember it, (3) they have to be able to translate the behavior into action (perhaps through practice), and (4) they have to be motivated to put that behavior into action.[15] When Ryan started practicing the piano with his children, he gave them a new and unusual behavior for them to notice. The children had labels for what he was doing because Amy was teaching them as well. Amy also helped them put their labeled behavior into action by having them practice each day. The degree to which they saw the fun that Ryan was having and found motivation in that remains an open question. Unfortunately, in recent months, Ryan has let his work and his other activities crowd out his piano practice. If he wants his children to benefit from his example, he will need to be more internally directed (in other words, living values of persistence and consistency), not just externally open.

Performing Artfully and Adaptively

RYAN: When we bought our first home my wife, Amy, was excited to decorate it. She knew she did not like the wallpaper, paint, chandeliers, or cupboards, but she had no idea what to do about them. She was often frustrated over her inability to make the house look the way she wanted it to. She approached decorating the home in an externally open state, and as a result, the journey she took as she learned to decorate is an example of influence through artful performance and collective mastery.

Amy learned how to decorate by reading books, watching home and garden shows on television, hiring an interior designer to teach her (not to decorate her home for her), hanging different-color paint chips on the wall, and painting rooms over and over until the shade was just right. She tried repainting or reupholstering furniture. She tore down cupboards and ceiling fans. She learned how to install a sink. She tried multiple strategies for every challenge.

Two years later, we were hunting for a new home. This time, she was completely different. She knew what to look for in the house, and when we looked inside homes, she could rattle off everything that would have to be done to make the house look nice. She no longer struggled to explain why she did not like the interior design of a home. She knew exactly what was wrong and how to fix it.

The road from novice to mastery that Amy took in interior design is the same road that architects, engineers, managers, psychotherapists, and other professionals take. Donald Schön studied professionals like these to see how they learn.[16] He found that the best professionals perform their craft artfully by reflecting on their work while they do it. In other words, they are externally open while they work. They come up with strategies, try them out (in their minds or in actuality), judge their quality (by extracting feedback from the task), and update their actions as they go along. When they are externally open, they develop a more accurate understanding of their situation,[17] they adapt their work more closely to the needs of the immediate situation,[18] and they innovate and come up with creative new ways to do the work.[19] This process, he argued, is what gives professional work its quality—what makes it artful.

The road to mastery that externally open people take can lift others by producing innovative and artful outcomes that inspire others. The poem *High Flight*, which we included in the introduction to this book, is an example of an inspiring outcome. The road to mastery can also lift others when we invite others to walk the road to mastery with us. When groups of people—like Schön's architects, engineers, managers, and psychotherapists—do their work together in an externally open way, they can develop a collective mastery in a particular domain. Research suggests, for example, that groups and organizations can develop collective capabilities in technical domains such as cardiac surgery, chemical adhesives development, and distributed organizing,[20] as well as in moral domains like courage and compassion.[21]

Collective mastery is not limited to formal groups. Amy often shares her growing mastery of internal design with others, and learns from others as well. She continues to watch, read, and talk to others. Whether formal or informal, communities of practice can lift each other by taking on challenges, being open to feedback from those challenges, and working together.

Sharing Knowledge and Celebrating Others' Successes

RYAN: About a year after Mason and Katie began learning to play the piano, Amy decided to see if Katie was up to the challenge of a more difficult piece. She asked Katie to start working on "Cuckoo." From Katie's effort to play "Cuckoo," I learned two more ways in which our externally open states can influence others.

Katie's first day of working on "Cuckoo" did not go well. Later in the evening Amy told me that it might have been too soon to ask Katie to play the song. I wondered if I could help Katie figure out how to play it, since I had struggled to learn it myself.

The next day, while Amy was out, I told Katie that it was time to practice the piano. Katie did not want to—her new song was too hard. "Katie," I said, "did you know that this was the first song that Mommy had me learn how to play?"

"No," she said. She was slightly more interested.

"It was. And it was hard for me too. But I can show you how I figured out how to play it."

Katie was willing to try that out. I showed her how I broke the song up into little pieces and practiced only a few notes at a time. I played those first few notes for her. I asked her to play the first few notes ten times. She did it, and did it pretty easily. We added a few more notes. After fifteen minutes, she had learned to play the first line and was proud of her accomplishment.

The next day I said to Katie, "Hey Katie, why don't you show your mom what you learned yesterday?" Katie walked proudly to the piano and played the first line of "Cuckoo." Amy was delighted and said, "Katie, that's wonderful! You did great! How did you learn that?"

"Daddy taught me!" she said.

That earned me some brownie points, and Amy immediately got to work helping Katie learn the rest of the song. Within two weeks she had it down, and she played it proudly at every opportunity for weeks afterward.

Because Ryan became externally open as he learned to play "Cuckoo," he was able to lift Katie in two ways. First, he lifted her by sharing knowledge. We cannot share knowledge that we do not have, and we gain knowledge by learning, which happens most effectively when we are in an externally open state. By learning to play "Cuckoo" and then teaching it to Katie, Ryan helped her become a better piano player. More importantly, perhaps, Ryan helped her become more confident in her ability to learn, something that should help her be externally open more often.

Helping Katie learn to play "Cuckoo" also gave Ryan an opportunity to celebrate Katie's success with her. People are less likely to celebrate others' successes with them when they are internally closed because they tend to feel diminished by the others' successes: if our abilities cannot change, then other people's successes make us less exceptional or more of a failure by comparison.[22] If we are externally open, we worry less about comparison, so we can celebrate others' successes. This strengthens our relationship with them, as discussed in chapter 8.

The Love of Performing

People can experience an externally open state by asking themselves (either before the activity or as they do the activity), "What are three (or four or five) strategies I could use to accomplish my purpose for this situation?" Externally open states lift us when we experience them because we believe that we can grow and improve, we take on challenges, we learn from feedback, we perform better in complex or uncertain activities, and we have fun doing all this. Our externally open states also tend to lift others because when we are externally open we free others from our judgmental labels, we act in ways that invite others to be externally open as well, we learn together and develop collective competencies, we gain new knowledge that we can share, and we are more likely to celebrate other people's successes with them.

An externally open state is a wonderful thing, but sometimes life requires us to focus on outcomes. What if we need to accomplish a goal now and we do not have time to learn how to do it better? Or what if we need to make an ethical decision? If it is a question of right or wrong, then wouldn't it be wrong to approach the situation open to the possibility of failure?

These are legitimate questions. For example, in the study we mentioned earlier in which Bunderson and Sutcliffe studied the business-unit management teams, being externally open was a good thing for these teams only to a point.[23] Too much of a focus on learning led to a decrease in performance, presumably because these teams needed to emphasize *using* knowledge as well as gaining knowledge. Similarly, when Anne Miner and her colleagues studied improvisation in the product-development activities of companies, they found that sometimes people kept improvising the designs of their products when the company needed them to freeze the product designs and begin to manufacture and sell them.[24] And sometimes ethical decisions need to be made, not deliberated on. In most cases, we know we should not lie, cheat, and steal. Seeking feedback is not likely to shed additional light on the situation.

There are limits, then, to how much challenge people should tackle and to how much feedback should be sought. Even so, we would argue that experiencing an externally open state is important most of the time for at least two reasons. First, when activities are complex and changing, people actually perform better in an externally open state. In a world that seems to be growing more complex and ambiguous by the moment, we are likely to encounter an increasing number of complex and changing activities. This is as true in dealing with ethical dilemmas as it is in performing activities. Learning may not be necessary for simple ethical decisions, but with economic distress, technological advancement, shifting demographics, globalization, and countless other forces affecting both our personal and professional lives, it seems that the moral questions of our day are growing more complex rather than less. If we believe our moral character is fixed and we avoid feedback because of this, then we will be ill-equipped to handle the challenges coming our way.[25]

The second reason why experiencing an externally open state is important is that—as with each of the characteristics of *lift*—we can take advantage of the benefits of an externally open state and avoid its disadvantages if we try to experience the other three characteristics of *lift* as well. For example, purposes can include deadlines that tell us when to stop gathering feedback. Values like efficiency or punctuality can help us know when to put feedback seeking on hold. And some of the stakeholders we empathize with are likely to push us to focus on execution when the time is appropriate. The four characteristics of *lift* help us from taking any particular component too far. Thus, having discussed each component individually, it is now time to explain how these characteristics fit together to help the people who experience them become a positive force in any situation.

⤲ Practices for Applying the Principles of Lift

When people want to become externally open, it can be difficult to come up with strategies or to stop worrying about impressing others or looking foolish. The following practices can help:

1. **Restate the praise or criticism we receive from others.** When people praise or criticize our inherent ability, we can reframe their comments to focus on effort and strategy.

2. **Get input.** If we have trouble coming up with strategies, we can ask others for suggestions, watch how other people approach the activity, and read books for suggestions.

3. **Name our fears.** When we feel pressure, stress, or fear, we can reduce that fear by naming it. Identifying and acknowledging pressure, stress, or fear reduces uncertainty and makes it easier to do something.

4. **Set learning goals for our extraordinary purposes.** Sometimes when we think about a result we want to create, we focus on what others will think about it. We can focus on this less by setting learning goals right after asking what result we want to create.

5. **List things we are grateful for and recall personal development journeys.** Thinking about times when we have overcome difficulties or developed new abilities can help us see that we can overcome challenges or develop abilities this time as well. And if we focus on what we are grateful for, in those journeys and in our lives now, we can reduce our concern over what others think. Gratitude does this by helping us think of our successes more humbly (so we are less likely to attribute them to our own ability), and by focusing us on factors that helped us succeed (this promotes learning).

chapter 11

The Integration of Positive Opposites

RYAN: In the spring of 2006, I spent a day and a half in Athens, Greece, training a group of managers from a global company on innovation. The first morning went well. During that afternoon, however, I asked the managers to split up into groups to work on an idea-generating task. As I explained the task to them, I could tell by their facial expressions that many of them did not want to do it. I thought that they would see the value of the task after they had gone through it, though, so I pressed on.

A few of the managers asked questions. They were polite, but it was clear that they did not think the exercise was relevant to them. One of the managers became particularly vocal. I expressed sympathy but told him that he would probably discover that he had learned from the task if he did it. He stood up, expressed his disagreement, and walked out of the room. The rest of the group performed the task, but the atmosphere in the room was tense. As

I walked among the groups I received many forced smiles and few signs of interest.

Eventually, the manager who walked out came back and joined his group. I talked to him. He explained his point of view in a calmer way. I acknowledged the legitimacy of his concerns and expressed appreciation for his willingness to come back and try the activity anyway. When the training session ended, the atmosphere was still tense and there was definitely no enthusiasm.

I could not sleep that night. I wallowed in my problems. I thought, "They need to learn how to come up with ideas. That's a fundamental step in innovating. The executives who hired me wanted me to train them on that. Why can't they trust me? I have expertise in this. That's why they hired me. If these managers rate me poorly, I'll lose this job. That would be so embarrassing. The executives who hired me will never trust me again, and I'll look stupid. Maybe I'm not that good at teaching after all." My imagination ran wild.

Ryan's thoughts that night had all the hallmarks of being comfort-centered, externally directed, self-focused, and internally closed. He wanted the managers to follow along with his teaching plan, but instead had the problem of how to deal with their discontent. He had let vague and indirect instructions from the people who hired him, emotional reactions from the managers, and other cues in the situation drive his behavior. He was worried about how this training session would affect him, his career, and his reputation instead of empathizing with how the managers and the other stakeholders in their company felt. He was afraid of negative feedback, and worried that this experience was a reflection of his fixed abilities.

RYAN: I recognized that I was in a comfort-centered, externally directed, self-focused, and internally closed state. Fortunately I knew what to do about it. I told myself that I had wallowed enough. Then I asked myself the four questions.

1. What result do I want to create?

I wanted to help the managers I was training to succeed at innovating in their company. I wanted them to be able to walk out of the room at lunchtime with clear ideas about what they were going to do differently to help their company be more innovative. I wanted them to be excited about implementing those ideas.

2. What would my story be if I were living the values I expect of others?

I had been expecting these managers to respect me for my expertise. I, however, had not shown them the same level of respect. They had expertise in their jobs. They knew where innovation was needed in their units. I needed to respect that expertise as I pursued my purpose. I began imagining a story for how I might do that. When I began teaching in the morning, I would ask them what they needed to know. I would respect their opinions and figure out how to give them ideas that would be relevant to their situations. I would also give them chances to talk about how they could apply those ideas in their situations.

3. How would I feel if I were experiencing this situation from other people's points of view?

When I asked myself this question, I felt bad about how my unwillingness to deviate from my teaching plan had frustrated the managers. I could empathize with their frustration, and as a result I wanted to do a better job tomorrow for *them*, not just for myself.

4. What are three (or four or five) strategies I could use to accomplish my purpose for this situation?

When I asked myself this question, I did two things. First, I thought of different ways that I could begin my training the next day. I wanted to learn more about their expertise and about what they wanted to know. I came up with different ways to begin the class. I was curious about which introduction would be best. I wanted feedback. I could not get feedback from the managers in my hotel room in the middle of the night, but I could imagine how each introduction might turn out, so that is what I did.

Imagining the introduction was the easy part. The second thing I needed to do was conduct a training session on innovation that focused on their needs. Until I asked my introductory questions, I would have no idea what their needs were. Therefore, after I asked my questions about what they wanted to learn, I would have to make up strategies and try them out in real time. I imagined speaking to them tomorrow, listening to their answers, trying out some strategies, and adapting to their feedback in real time. It was intimidating, but I was comforted by the fact that I now felt real concern for them and I wanted to learn from them about how I could best meet their needs.

The next morning I walked into the classroom. I opened the class by saying, "Yesterday afternoon I asked you to participate in an idea-generating activity that many of you did not want to do. If I understand correctly, those of you who did not want to do the activity did not want to do it because you did not feel that generating ideas is an issue for you in your jobs. I believe in adapting my teaching to the needs of the people I am working with, and I failed to do that yesterday. I am sorry. This morning I want to work together with you to create a training session that will be maximally useful to you for innovating successfully in your jobs. To do that, I need to know what you need to know. So to start out this morning, I'd like to ask you to tell me, 'What do you need to know in order to innovate successfully in your organization?'"

When I said this, the managers raised their hands. Each of them told me what they wanted to know, and I wrote all of their answers on a flip chart. When they finished, it was clear that almost all of them had the same problem. They did not have many problems coming up with ideas that could help them in their work. Their problem was in getting their ideas implemented. In one form or another, all of the managers wanted to know how they could influence others in ways that would help them get their best ideas implemented.

Now that I knew what they needed, I paused and thought for a moment. Then I decided to skip over dozens of slides. Instead I selected twelve slides that focused on how to get innovations implemented in organizations. As I presented them, the managers became increasingly enthusiastic. Given how much they liked the concepts I was presenting, I suggested that each person select one of the concepts, form a group with others, tell the other people in the group how they might apply that principle to get one of their own ideas implemented, and then get suggestions from others in the group about how they could improve their efforts even further. The managers broke into groups, and the groups buzzed with energy as they discussed these ideas.

The morning flew by. At the end of it, managers announced to each other the things that they were going to do differently when they returned to their offices. After we finished, the manager who had walked out on my training session during the previous afternoon came up to talk to me. He shook my hand and said, "Thank you. That was fabulous. If we could do what you did this morning in our company, we would not need any training in innovation."

We share the story of Ryan's training session for two reasons. First, we share it because it integrates the concepts we reviewed in chapters 3 through 10; it describes how a person who is comfort-centered, externally driven, self-focused, and internally closed can become purpose-centered, internally driven, other-focused, and externally open. Second, we share it because it is an illustration of the subtitle of this book, of how to become a positive force in any situation. This claim—that a person can become a positive force in any situation—is audacious. We need to explain why we would make such an audacious claim. Therefore, we close this book by discussing each point in the claim: What is it about the four characteristics of lift that make lift so *positive*? What is it about these four characteristics that helps a person become a *force*, or an influence, upon others? Do these four characteristics really apply in *any* situation? And why is this focus on *situations* so important? By discussing these questions, we learn how these principles work together and what we can do to take advantage of them.

Becoming Positive

The first step in understanding how the four characteristics of lift work together is to summarize the principles behind each characteristic.

We do this in Table 11.1. The titles across the top of the columns are the four characteristics of lift. The rows include the thoughts and feelings that make up each of the four characteristics, the obstacles that prevent people from experiencing each characteristic, the question that helps people experience each characteristic, and the influence that people who experience each characteristic usually have on others.

Now, to see how the four characteristics of lift work together, imagine that Ryan had not clarified his purpose before the final half-day of training. Instead, imagine that he spent the night trying to solve the problem of how to teach idea generation to managers who did not think they needed to learn it. In this case, even if Ryan respected the expertise of the managers he was training (internal direction), he would have tried to figure out how to adapt his teaching on idea generation to help them see how it could be useful to their jobs rather than tried to figure out what they needed to know to innovate successfully. Even if he had empathized with their frustrations (other-focus), he probably would have tried to find a way to make his training on idea generation less frustrating and more useful. And even if he had come up with multiple strategies for how to approach the teaching (external openness), they would have been strategies for how to teach idea generation. Clarifying our purpose lifts us out of our problems and gives us meaning, direction, and energy for our activities. No matter how much integrity, empathy, and artfulness we use, if we let our problems define our situation we are unlikely to see the opportunities that come when we focus on purpose. We may even exacerbate the problems.

Similar problems arise with each characteristic of *lift*. If Ryan had clarified his purpose, empathized with the managers, and tried out different strategies without developing a story about living his values, he might have regressed into the automatic patterns of hierarchical teacher-student relationships. If he had clarified his purpose, thought through how he would act consistently with his values, and tried out different strategies without trying to empathize with the managers, then his effort to teach to their needs might have felt forced or contrived to them. And if he had clarified his purpose, thought through

Table 11.1 Summary of the Four Characteristics of Lift

	Purpose-Centered	Internally Directed	Other-Focused	Externally Open

Thoughts and feelings that define this state	1. Specific, positive, challenging, self-chosen goals
	2. Energy
	3. Focus
	4. A clear definition of the situation that directs action and gives meaning
		1. Dignity
		  a. Strength
		  b. Freedom
		  c. Stories that describe how and explain why a person should act consistently with personal values
		2. Calmness, comfort
		3. A more complex understanding of the situation
			1. Empathy
			2. Rapport
			3. Energy
			4. Calmness
				1. A belief that people's abilities and characteristics can be developed
				  a. Desire for challenge
				  b. Interest in feedback
				2. Confidence
				3. Enjoyment (fun)

Obstacles to being in this state	1. Expectations learned in previous situations or from others	1. Automatic responses to cues in a person's context
		2. Self-justification
			1. Ignoring invitations to empathize
			2. Self-justification
				1. The belief that people's abilities and characteristics are relatively fixed
				  a. Praise for ability or characteristics
				  b. Competitive goals

Question that helps people experience this state	What result do I want to create?	What would my story be if I were living the values I expect of others?	How would I feel if I were experiencing this situation from other people's points of view?	What are three (or four or five) strategies I could use to accomplish my purpose for this situation?

Influences that this state has on others	1. More complex and creative thinking
	2. More importance is attributed to the situation
	3. Energy
	4. The attraction and creation of resources
	5. Higher performance, which creates legitimacy for the purpose being pursued
		1. Elevation—the desire to live one's own highest values
		2. Comfort
		3. Higher performance, which creates legitimacy for the purpose being pursued
			1. Security/safety
			2. Increased willingness to take risks, including:
			  a. Acting with integrity
			  b. Resilience
			  c. Trust
			  d. Learning and experimentation
			3. Higher performance, which creates legitimacy for the purpose being pursued
				1. Freedom from labels
				2. Openness to challenge and feedback
				3. Higher performance, which creates legitimacy for the purpose being pursued
				4. Communities of practice
				5. Knowledge to share
				6. Joy in others' success

how he would act consistently with his values, and empathized with the managers' frustration without trying out different strategies, then he might have been more intimidated by feedback and less able to adapt to their needs and deliver to them the training that was most useful to them.

Integrating the Experiences

The exclusion of one characteristic of *lift*, then, can dampen the positivity of our experience and our influence. Our experience with these characteristics is the most positive, in contrast, when they are integrated, whether the situation involves a mechanic repairing a car, a person visiting a neighbor, an accountant trying to figure out how to state earnings, or people engaged in any activity. When we experience all four characteristics of *lift*, these characteristics reinforce the positive and lessen the negative effects of the other characteristics, both in their influence and in our psychological state.

When Ryan decided that the result he wanted to create in the last half-day of his innovation training was to help the managers be successful at and get excited about innovating, his purpose reinforced the other three characteristics. It reinforced his desire to live consistently with his values because his purpose made the activity more meaningful; he was trying to help the managers make a difference in their company, not just to make them understand concepts. We are more likely to want to live our values as we pursue our goals if those goals are meaningful to us. After all, if a purpose really matters, it should be done with integrity and done well.

Ryan's purpose also reinforced his efforts to empathize with people by defining the situation for him. Without a definition of the situation, he may have empathized with people whose feelings were not relevant to the situation, or he may have failed to empathize with people who were relevant to the situation. For example, because his purpose was to help the company as well as the managers, he could empathize with others in the company as well.

Ryan's purpose also helped him identify strategies, seek feedback, and learn from the situation. If Ryan had not had a purpose, his strategies would have focused on motivating the managers to learn how to come up with ideas, and he probably would have learned the wrong things. Also, it is easier to develop strategies to achieve clear purposes. Thus, a clear, meaningful purpose reinforced Ryan's experience of each of the other characteristics of lift.

Just like clear purposes, internally directed, other-focused, and externally open states can reinforce the other three characteristics. The internally directed state can reinforce the other-focused state by questioning the validity of the justifications that keep us from empathizing with others. The stories that we have in an internally directed state can also give us a starting point for developing the strategies of an externally open state. And, because values are meaningful goals in their own right, incorporating these values into our purpose for our activities can also help make those activities more meaningful. For example, as Ryan became more internally directed, he found it easier to empathize with the managers he was training, he based his ideas for how to approach the next day on his story of asking them what they wanted to learn, and he adapted his purpose so that he would help the managers succeed in a way that respected their expertise.

The other-focused state can help us be externally open because we usually want to learn the perspectives, knowledge, and insights of the people we care about. The other-focused state reinforces the meaningfulness of our purposes because we incorporate the feelings and needs of the people we empathize with into our purpose. The other-focused state can also help us be internally directed because our empathy for others melts away our justifications and connects us to some of our deepest values. For example, as Ryan became other-focused in preparing for the training session, he felt motivated to get the feedback he needed to understand the managers' feelings more deeply, his desire to help the managers increased, and he wanted to help them in a way that respected their expertise.

The externally open state can also reinforce the other characteristics. The strategies of the externally open state help us accomplish the goals of a purpose-centered state, and the feedback we receive gives us insight into how to adapt our purposes to our unfolding situations. Also, by creating and comparing multiple strategies, we can see which strategies are most consistent with our values and whether we need to update our understanding of what those values mean. Finally, the feedback we receive in an externally open state can help us see and understand the people with whom we are trying to empathize in deeper and more nuanced ways. For example, as Ryan became more externally open in his training, he refined his purpose further by focusing on implementation and influence. He respected the managers' expertise more fully by listening to feedback about their needs and adapting the training accordingly. He also empathized more fully by paying attention and adapting to their needs and feelings throughout the presentation. These processes are similar each time we integrate these characteristics: we feel uplifted by a clear, meaningful purpose, the dignity of acting consistently with our values, the empathy of caring for others, and the curiosity and interest of learning and trying new things.

Integrating the Influence

The integration of the four characteristics of *lift* affects how positive our influence is on others as well as how positive our personal experience is. For starters, each of the characteristics of lift, for different reasons that we discussed in chapters 4, 6, 8, and 10, tends to improve a person's performance on the activities in which they experience these states. When these characteristics are combined, we can expect that people who experience lift will tend to perform well in the activities in which they are participating. High performance tends to draw attention, attract people, make activities legitimate, and draw resources. This is why, for example, when Ryan finished his final training session, the participants wanted to use the ideas they received and the manager who had walked out the day before wanted to compliment him. Sometimes people become jealous of those who achieve high performance, but this possibility is less likely when the high-performing person is other-focused. When high performers are other-focused, people usually know that the high performers care for them and the high performers often include others in their activities.

Other types of influence from each of the characteristics of lift also reinforce each other. For example, we usually feel inspired to live our values more fully when we watch the actions of a person who is in an internally directed state. We are even more likely to act on that inspiration, though, if the person we are watching also empathizes with us, helping us feel secure. Further, our value-laden action will probably become more sophisticated if that internally directed, externally open person is also purpose-centered. And because that person is externally open, his or her desire to learn will invite us to participate in a community of practice, where we can learn together how to live our values. The managers in Ryan's training seminar appeared to do this. When he left they were all sharing ideas about how they would implement concepts from the training with each other. They acted as though they felt excited about using these concepts and secure in taking the risks the concepts implied. Ryan's final session with them had had an integrated, positive, and reinforcing influence on all involved.

What Is Positive?

The integration of the four characteristics of lift also helps us address an important question about our claim that people who experience lift have a positive influence. Namely, how can we claim that a person has positive influence when everyone has a different perspective on what is "positive?" For example, when Ryan trained the managers in Greece, there may have been a few of them who did not think the training was positive. The positivity of a person's influence is a value judgment. If everyone has different values, then it seems that there must always be trade-offs in how positive a person's influence is.

It is because of this potential for trade-offs that the integration of positive opposites in our framework for lift is so important. Lift requires us to focus on what others feel as well as on what we want. It requires us to hold ourselves up to enduring values and standards while also using feedback to adapt to unfolding situations. These positive opposites, and the effort it takes for us to integrate the trade-offs they imply, suggest that we need to think about influence differently.

Normally we tend to think of influence as flowing in one direction, from the influencer to the person or people being influenced. If a person is other-focused and externally open, however, we may be better off thinking about influence as a conversation. As in a conversation, people who experience *lift* influence others in part because they are concerned about all of the people who are affected by the situation (other-focused) and they are anxious to receive feedback from these people (externally open). This means that when we experience lift, we are influenced by others as well as influencing them. Their beliefs about what is positive will inform our beliefs; will be incorporated into our thoughts, feelings, and actions; and will be updated as we continue to receive feedback.

When Ryan asked the managers in the innovation training what they wanted to learn, he used this conversational approach to influence. He incorporated their ideas about what would make the situation positive with his own ideas. Their perspectives about what was positive did not overwhelm his. He still knew what result he wanted to create and which of his personal values would guide his efforts. He was also able to increase the positivity of his influence, however, by making his influence conversational. In fact, it is often when we are seeking to be influenced that we are most influential. When we do this, we learn together how to embrace and integrate trade-offs rather than succumb to them.

The Implications of Positivity

The importance of positivity and conversation becomes especially clear when we consider the research of Marcial Losada. A number of years ago, Losada worked as the director of Electronic Data Systems Center for Advanced Research. Within this center, Losada had a laboratory called the "Capture Lab," where he and his colleagues would bring in business-unit leadership teams and watch their strategic planning meetings.[1]

Using two-way mirrors, microphones, and special software, Losada recorded the time of every comment the members of the business teams uttered, then coded each comment's type. He used a positive-negative code to identify comments as either supportive, encouraging, or appreciative, or as disapproving, sarcastic, or cynical; an inquiry-advocacy code to identify comments as either exploring a position or arguing for a position; and a self-other code to identify comments as either focusing inward (on the speaker, the speaker's group, or the speaker's company) or outward (on a person or group outside of the room or on another company). He divided the management teams into high-, mixed-, and low-performing groups, on the basis of both the profitability and customer satisfaction these teams achieved and how the team members were rated by others in their company. He plotted each team's positivity-negativity, inquiry-advocacy, and self-other scores over time. Then he made an interesting discovery.

When Losada plotted the teams' positivity-negativity, inquiry-advocacy, and self-other scores across time, he found that the pattern formed by the fifteen high-performing teams was a butterfly-shaped pattern. This pattern, originally discovered by Edward Lorenz, is a trajectory that does not repeat itself and does not end at a single, particular set of values.[2] It represents a system that is neither rigidly ordered nor completely disordered, making it an excellent system for learning and adaptation. The size and shape of this pattern suggests that these teams' conversations had high and balanced amounts of inquiring and advocating, high and balanced amounts of focusing inward and focusing outward, and 5.6 times as many times positive things said as negative things. These teams were never repetitive and were much more expansive in their conversational experience than the twenty-six mixed- and nineteen low-performing teams.

In contrast with the high-performing teams, the conversations of the mixed-performing teams had a pattern that started out like the pattern in the high-performing teams, but they were less broad and they eventually fell into a pattern that recurred over and over. The conversations of the low-performance teams simply spiraled down to a single point and stopped—like the flat line on a heart monitor when someone dies.

These observations suggest that the reason the high-performing teams performed so well is that they were much more expansive and original in the way they interacted. They balanced creativity and structure in ways that created exceptional learning and performance.

Losada's discoveries did not end there. He was intrigued by the 5.6-to-1 ratio of positivity-to-negativity he found in the high-performing teams. Then, as he read literature throughout the social sciences, he found out that John Gottman and his colleagues had used positivity-negativity ratios to study a different social unit: marriages.[3] By observing the conversations of married couples, Gottman found that those couples who had a positivity-to-negativity ratio of 5 to 1 had happy, productive, and enduring marriages whereas the couples whose marriages ended in divorce had less than one positive comment for every negative comment.

Losada returned to the equations he used to model the chaotic attractor and looked at the ratios more closely.[4] His model suggested that the behavior of all the variables in the model can be described with only the positivity-negativity ratio. In other words, he could predict the performance of the business units—and the success of the marriages—on the basis of the ratio of positive-to-negative things that the people in these teams and marriages said to each other.

Losada found an explanation for this pattern when he met Barbara Fredrickson, whose work on positive emotions is described in chapter 4. Fredrickson's research suggests that positive emotions serve two functions.[5] First, positive emotions broaden the repertoire of thoughts and actions that a person has available in any given situation. For example, when Ryan felt empathy for the managers he was training, he was also able to pay attention to a broader array of cues. And when he started improvising and having fun in the actual training session, he was able to think of and even combine activities that he had not considered before.

A second function of positive emotions is the building of enduring resources for the people who experience them. For example, in the innovation training session, Ryan created constructive relationships where he might have had no relationships or negative relationships. He also came up with new ways to present innovation and new developmental activities, all of which he can use again in the future. In other words, Fredrickson's theory suggests that the reason why Losada's business teams and Gottman's married couples were so successful was that their positivity enabled them to consider a wide range of possibilities and to build resources that they could use to weather bad times and flourish during good times.

Fredrickson and Losada took this research two steps further.[6] First, in a journaling study of emotions experienced by college students, they found that the same patterns that occur in business teams and married couples also occur in individuals' lives: flourishing college students experienced a positivity-to-negativity ratio of 3.2. Languishing college students experienced a ratio of 2.3. Given these findings, Losada reexamined Lorenz's equations and found that we can expect people to move between languishing and flourishing at a ratio of 2.9 (or, for practical purposes, 3). In other words, if people experience more than three times as much positivity as negativity in their lives, work, and relationships, they are likely to flourish. If they experience less than three times as much positivity as negativity, they are likely to languish.

It is important to note that the ratio for human flourishing is not 3 to 0. Negativity still exists in these individual lives, married relationships, and business teams. In fact, when Fredrickson and Losada examined the Lorenz equations to see if there was an upper limit for too much positivity, they found that the butterfly-shaped dynamics in their model begin to erode when the positivity-to-negativity ratio exceeds 11.6. Above this threshold, the pattern begins to contract and then to repeat itself over and over. This suggests a need for appropriate negativity in human lives, relationships, and groups. We say "appropriate" negativity because research also indicates that some kinds of negativity are much more corrosive than others. Gottman, for example, found that some conflict in a marriage is a good thing, but that expressions of disgust or contempt can be exceedingly damaging.[7]

Positivity and negativity, then, play a critical role in influencing the positivity of our personal experience and our influence on others. If we examine Table 11.1, we can see that when we experience all four of the characteristics of *lift*, we are likely to also experience healthy ratios of positivity to negativity and to inspire similar ratios in others. On the positive side, people who experience *lift* are likely to feel energized about their goals, peace about the consistency between their values and their actions, love for other people, an interest in learning, and enjoyment of their activities. They may also experience some distress if they are initially the only ones who pursue their goals, some brief fear or guilt if they need to make changes in order to act consistently with their values, sadness if the people they empathize with are suffering, or frustration over some negative feedback. Overall, though, people who experience *lift* are likely to have a fairly high ratio of positivity to negativity.

The influence that people who experience *lift* will have on others also tends to include a fairly high ratio of positivity to negativity. Part of this comes through emotional contagion, as others pick up on the emotions of those who are experiencing *lift*. But these people are also likely to experience the confidence that comes from joining a winning and legitimate course of action, the elevation of seeing people act in virtuous ways, the security of being with people who care, the interest of gaining new knowledge, and so forth. There can also be some negativity for these people, who now think more complexly, take risks, and take on more challenges, but overall we can expect these people to experience a relatively high ratio of positivity to negativity.

Emotions, of course, are not the only things that make *lift* a positive force. Thoughts—such as goals, complexity, stories, beliefs, knowledge, and freedom from labels—also play critical roles in making lift a positive force, as we explained when we discussed the integration of the four characteristics. We introduced the work of Losada, Fredrickson, and Gottman simply to show the importance of emotions for influence and the importance of balancing positive and negative emotions in ways that facilitate this positive influence.

Becoming a Force

This book is about becoming about a positive influence—a positive force. Our psychological states influence others whether we intend them to or not. The things we think and feel provide cues for people to interpret. They also influence our actions, the ways we do those actions, and the outcomes of our actions, thereby providing more cues for people to interpret. We think, feel, act, and create outcomes all the time. We cannot escape our influence.

Even though other people have to make sense of our thoughts, feelings, actions, and outcomes, they choose for themselves *how* they will make sense of them. In other words, part of what makes our influence positive when we experience *lift* is that although we may *be* a force, we seldom, if ever, try to force the way other people think or act. We are not likely to try to control or manipulate others when we experience *lift*. We may take aggressive action. We may even seek to persuade others to adopt our point of view or to take particular actions. But even if we are aggressive or persuasive, our empathy for others will usually prevent us from trying to control or manipulate them. Our desire to learn and receive feedback makes us unlikely to assume that we have sufficient knowledge to force others to do what we think. And our desire to live consistently with our values—especially if those values include virtues like respect or freedom—is also likely to prevent us from forcing our will on others.

There are some exceptions in which we may use force when we experience *lift*. For example, if someone tries to hurt himself or herself or another person, then we may try to stop that person. Events like these, however, are the exceptions rather than the rules. When we experience *lift*, we may apply negative consequences to poor actions that other people take, but this will generally be done to help them learn, not to force their behavior. When we experience *lift*, we try to be our best selves, allowing this best self to attract others to think and act in positive ways. Or we seek to learn about others and see how other's interests can be integrated with our own in a mutually beneficial way. For example, when Ryan's training session went poorly, it was at least in part because he tried to force the training that he had planned upon those managers. The next morning, when he was experiencing *lift*, he tried to learn their perspectives, integrate their desires with his, and exemplify the kind of innovating that he hoped to inspire in them.

If our influence is found in the thoughts, feelings, actions, and outcomes that others interpret and respond to when we experience *lift*, then our influence is separate from the way other people respond to us. We discussed this separation briefly at the end of chapter 6. In that discussion, we mentioned people—like Mahatma Gandhi and Abraham Lincoln—who were trying to act in ways that were consistent with their values and were killed for it. These men exerted positive influence. They thought, felt, acted, and generated results that invited others to respond in positive and constructive ways. Other people, however, chose to interpret and respond to those cues in negative or even destructive ways. This does not mean that their influence was negative, even though other people's responses to that influence were.

Our influence can be negative when we experience *lift*, however, when our actions generate unintended negative outcomes. For example, a colleague of ours shared a story with us about how he placed adhesive, nonstick tape on the treads of the wooden stairs at his back door. He did this to make the stairs less slippery and safer for his family. When the weather got cold, though, the tape contracted and pulled the paint off the stairs. Shortly afterward, when he walked down those stairs, he tripped on the loose tape and bumped down the stairs on his back. In other words, the actions that he took with the intention to make the stairs safer actually had the opposite effect. His influence on others in this situation was negative, even though the thoughts and feelings he had when installing the plastic were positive.

The influence of our colleague who put tape on his stairs was negative, even if it was unintended (and even if it only influenced himself). The duration of this negative influence, however, was short-lived. Because our colleague was externally open, he paid attention to the feedback he received about the safety of his tape (as he fell down the stairs) and took action to remedy his mistake. Thus, even though his immediate influence on the situation may have been negative, his openness to feedback made his long-term influence positive. This is one reason why being externally open is so important. If people who are externally open have unintended negative influences on others, their willingness to receive and use feedback will tend to make even their unintended negative influence positive in the long run.

Any Situation?

If people who experience lift can generate unintended negative consequences, then is it really fair for us to claim that people in this state will be a positive influence in any situation? What if there are other exceptions as well? We do not know of any other exceptions to our claim, but from a scientific point of view, we have to say that we cannot know for sure that the long-range influence of people who experience lift will always be positive. We have not studied the influence of lift in a wide enough array of situations to make that claim. We believe that scholars should continue to study the topics of positive influence and psychological states. We suspect that research on the topic will refine and update the principles and frameworks we have proposed.

Although we expect continued research to refine and update these frameworks and principles, we are also confident that future research will largely support our claims. We believe this for two reasons. First, many—if not most—of the concepts we described are relatively fundamental in their nature. They tap into biological, psychological, and sociological principles that form the basis of attention, automatic responses, assumptions, resourcefulness, emotions, relationships, expectations, and effectiveness. Second, we have applied these principles ourselves and many of our colleagues have also applied them in numerous and varied situations. With each application, we have become more and more confident that people who experience lift will be a positive force in any situation.

In an earlier draft, our subtitle for this book was "Becoming a Positive Force in Every Situation." However, we decided to use the word "any" instead of "every" because we realize that there is an array of forces that tend to push us into comfort-centered, externally directed, self-focused, and internally closed states without us even realizing it. It is probably unrealistic to expect a person to be a positive force in every situation. We can become a positive force in more and more situations, however, and it is certainly possible to be a positive force in any situation.

The Importance of Situations

Our use of the word "any" instead of the word "every" also highlights another important distinction in how we think about influence and behavior. To claim that people can experience lift in every situation would imply that lift is an enduring personality trait rather than a psychological state. Traits, as people often use the term, are patterns of behavior that are consistent across situations.[8] States, in contrast, tend to change from situation to situation.

This is not a book about traits—at least according to this common use of the term. Labeling people's traits can help people gain personal insights, but it also comes with a danger. When we label ourselves or others as engaging in the same behavioral patterns across situations, we can get trapped in those behaviors without realizing it.

Consider, for example, the Myers-Briggs Type Indicator. This instrument classifies people into categories such as introverted (I) versus extroverted (E) and judging (J) versus perceiving (P). Those who use instruments like this to train others usually tell them that these categories are general tendencies rather than universal descriptions. Our experience, however, is that once people receive this training, they tend to treat these labels as universal descriptions. We have sat in many meetings when people who disagree with each other will say something like, "Well that's because you are an 'I' and I am a 'J'." When people do this, they are usually trying to be open-minded by accounting for differences in other people. These kinds of comments have another effect as well, though: they exhibit the internally closed belief "Our traits are fixed, there's nothing we can do about it, so we'll just have to try to find some way to work around it."

BOB: An alternative to fixed labels is to think of ourselves in terms of temporary states. For example, one day I was designing a course with Phil, a colleague of mine. As we began to discuss the logistics of the course, Phil threw his hands up in the air and said, "I'm not very useful when it comes to these kinds of things—I'm just not detail oriented enough."

"That's interesting," I said. "I would tend to disagree."

Phil was surprised. Most people who knew Phil would agree with his statement. He does seem to focus much more on the "big picture" than on details. He replied, "Really?"

"Yes," I said. "For example, I've seen you when you compose music. When you do that, your attention to detail is extraordinary. That suggests to me that if you really care about something, you are entirely capable of taking care of even the finest of details."

Phil looked at me for a second and then said, half-jokingly, "I hate it when you do that."

Phil hates it when Bob points out examples that contradict his claims about what kind of person he is because Phil has learned to use labels for his personality traits as a way to get out of doing things he does not like to do. Most of the time that is fine. Phil excels at "big-picture" activities. Sometimes, however, we need him to focus on details. If Bob did not point out that his labels are only labels, then we would lose out on the value of what Phil has to offer in those situations.

I Am Part of My Situation and My Situation Is Part of Me

Phil's unusual tendency to become detail oriented when he works on musical compositions illustrates a principle that we first discussed in chapter 5. In chapter 5, we reviewed studies like the experiments in which people administered shocks to others and the Good Samaritan study. Studies like these help us to understand that who we are at any moment—the thoughts and feelings that compose our psychological states—depends in part on the situation we are in. We cannot separate ourselves from our situation. And, as the obedience study, the Good Samaritan study, and the story about Phil's musical compositions suggest, our behaviors are often driven as much by our situation as they are by our personality.

Human beings tend to respond to particular types of situations with particular types of responses. These automatic responses often make choosing other behaviors quite difficult. The four questions that we introduced in this book, however, can help. They do not help us by making it easier to choose different behaviors—at least not directly. They help because they change the situation, and by changing the situation, they change who we are.

The question "What result do I want to create?" redefines problem situations as situations of purpose. This transforms us from comfort-seekers to creators of opportunity. The question "What would my story be if I were living the values I expect of others?" changes the situation by creating a new story. We are then no longer an object in the old story, but the subject of the new story. The question "How would I feel if I were experiencing this situation from other people's points of view?" introduces other people's definitions of the situation into ours. This transforms us from being individuals into being members of communities. And the question "What are three (or four or five) strategies I could use to accomplish my purpose for this situation?" reframes the situation from being an obligation to perform to an opportunity to learn, turning us from performers into learners. When situations change, we change as well, taking on new identities and a new range of possible actions.

If we change the situation we are participating in and create a new range of possible actions, we are also likely to have new insights and intuitions into the situation. For example, in chapter 1 we told the story about how Ryan's son, Mason, became angry and irritable after beginning kindergarten. In a bad moment, when Mason hoarded the food on the table, Ryan used the principles from this book and experienced *lift*. When he did, a thought popped into his head: "Read to him anyway." This thought seemed bizarre. Why should Ryan reward Mason for bad behavior? What would that teach him? The impulse felt right, though, so Ryan acted on his intuition. Mason melted, apologized, hugged him, and began behaving better.

Intuitions like the one Ryan had with Mason depend on the situation we are in. Research suggests that when we experience intuition, our unconscious minds pick up on relevant cues in our situation, associate those cues with similar situations we have experienced, and give us a feeling about what an appropriate response to the current situation might be.[9] Our unconscious minds, however, may or may not be correct.

Whether or not our unconscious minds are correct depends on a number of factors, such as our definition of the situation (and therefore what kind of cues we notice), the quality and frequency of the feedback we receive, how much practice we have in this kind of situation, the complexity of our understanding of the situation, and the degree of judgment involved in the activity. Much research remains to be done before we fully understand intuition, but it is interesting to note that many of the factors that affect the appropriateness of a person's intuition are captured in the four characteristics of lift. Purpose defines the situation. Stories suggest new ways for us to practice behaving. Empathy for people affected by the situation increases the complexity of our understanding. And a belief that our situation-relevant abilities can be improved increases the quality and frequency of the feedback we receive about the situation.

In general, the four characteristics of lift dispose us to receive intuition that is high in purpose, integrity, love, and learning. We suspect, as a result, that intuition received when a person is experiencing lift is likely to be intuition of very high quality. This appears to have been the case in Ryan's experience with Mason, and it also appears to have been the case with Ryan's intuition about how to change the innovation training in Greece.

Onward and Upward

After the Wright brothers' successful flight in Kitty Hawk, they announced to the press that the age of the flying machine had come. They had flown the first airplane in human history, but they were not finished. Their airplane had flown only in straight lines and landed on the soft sands of Kitty Hawk. Therefore, in 1904, the Wright brothers began flying their new airplanes in a cow pasture in Ohio. They added weight to the front of the airplane to improve stability and moved the elevator farther forward so that it would be less sensitive. Finally, on October 20, 1904, they flew their first circular flight for one minute and thirty-six seconds. By 1905, they built an airplane that flew for thirty-nine minutes. This airplane could be used for practical purposes. The Wright brothers sought a patent and began looking for customers so they could commercialize their invention. They harnessed the aerodynamic force of lift. They changed our world forever, but they did not stop improving their understanding and application of these principles.

As we have suggested, the principles for harnessing the psychological state of *lift* are analogous to the Wright brothers' harnessing the aerodynamic force of lift. And like the Wright brothers, the effort to do this is a lifelong journey for each of us. The experience Ryan had when training the managers in Greece, for example, was just one step in this journey. The effort to understand and apply the principles of positive influence began before either of us was born. It developed as philosophers explored the question of what is "good," and as scientists explored the topics of influence and psychological states. It continued as Bob began studying change and, with his colleagues, developed the competing-values framework.

RYAN: My interest in positive influence began early. When I was five years old, one of my teachers asked me to give a three-minute speech in class. My teachers often had students do this, so I did not think much about it. My father, however, took the assignment seriously. He taught me how to write a speech and made me write the speech myself. Then he had me memorize it and practice giving it from the top of a stool. I thought this was odd, but did what my father asked. After I gave the speech, one of the teachers sent me a letter in the mail telling me how moved he was by it. The speech had a positive effect.

My father never told me what I should do for a career (in fact, he seemed a little surprised when I told him I had decided to be a professor like him), but I learned early on to care about teaching, professional or otherwise. I learned that teaching is influence. This means that when we teach we have a responsibility to ensure that our influence is positive.

As we have studied influence and psychological states, we have learned that teaching happens more than most of us ever realize. All of us are regularly, if not constantly, teaching others on the basis of who we are, and all of us have a choice: we can choose to be the kind of people who drag others down or to be the kind of people who lift. We, like the Wright brothers, still have far to go on this adventure. Our choice, however, and hopefully yours, is to lift.

Introduction

1. For a brief history of John Gillespie Magee, Jr. and his poem, *High Flight*, see http://en.wikipedia.org/wiki/John_Gillespie_Magee,_Jr.

2. Magee passed away in a flight accident shortly after writing this poem. He wrote it on the back of a letter to his parents. The original copy is kept in the Library of Congress. In the 1982 winter issue of *This England* magazine, a friend of the Magee family named Dr. A. H. Lankester, with help from members of Magee's family, wrote a tribute article to John Magee that included a copy of this poem. The editors of the magazine added, "We are pleased to grant permission for the article to be reprinted in any other publication, without fee, providing acknowledgment is made to *This England* and a copy of the publication forwarded to us for our archives; *This England*, P.O. Box 52, Cheltenham, Gloustershire, England GL50 1YQ."

3. In the past, when we have discussed the concept of *lift*—primarily with business executives—we called it "the fundamental state of leadership." See R. E. Quinn, *Building the Bridge as You Walk on It: A Guide for Leading Change* (San Francisco: Jossey-Bass, 2004); and R. E. Quinn (2005), "Moments of Greatness: Entering the Fundamental State of Leadership," *Harvard Business Review* 83(7): 74–83. We used that phrase because this concept helps leaders find the courage and direction they need to lift themselves and the people they are responsible for to higher levels of effectiveness. The word "leadership," however, can also be limiting. "Leadership" is a word that ignites immediate interest in business, government, and other organizations, but people who do not hold formal leadership positions are less likely to think that a book about leadership applies to them. Parents, children, coaches, teachers, friends, engineers, doctors, salespeople, politicians, philanthropists, and people from all walks of life want to have a positive influence on others, though, even if they are not in formal leadership positions. Therefore, to make the

concepts of this book accessible to the widest audience possible, both in business and in life generally, we have adopted the more general term *lift*. *Lift* is a concept that can be used by anyone in any situation.

4. When we tell stories about other people, we usually change the names of the people and organizations involved to protect their privacy. Exceptions to this occur if the name of a person in a story is obvious because of a relationship we have with them (such as our wives or children) or if the story is one that is in the public record.

Chapter 1

1. Much of the scientific research on influence tends to focus on tactics like these. Examples of research that examines tactics of influence includes D. Kipnis and S. M. Schmidt (1988), "Upward-Influence Styles: Relationships With Performance Evaluations, Salary, and Stress," *Administrative Science Quarterly*, 33(4): 528–543; D. Kipnis, S. M. Schmidt, and W. Ian (1988), "Intraorganizational Influence Tactics: Explorations in Getting One's Way," *Journal of Applied Psychology* 65(4): 440–4532; and G. Yukl and C. M. Falbe (1990), "Influence Tactics and Objectives in Upward, Downward, and Lateral Influence Attempts," *Journal of Applied Psychology* 75: 132–140. Popular books that summarize tactics like these include Robert Cialdini's *Influence: The Psychology of Persuasion* (rev. ed.) (New York: Collins Business, 2006) and *Yes! 50 Scientifically-Proven Ways to Be Persuasive* (New York: Free Press, 2008). Literature like this seldom considers the ethics of influence tactics. If it mentions ethics at all, it usually tells readers only to use these principles ethically.

2. This story was recorded first in R. E. Quinn, *Change the World: How Ordinary People Can Accomplish Extraordinary Results* (San Francisco: Jossey-Bass, 2000), 123–124.

3. For example, research suggests that when one person speaks to another, listeners receive 12.5 times as much information, on average, from the speakers' nonverbal cues as they do from the speaker's words, and that people believe the nonverbal cues more than they believe the verbal ones. This makes unexpected nonverbal cues even more important for people to make sense of than the verbal ones. See J. K. Burgoon, "Nonverbal Signals," in M. L. Knapp and G. R. Miller (eds.), *Handbook of Interpersonal Communication*, vol. 2 (Thousand Oaks, CA: Sage, 1994), 229–285; and J. K. Burgoon, "Nonverbal Communication Research in the 1970s: An Overview," in D. Nimmo (ed.), *Communication Yearbook* (New Brunswick, NJ: Transaction Books, 1980), 179–197.

4. Scientists call this process "emotional contagion." For a description of the process, see E. Hatfield, J. T. Cacioppo, and R. L. Rapson, "Primitive Emotional Contagion," in M. S. Clark (ed.), *Emotion and Social Behavior:*

Vol. 14. Review of Personality and Social Psychology (Newbury Park, CA: Sage, 1992), 151–177.

5. For example, Donald A. Schön describes how the reflection with which professionals do their work affects how artfully their decisions are made in his 1983 book *The Reflective Practitioner: How Professionals Think in Action* (New York: Basic Books). Isen's research on emotions and creativity suggest that people will make more creative decisions or perform more creatively depending on their psychological states. (See A. M. Isen, "Positive Affect and Creativity," in S. Russ [ed.], *Affect, Creative Experience, and Psychological Adjustment* [Philadelphia: Bruner/Masel, 1999], 3–7.) Other examples can be given as well.

6. Large and small successes and other extraordinary results draw attention and add legitimacy to what a person is doing, as pointed out by Jim Collins's 2001 book *Good to Great: Why Some Companies Make the Leap . . . and Others Don't* (New York: Harper Business) and Karl Weick's 1984 article "Small Wins: Redefining the Scale of Social Problems," *American Psychologist* 39(40–49).

7. See, e.g., M. Emirbayer (1997), "Manifesto for a Relational Sociology," *American Journal of Sociology* 103(2): 281–317.

8. For a good description of how intuitions like these work, see E. Dane and M. G. Pratt (2007), "Exploring Intuition and Its Role in Managerial Decision Making," *Academy of Management Review* 32(1): 33–54.

9. See K. S. Cameron, J. E. Dutton, and R. E. Quinn, *Positive Organizational Scholarship: Foundations of a New Discipline* (San Francisco: Berrett-Koehler, 2003).

10. See M. E. P. Seligman, *Authentic Happiness: Using the New Positive Psychology to Realize Your Potential for Lasting Fulfillment* (New York: Free Press, 2002).

Chapter 2

1. Our history of the Wright brothers' quest to build a flying machine comes from the Web sites of the Smithsonian National Air and Space Museum (http://www.nasm.si.edu/wrightbrothers/fly/1900/designing.cfm), NASA (http://www.grc.nasa.gov/WWW/K12/airplane/lift1.html), Wright Brothers Aeroplane Co. (http://www.first-to-fly.com/Adventure/Workshop/lift_and_drift.htm), and Failure Magazine (http://www.failuremag.com/arch_science_wright_brothers.html).

2. R. E. Quinn and J. Rohrbaugh (1983), "A Spatial Model of Effectiveness Criteria: Towards a Competing Values Approach to Organizational Analysis," *Management Science* 29(3): 363–377.

3. See K. S. Cameron and R. E. Quinn, *Diagnosing and Changing Organizational Culture: Based on the Competing Values Framework* (Reading, MA:

Addison-Wesley, 1999); K. S. Cameron, R. E. Quinn, J. DeGraff, and A. V. Thakor, *Competing Values Leadership: Creating Value in Organizations* (Northampton, MA: Edward Elgar Publishing, 2006); J. DeGraff and S. E. Quinn, *Leading Innovation: How to Jump Start Your Organization's Growth Engine* (New York: McGraw-Hill, 2007); S. Hart and R. E. Quinn (1993), "Roles Executives Play: CEOs, Behavioral Complexity, and Firm Performance," *Human Relations* 46(5): 543–574; R. E. Quinn and K. S. Cameron (1983), "Organizational Life Cycles and Shifting Criteria of Effectiveness: Some Preliminary Evidence," *Management Science* 29(1): 33–51; R. E. Quinn, S. R. Faerman, M. P. Thompson, and M. R. McGrath, *Becoming a Master Manager: A Competency Framework* (Hoboken, NJ: Wiley, 2003); and R. E. Quinn, H. W. Hildebrandt, P. S. Rogers, and M. P. Thompson (1991), "A Competing Values Framework for Analyzing Presentational Communication in Management Contexts," *The Journal of Business Communication* 28(3): 213–232.

4. P. R. and N. Nohria, *Driven: How Human Nature Shapes Our Choices* (San Francisco: Jossey-Bass, 2002).

5. S. H. Schwartz, "Universals in the Content and Structure of Values: Theoretical Advances and Empirical Tests in 20 Countries," in M. P. Zanna (ed.), *Advances in Experimental and Social Psychology*, vol. 25 (San Diego, CA: Academic Press, 1992), 1–65.

6. K. Benziger, *Thriving in Mind: The Art and Science of Using Your Whole Brain* (New York: K B A Pub., 2004).

7. A. P. Fiske, *Structures of Social Life: The Four Elementary Forms of Human Relations* (New York: Free Press, 1993).

8. K. Wilbur, *A Theory of Everything: An Integral Vision of Business, Politics, Science, and Spirituality* (Boston: Shambhala, 2001).

9. R. E. Quinn, *Deep Change: Discovering the Leader Within* (San Francisco: Jossey-Bass, 1996).

10. Perhaps some of the most prominent works for describing these philosophies are John Stuart Mill's *Utilitarianism* (Boston: Willard Small, 1899); Aristotle's *Nicomachean Ethics* (translated by T. Irwin) (Indianapolis, IN: Hackett, 2000) (for virtue ethics); Immanuel Kant's *Groundwork of the Metaphysics of Morals* (translated by H. J. Paton) (New York: Harper Torchbooks, 1964); and John Dewey's *Human Nature and Conduct: An Introduction to Social Psychology* (New York: Henry Holt, 1922) (for pragmatism).

Chapter 3

1. J. T. Noteboom (2001), "Activation of the Arousal Response and Impairment of Performance Increase With Anxiety and Stressor Intensity," *Journal of Applied Physiology* 91: 2093–2101.

2. M. H. Ashcraft and E. P. Kirk (2001), "The Relationships Among Working Memory, Math Anxiety, and Performance," *Journal of Experimental Psychology: General* 130(2): 224–237.

3. B. M. Elzinga and K. Roelofs (2005), "Cortisol-Indused Impairments of Working Memory Require Acute Symapthetic Activation," *Behavioral Neuroscience* 119(1): 98–103.

4. The effects of tension on performance can be summarized by what has come to be called the Yerkes-Dodson Law, based on R. M. Yerkes and J. D. Dodson's 1908 paper "The Relation of Strength of Stimulus to Rapidity of Habit-Formation," *Journal of Comparative Neurology and Psychology* 18: 459–482. This "law" suggests that the relationship between the tense activation people feel and how well they perform in their activities is shaped like an upside-down U. In other words, people initially perform better as their tense activation increases. Once the tense activation they feel passes a certain threshold, however, more tense activation leads to a decrease in performance. How much tense activation people feel about an activity depends, of course, on how good they are at performing that activity. When people experience high levels of tense activation, their performance level decreases because of hyperfocus; jerky, erratic, or habitual behavior; diminished working memory; the fight-or-flight response; rigidity in the face of threat; and so forth. Additional research on this law and on the effects of high levels of tense activation includes R. P. Barthol and N. D. Ku (1959), "Regression Under Stress to First Learned Behavior," *Journal of Abnormal and Social Psychology* 59: 134–136; P. L. Broadhurst (1957), "Emotionality and the Yerkes-Dodson Law," *Journal of Experimental Psychology* 54: 345–352; W. B. Cannon, *Bodily Changes in Pain, Hunger, Fear and Rage: An Account of Recent Researches Into the Function of Emotional Excitement* (New York: Harper & Row, 1963); G. Mandler, *Mind and Body: Psychology of Emotion and Stress* (New York: Norton, 1984); B. M. Staw, L. E. Sandelands, and J. E. Dutton (1981), "Threat-Rigidity Effects in Organizational Behavior: A Multilevel Analysis," *Administrative Science Quarterly* 26(4): 501–524; and R. E. Thayer, *The Biopsychology of Mood and Arousal* (New York: Oxford University Press, 1989).

5. For a detailed analysis of the impact that tension had on the events that unfolded in the Los Rodeos airport, see K. E. Weick (1990), "The Vulnerable System: An Analysis of the Tenerife Air Disaster," *Journal of Management* 16(3): 571–593.

6. Mandler, *Mind and Body: Psychology of Emotion and Stress.*

7. G. F. Smith (1988), "Towards a Heuristic Theory of Problem Structuring," *Management Science* 34: 1489–1506.

8. M. Snyder and W. B. Swann (1978), "Hypothesis-Testing Processes in Social Interaction," *Journal of Personality and Social Psychology* 36(11): 1202–1212.

9. C. Lord and M. Lepper (1979), "Biased Assimilation and Attitude Polarization: The Effects of Prior Theories on Subsequently Considered Evidence," *Journal of Personality and Social Psychology* 37: 2098–2109.

10. D. Westen, B. Pavel, K. Harenski, C. Kilts, and S. Hamann (2006), "Neural Bases of Motivated Reasoning: An fMRI Study of Emotional Constraints on Partisan Political Judgment in the 2004 U.S. Presidential Election," *Journal of Cognitive Neuroscience* 18(11): 1947–1958.

11. K. E. Weick, *Sensemaking in Organizations* (Thousand Oaks, CA: Sage, 1995).

12. R. Fritz, *The Path of Least Resistance: Learning to Become the Creative Force in Your Own Life* (New York: Fawcett, 1989).

Chapter 4

1. See H. Garfinkel, *Studies in Ethnomethodology* (Englewood Cliffs, NJ: Prentice Hall, 1967). Other, related examples can be found in E. J. Langer, *Mindfulness* (Reading, MA: Addison-Wesley, 1989) and G. R. Salancik (1979), "Field Simulations for Organizational Behavior Research," *Administrative Science Quarterly* 24: 638–649.

2. For the complete story in Thurman's own words, see R. Thurman (1958), "The Countess and the Impossible," *Reader's Digest* (June), 107–110.

3. G. A. Nix, R. M. Ryan, J. B. Manly, and E. L. Deci (1999), "Revitalization Through Self-Regulation: The Effects of Autonomous and Controlled Motivation on Happiness and Vitality," *Journal of Experimental Social Psychology* 35(3): 266–284.

4. S. R. Marks (1977), "Multiple Roles and Role Strain: Some Notes on Human Energy, Time, and Commitment," *American Sociological Review* 42(6): 921–936.

5. See K. H. Moffit and J. A. Singer (1994), "Continuity in the Life Story: Self-Defining Memories, Affect, and Approach/Avoidance Personal Strivings," *Journal of Personality* 62(1): 22–43; and J. A. Singer (1990), "Affective Responses to Autobiographical Memories and Their Relationship to Long-Term Goals," *Journal of Personality* 58: 535–563. There are also advantages to negative goals. Some researchers (such as J. Brockner and E. T. Higgins [2001], "Regulatory Focus Theory: Its Implications for the Study of Emotions in the Workplace," *Organizational Behavior and Human Decision Processes* 86: 35–66; and N. Schwarz and G. Bohner, "Feelings and Their Motivational Implications: Moods and the Action Sequence," in P. M. Gollwitzer and J. A. Bargh [eds.], *The Psychology of Action: Linking Cognition and Motivation to Behavior* [New York: Guilford Press, 1996], 119–145) have found that negative goals increase vigilance, systematic and analytical processing, and the prevention and detection of error. In practice, people often use multiple goals in a single activity. For example, Thurman's superordinate goal of mowing a

five-dollar lawn may have consisted of several subordinate goals, both positive and negative, such as "don't miss any corners" and "trim the walkway."

6. J. Tomaka, J. Blascovich, R. M. Kelsey, and C. L. Leitten (1993), "Subjective, Physiological, and Behavioral Effects of Threat and Challenge Appraisal," *Journal of Personality and Social Psychology* 65(2): 248–260.

7. E. A. Locke and G. P. Latham (1990), *A Theory of Goal Setting and Task Performance* (Englewood Cliffs, NJ: Prentice Hall).

8. R. W. Quinn (2006), "Flow in Knowledge Work: High Performance Experience in the Design of National Security Technology," *Administrative Science Quarterly* 50(4): 610–641.

9. C. E. Cohen and E. B. Ebbeson (1979), "Observational Goals and Schema Activation: A Theoretical Framework for Behavior Perception," *Journal of Experimental Social Psychology* 15: 305–329.

10. See E. A. Locke and J. F. Bryan (1969), "The Directing Function of Goals in Task Performance," *Organizational Behavior and Human Performance* 4: 35–42; N. E. Adler and D. Goleman (1975), "Goal Setting, T-Group Participation, and Self-Rated Change: An Experimental Study," *Journal of Applied Behavioral Science* 11(2): 197–208; J. R. Terborg and H. E. Miller (1978), "Motivation, Behavior, and Performance: A Closer Examination of Goal Setting and Monetary Incentives," *Journal of Applied Psychology* 63(1): 29–39; W. F. Nemeroth and J. Cosentino (1979), "Utilizing Feedback and Goal Setting to Increase Performance Appraisal Interviewer Skills of Managers," *Academy of Management Journal* 22: 566–576; E. Z. Rothkopf and M. J. Billington (1979), "Goal-Guided Learning From Text: Inferring a Descriptive Processing Model From Inspection Times and Eye Movements," *Journal of Educational Psychology* 71(3): 310–327; and E. A. Locke, D. O. Chah, S. Harrison, and N. Lustgarten (1989), "Separating the Effects of Goal Specificity From Goal Level," *Organizational Behavior and Human Decision Processes* 43: 270–287.

11. K. E. Weick, *The Social Psychology of Organizing* (New York: McGraw-Hill, 1979).

12. G. F. Lanzara (1983), "Ephemeral Organizations in Extreme Environments: Emergence, Strategy, Extinction," *Journal of Management Studies* 20(1): 71–95.

13. For additional evidence regarding people's tendencies to preserve their expectations, see research on the status quo bias (W. Samuelson and R. Zeckhauser [1988], "Status Quo Bias in Decision Making," *Journal of Risk and Uncertainty* 1: 7–59) and the omission bias (I. Ritov and J. Baron [1990], "Status Quo and Omission Bias," *Journal of Risk and Uncertainty* 5: 49–62).

14. S. Moscovici and C. Faucheux, "Social Influence, Confirming Bias, and the Study of Active Memories," in L. Berkowitz (ed.), *Advances in Experimental Social Psychology*, vol. 6 (New York: Academic Press, 1972), 149–202. See also C. Nemeth and C. Chiles (1988), "Modelling Courage: The Role

of Dissent in Fostering Independence, *European Journal of Social Psychology* 18: 275–280.

15. L. Van Dyne and R. Saavedra (1996), "A Naturalistic Minority Influence Experiment: Effects on Divergent Thinking, Conflict, and Originality in Work-Groups," *British Journal of Social Psychology* 35: 151–167.

16. Nemeth and Chiles, "Modelling Courage: The Role of Dissent in Fostering Independence."

17. For a review of the relationship between goals and persistence, see Locke and Latham, *A Theory of Goal Setting and Task Performance.*

18. J. Pfeffer, *Managing With Power: Politics and Influence in Organizations* (Boston, MA: Harvard Business School Press, 1992).

19. The commonality of emotional cues around the world is limited to facial expressions. The commonality of facial expressions and their meanings across cultures, however, is quite striking. Paul Ekman found these commonalities by traveling to some of the most remote places in the world and comparing facial expressions. The involuntary movements of muscles in the face correspond to particular emotions. For example, the Duchene, or authentic, smile is a sign of happiness everywhere. See P. Ekman, *Telling Lies: Clues to Deceit in the Marketplace, Politics, and Marriage* (New York: W. W. Norton, 1992). See also Hatfield, Cacioppo, and Rapson, "Primitive Emotional Contagion." A meta-analysis of research on the accuracy of emotion recognition confirms this finding, but also adds that average accuracy is higher when assessed by people from the same culture. See H. A. Elfenbein and N. Ambadi (2002), "On the Universality and Cultural Specificity of Emotion Recognition: A Meta-Analysis," *Psychological Bulletin*, 128: 203–235.

20. See R. N. Emde (1983), "The Prepresentational Self and Its Affective Core," *The Psychoanalytic Study of the Child* 38: 165–192.

21. F. Strack, L. L. Martin, and S. Stepper (1988), "Inhibiting and Facilitating Conditions of the Human Smile: A Nonobtrusive Test of the Facial Feedback Hypothesis," *Journal of Personality and Social Psychology* 54(5): 768–776.

22. B. L. Fredrickson and C. Branigan (2005), "Positive Emotions Broaden the Scope of Attention and Thought-Action Repertoires," *Cognition and Emotion* 19(3): 313–332.

23. C. E. Waugh and B. L. Fredrickson (2006), "Nice to Know You: Positive Emotions, Self-Other Overlap, and Complex Understanding in the Formation of New Relationships," *Journal of Positive Psychology* 1(2): 93–106.

24. K. J. Johnson and B. L. Fredrickson (2005), " 'We All Look the Same to Me': Positive Emotions Eliminate the Own-Race Bias in Face Recognition," *Psychological Science* 16(11): 875–881.

25. A. M. Isen, "Positive Affect and Creativity," 3–17. It is important to note, here, that the story of creativity is more complex than just "positive

emotions make people more creative." Other factors, including negative emotions, can also play a role (see, e.g., J. M. George and J. Zhou [2002], "Understanding When Bad Moods Can Foster Creativity and Good Moods Don't: The Role of Context and Clarity of Feelings," *Journal of Applied Psychology* 87: 687–697). Our point in citing the work on the relationship between positive emotions and creativity is simply to provide further evidence for the general observation that positive emotions tend to broaden the thoughts and actions that people have available to them and help them build enduring resources.

26. W. Baker, R. Cross, and M. Wooten, "Positive Organizational Network Analysis and Energizing Relationships," in Cameron, Dutton, and Quinn (eds.), *Positive Organizational Scholarship: Foundations of a New Discipline*, 328–342.

27. Locke and Latham, *A Theory of Goal Setting and Task Performance*.

28. Collins, *Good to Great: Why Some Companies Make the Leap . . . and Others Don't*, 6.

29. Ibid., 176.

30. Weick, "Small Wins: Redefining the Scale of Social Problems." The quote is from page 43.

31. Fritz, *The Path of Least Resistance: Learning to Become the Creative Force in Your Own Life*, 135–136.

Chapter 5

1. M. Rokeach, *The Nature of Human Values* (New York: Free Press, 1973).

2. S. Milgram, *Obedience to Authority* (New York: Harper, 1974).

3. Scientists and ethicists have engaged in extensive debates over how ethical Milgram's experiments were. We mention some of this debate in chapter 6. Because of these experiments, and others like them, universities and other research institutions now have much stricter controls over what kinds of research can be conducted. Milgram conducted this research primarily in the 1960s.

4. Examples include T. Blass (1991), "Understanding Behavior in the Milgram Obedience Experiment: The Role of Personality, Situations, and Their Interactions," *Journal of Personality and Social Psychology* 60: 398–413; and S. A. Haslam and S. Reicher (2007), "Beyond the Banality of Evil: Three Dynamics of an Interactionist Social Psychology of Tyranny," *Personality and Social Psychology Bulletin* 33: 615–622.

5. J. Darley and B. Latane (1968), "Bystander Intervention in Emergencies: Diffusion of Responsibility," *Journal of Personality and Social Psychology* 8(4): 377–383. Darley and Latane developed this experiment in response

to a story about a woman named Kitty Genovese who was mugged and killed in broad daylight on the streets of New York in view of a large number of people (the number of people is disputed) who did not help her in spite of her calls for help. A newspaper article (M. Gansberg, "37 Who Saw Murder Didn't Call the Police," *New York Times*, March 27, 1964, 1) claimed that thirty-seven people witnessed the woman get attacked three times over the course of thirty minutes, and that none of the witnesses did anything to help her. Evidence found later suggests that the claims of the original article may not be entirely true (see R. Manning, M. Levine, and A. Collins [2007], "The Kitty Genovese Murder and the Social Psychology of Helping: The Parable of the 38 Witnesses," *American Psychologist* 62: 555–562.), but the research it inspired is both rigorous and path-breaking and has contributed significantly to our understanding of why people who value helpfulness may choose to not be helpful.

6. J. M. Darley and C. D. Batson (1973), "From Jerusalem to Jericho: A Study of Situational and Dispositional Variables in Helping Behavior," *Journal of Personality and Social Psychology*, 27: 100–119.

7. M. Shih, T. L. Pittinsky, and N. Ambady (1999), "Stereotype Susceptibility: Identity Salience and Shifts in Quantitative Performance," *Psychological Science* 10(1): 80–83.

8. J. A. Bargh, M. Chen, and L. Burrows (1996), "Automaticity of Social Behavior: Direct Effects of Trait Construct and Stereotype Activation on Action," *Journal of Personality and Social Psychology* 71(2): 230–244.

9. Ibid.

10. J. A. Bargh and T. L. Chartrand (1999), "The Unbearable Automaticity of Being," *American Psychologist* 53(7): 462–479.

11. C. Tavris and E. Aronson, *Mistakes Were Made (but Not By Me): Why We Justify Foolish Beliefs, Bad Decisions, and Hurtful Acts* (Orlando, FL: Harcourt, 2007), 32.

12. L. Festinger, *A Theory of Cognitive Dissonance* (Stanford, CA: Stanford University Press, 1957).

13. A. Buckley and B. Kleiner (2002), "The Accuracy of Eyewitness Testimony," *Managerial Law* 44(1/2): 86–91; and B. C. Feeney and J. Cassidy (2003), "Reconstructed Memory Related to Adolescent-Parent Conflict Interactions: The Influence of Attachment-Related Perceptions and Changes in Perceptions Over Time," *Journal of Personality and Social Psychology* 85: 945–955.

14. S. Freud, *An Outline of Psychoanalysis* (London: Balliere, 1940).

15. We focus here on the tendency to develop automatic reactions to external cues. It is important to note, however, that people can consciously choose to do things that are inconsistent with their values. Often, they will justify these actions, either changing their values or hiding the inconsistency from themselves through justification.

Chapter 6

1. T. L. Webb and P. Sheeran (2003), "Can Implementation Intentions Help to Overcome Ego-Depletion?" *Journal of Experimental Social Psychology* 39: 279–286.

2. The leading researcher on the topic of implementation intention is Peter Gollwitzer. His work includes P. M. Gollwitzer (1993), "Goal Achievement: The Role of Intentions," *European Review of Social Psychology* 4: 141–185; P. M. Gollwitzer and V. Brandstaetter (1997), "Implementation Intentions and Effective Goal Pursuit," *Journal of Personality and Social Psychology* 73: 186–199; P. M. Gollwitzer and B. Schaal (1998), "Metacognition in Action: The Importance of Implementation Intentions," *Personality and Social Psychology Review* 2: 124–136; and P. M. Gollwitzer, K. Fujita, and G. Oettingen, "Planning and the Implementation of Goals," in R. F. Baumeister and K. D. Vohs (eds.), *Handbook of Self-Regulation: Research, Theory and Applications* (New York: Guilford Press, 2004), 211–228.

3. G. R. Maio, J. M. Olson, L. Allen, and M. M. Bernard (2000), "Addressing Discrepancies Between Values and Behavior: The Motivating Effect of Reasons," *Journal of Experimental Social Psychology* 37: 104–117.

4. For example, see Rokeach, *The Nature of Human Values*; S. H. Schwartz, "Value Priorities and Behavior: Applying the Theory of Integrated Value Systems," in C. Seligman, J. M. Olson, and M. P. Zanna (eds.), *Values: The Ontario Symposium*, vol. 8 (Mahwah, NJ: Erlbaum, 1996), 1–24; and C. Seligman and A. Katz, "The Dynamics of Value Systems," in Seligman, Olson, and Zanna (eds.), *Values: The Ontario Symposium*, vol. 8, 53–75.

5. This experiment can also be found in Maio, Olson, Allen, and Bernard, "Addressing Discrepancies Between Values and Behavior: The Motivating Effect of Reasons."

6. J. Loehr, *The Power of Story: Rewrite Your Destiny in Business and in Life* (New York: Free Press, 2007). For additional evidence on how stories can motivate action, see A. M. Grant (2008), "The Significance of Task Significance: Job Performance Effects, Relational Mechanisms, and Boundary Conditions," *Journal of Applied Psychology* 93: 108–124; and A. M. Grant (2008), "Employees Without a Cause: The Motivational Effects of Prosocial Impact in Public Service," *International Public Management Journal* 11: 48–66. Participants in Grant's studies increased their effort, persistence, performance, and productivity after hearing stories of how their work benefited others.

7. Rokeach, *The Nature of Human Values*.

8. A. J. Greimas, *On Meaning: Selected Writings in Semiotic Theory* (Amsterdam and Philadelphia: John Benjamins, 1988).

9. J. D. Margolis (2001), "Responsibility in an Organizational Context," *Business Ethics Quarterly* 11(3): 431–454.

10. D. Baumrind (1964), "Some Thoughts on Ethics of Research: After Reading Milgram's 'Behavioral Study of Obedience,'" *American Psychologist* 19: 421–423.

11. Milgram, *Obedience to Authority*, 197. Milgram actually defended his research on a number of other points as well. He argued that he and his research assistants took measures to protect participants, that they told participants they could withdraw at any time, that the deception in the experiment was necessary to address the research question, that they explained the deception to the participants as soon as the experiment was over, and that follow-up surveys with participants suggested that participation had not harmed them, but in fact, in some cases, was life-altering for them in a positive way.

12. Margolis, "Responsibility in an Organizational Context," 441.

13. C. Peterson and M. E. P. Seligman, *Character Strengths and Virtues: A Handbook and Classification* (Washington, DC and New York: American Psychological Association and Oxford University Press, 2004).

14. American Psychiatric Association, *Diagnostic and Statistical Manual of Mental Disorders* (4th ed.) (Arlington, VA: American Psychiatric Publishing, 2000).

15. R. F. Baumeister, E. Bratslavsky, M. Muraven, and D. M. Tice (1998), "Ego Depletion: Is the Active Self a Limited Resource?" *Journal of Personality and Social Psychology* 74(5): 1252–1265.

16. P. Sheeran, "Intention-Behavior Relations: A Conceptual and Empirical Review," in M. Hewstone and W. Stroebe (eds.), *European Review of Social Psychology*, vol. 12 (Chichester, England: Wiley, 2002), 1–36.

17. C. R. Rogers, *On Becoming a Person* (Boston: Houghton Mifflin, 1961), 122.

18. Ibid., 180.

19. The quotes in this story can be found in the transcript of Oprah's January 26, 2006 show. A longer description and analysis of this story can be found on pages 213 through 216 of Tavris and Aronson, *Mistakes Were Made (but Not By Me): Why We Justify Foolish Beliefs, Bad Decisions, and Hurtful Acts.*

20. M. C. Worline, A. Wrzesniewski, and A.Rafaeli, "Courage and Work: Breaking Routines to Improve Performance," in R. Klimoski and R. Kanfer (eds.), *Emotions in the Workplace: Understanding the Structure and Role of Emotions in Organizational Behavior* (San Francisco, CA: Jossey-Bass, 2002).

21. J. Haidt (2000), "The Positive Emotion of Elevation," *Prevention and Treatment* 3(3), online at http://content.apa.org/journals/pre/3/1/3.

22. Rogers, *On Becoming a Person.*

23. K. M. Sheldon and A. J. Elliott (1999), "Goal Striving, Need Satisfaction, and Longitudinal Well-Being: The Self-Concordance Model," *Journal of Personality and Social Psychology* 76(3): 482–497.

24. W. Mischel, Y. Shoda, and P. K. Peake (1988), "The Nature of Adolescent Competencies Predicted by Preschool Delay of Gratification," *Journal of Personality and Social Psychology* 54(4): 687–696.

25. Kim Cameron and his colleagues have begun to study the relationship between virtues and performance (e.g., K. S. Cameron, D. Bright, and A. Caza [2004], "Exploring the Relationships Between Virtuousness and Performance," *American Behavioral Scientist* 47[6]: 766–790). Also relevant to the issue of virtuous business and performance, however, is the question of how well a company and its members engage in self-regulation. For example, Jim Collins's research suggests that a "culture of discipline" is a condition that is necessary for companies to move from good performance to great performance (see Collins, *Good to Great: Why Some Companies Make the Leap . . . and Others Don't).*

Chapter 7

1. M. Buber, *I and Thou* (W. Kaufmann, trans.) (New York: Simon & Schuster, 1990). We focus on Buber here because his philosophy concentrated on specific psychological states. Immanuel Kant, however, was the philosopher to introduce, in 1785, the idea that morality is dependent on treating the humanity in others and in oneself as an end and never merely as a means. See I. Kant, *Grounding for the Metaphysics of Morals*, 3d ed., J. W. Ellington, trans. (Indianapolis, IN: Hackett, 1993).

2. C. D. Batson (1990), "How Social an Animal? The Human Capacity for Caring," *American Psychologist* 45(3): 336–346.

3. D. A. Quinney (1997), "Daniel Bernoulli and the Making of the Fluid Equation," +*plus magazine*, from http://plus.maths.org/issue1/bern/index .html.

4. W. D. Hutchinson, K. D. Davis, A. M. Lozano, R. R. Tasker, and J. O. Dostrovsky (1999), "Pain-Related Neurons in the Human Cingulate Cortex," *Nature Neuroscience* 2: 403–405.

5. The participants in this study were patients suffering from psychiatric diseases. These patients required brain surgery, so they were already undergoing the surgical procedure necessary for Hutchinson and his colleagues to study their brains with microelectrodes. The patients agreed to participate in the study and were told they could withdraw at any time.

6. J. S. Morris, A. Öhman, and R. J. Dolan (1998), "Conscious and Unconscious Emotional Learning in the Human Amygdala," *Nature* 393: 467–470.

7. P. J. Whalen, L. M. Shin, and S. C. McInerney (2001), "A Functional MRI Study of Human Amygdala Responses to Facial Expressions of Fear Versus Anger," *Emotion* 1(1): 70–83.

8. N. H. Frijda (1988), "The Laws of Emotion," *American Psychologist* 43(5): 349–358.

9. S. D. Preston and F. B. M. de Wall (2002), "Empathy: Its Ultimate and Proximal Bases," *Behavioral and Brain Sciences* 25: 1–72.

10. Communication scholars point out that we cannot know other people's intentions when we communicate with them. Some scholars, like François Cooren (*The Organizing Property of Communication* [Amsterdam/Philadelphia: John Benjamins, 2000], explain that even though we cannot understand others' intentions, we get by relatively effectively most of the time because of our ability to use the context to help us interpret people's messages. We would argue that emotions are often the most important contextual cues that humans have to help them with these interpretations (see, e.g., R. W. Quinn and J. E. Dutton [2005], "Coordination as Energy-in-Conversation," *Academy of Management Review* 30[1]: 36–57).

11. Sometimes, some of the nuance that we add to our empathy is inaccurate or inappropriate because some element or elements of our mental models are inappropriate. If this happens, we will often feel inclined to update our mental models to make them more accurate because of the empathy we feel for others. It is important, however, to acknowledge that this system is imperfect, making learning and adaptation as important as empathy.

12. K. N. Ochsner, K. Knierim, D. H. Ludlow, J. Hanelin, T. Ramachandran, G. Glover, and S. C. Mackey (2004), "Reflecting Upon Feelings: An fMRI Study of Neural Systems Supporting the Attribution of Emotion to Self and Other," *Journal of Cognitive Neuroscience* 16(10): 1746–1772.

13. C. T. Warner, *Bonds That Make Us Free: Healing Our Relationships, Coming to Ourselves* (Salt Lake City, UT: Shadow Mountain, 2001). Also, for an excellent application of Warner's ideas to business settings, see The Arbinger Institute, *Leadership and Self-Deception: Getting Out of the Box* (San Francisco: Berrett-Koehler, 2002).

14. B. M. Staw, S. G. Barsade, and K. W. Koput (1997), "Escalation at the Credit Window: A Longitudinal Study of Bank Executives' Recognition and Write-Off of Problem Loans," *Journal of Applied Psychology* 82(1): 130–142. For further research on justification and the escalation of commitment, see G. R. Salancik, "Commitment and the Control of Organizational Behavior and Belief," in B. M. Staw and G. R. Salancik (eds.), *New Directions in Organizational Behavior* (Chicago: St. Clair, 1977), 1–54; and K. E. Weick, *Sensemaking in Organizations*.

15. See R. Collins, *Interaction Ritual Chains* (Princeton, NJ: Princeton University Press, 2004).

16. S. L. Gable, G. C. Gonzaga, and A. Strachman (2006), "Will You Be There for Me When Things Go Right? Supportive Responses to Event Disclosures," *Journal of Personality and Social Psychology* 91(5): 904–917.

17. On the difficulty of mental control, see D. M. Wegner (1994), "Ironic Processes of Mental Control," *Psychological Review* 101(1): 34–52. On the

costs of emotional suppression, see E. Kennedy-Moore and J. C. Watson (2001), "How and When Does Emotional Expression Help?" *Review of General Psychology* 5(3): 187–212. Paul Ekman's 1992 work—*Telling Lies: Clues to Deceit in the Marketplace, Politics, and Marriage* (New York: W. W. Norton)— is also relevant here, showing how the face reveals lies in the micromovements of its muscles.

18. Morris, Öhman, and Dolan, "Conscious and Unconscious Emotional Learning in the Human Amygdala."

19. For research on how emotional suppression inhibits the development of new relationships, see E. Butler, B. Egloff, F. H. Wilhelm, N. C. Smith, E. A. Erickson, and J. J. Gross (2003), "The Social Consequences of Expressive Suppression," *Emotion* 3: 48–67.

20. R. F. Baumeister and M. R. Leary (1995), "The Need to Belong: Desire for Interpersonal Attachments as a Fundamental Human Motivation," *Psychological Bulletin* 117(3): 497–529.

21. N. I. Eisenberger, M. D. Lieberman, and K. D. Williams (Oct. 10, 2003), "Does Rejection Hurt? An fMRI Study of Social Exclusion," *Science* 302(5643): 290–292.

22. See, e.g., Mandler, *Mind and Body: Psychology of Emotion and Stress.*

23. M. R. Leary, C. Springer, L. Negel, E. Ansell, and K. Evans (1998), "The Causes, Phenomenology, and Consequences of Hurt Feelings," *Journal of Personality and Social Psychology* 74(5): 1225–1237.

24. See M. D. S. Ainsworth, S. Bell, and D. Slayton, "Infant-Mother Attachment and Social Development: Socialization as a Product of Reciprocal Responsiveness to Signals," in M. P. M. Richards (ed.), *The Integration of a Child Into a Social World* (Cambridge, UK: Cambridge University Press, 1974), 99–135; F. J. Bernieri, S. Reznick, and R. Rosenthal (1988), "Synchrony, Pseudosynchrony, and Dissynchrony: Measuring the Entrainment Process in Mother-Infant Interactions," *Journal of Personality and Social Psychology* 54(2): 243–253; J. Bowlby, *A Secure Base: Parent-Child Attachment and Human Development* (New York: Basic Books, 1990); T. Field, "Attachment as Psychobiological Attunement: Being on the Same Wavelength," in M. Reite and T. Field (eds.), *The Psychobiology of Attachment and Separation* (Orlando, FL: Academic Press, 1985), 415–454; and A. Schore, *Affect Regulation and the Origin of the Self: The Neurobiology of Emotional Development* (Hillsdale, NJ: Erlbaum, 1994).

Chapter 8

1. Ochsner et al.,"Reflecting Upon Feelings: An fMRI Study of Neural Systems Supporting the Attribution of Emotion to Self and Other."

2. The three parts of the brain that were activated were the medial prefrontal cortex, the superior temporal gyrus, and the posterior cingulate.

3. See, e.g., Hutchinson et al., "Pain-Related Neurons in the Human Cingulate Cortex."

4. It is also worth noting that in addition to choosing the words of this question carefully, we were careful about what words we would *not* include in this question. In particular, this question does not ask, "How would *I* feel if I were experiencing this situation from the perspective of others?" This is because Daniel Batson and his colleagues have found that we experience empathy when we ask how another person feels, but when we ask how we would feel in the same situation we feel both empathy and personal distress (see C. D. Batson, S. Early, and G. Salvarani [1997], "Perspective Taking: Imagining How Another Feels Versus Imagining How You Would Feel," *Personality and Social Psychology Bulletin* 23[7]: 751–757). This is an important distinction, because when we feel empathy, we feel compelled to help other people for their sake, but when we feel empathy and distress, our desire to help those people is motivated more by self-focused interests.

5. See C. D. Batson, *The Altruism Question: Toward a Scientific Answer* (Mahwah, NJ: Erlbaum, 1991); D. L. Krebs (1970), "Altruism—An Examination of the Concept and a Review of the Literature," *Psychological Bulletin* 73(4): 258–302.

6. See C. T. Warner, *Bonds That Make Us Free: Healing Our Relationships, Coming to Ourselves* (Salt Lake City, UT: Shadow Mountain, 2001), 197, for a more extensive discussion of how this process works.

7. It can also be harder to be other-focused when the expectations that define our situation are self-focused. For example, Nicholas Epley and his colleagues conducted a series of experiments in which they asked participants with competing interests to consider the perspectives of the other participants (see N. Epley, E. M. Caruso, and M. H. Bazerman [2006], "When Perspective Taking Increases Taking: Reactive Egoism in Social Interaction," *Journal of Personality and Social Psychology* 91[5]: 872–889). Instead of acting more fairly, the participants who considered the other participants' perspectives acted less fairly, even after clearly stating what they believed fair actions would be. Epley and his colleagues found that considering other participants' perspectives led to unfair behavior because participants who considered other participants' perspectives realized that it was in the other participants' interest to act unfairly as well. Considering other people's perspectives in competitive situations, they concluded, makes people more likely to act more selfishly, not less.

These experiments could be used to explain the behavior of most of the people in Hugh's company. They quickly realized what other people's interests were and acted in selfish ways. These experiments do not, however, explain how or why Hugh came to feel and act so differently. We would argue that there are two major differences between the Epley experiments and Hugh's experience. Epley and his colleagues did not require their participants to question their own virtue. They also asked their participants to focus on the other participants' perspectives, rather than on their feelings. Questioning one's justifications in a competitive context helps people see the problems as stemming, at least in part, from their own justifications, and it also helps them see how others are laboring under similarly faulty justifications. It is easier to feel empathy for people who are struggling with something that we have struggled with ourselves. We suspect that this is why Hugh felt a need to challenge his co-workers as well as to offer his support: he felt a desire to help them free themselves from their faulty justifications.

8. Rogers, *On Becoming a Person*.

9. R. E. Freeman, J. S. Harrison, and A. C. Wicks, *Managing for Stakeholders: Survival, Reputation, and Success* (New Haven, CT: Yale University Press, 2007).

10. The story of BankBoston and First Community Bank can be found in R. M. Kanter (1999), "From Spare Change to Real Change: The Social Sector as a Beta Site for Business Innovation," *Harvard Business Review* 77(3): 122–135.

11. N. H. Frijda, P. Kuipers, and E. Schure (1989), "Relations Among Emotion, Appraisal, and Emotional Action Readiness," *Journal of Personality and Social Psychology* 57: 212–228.

12. See Batson, *The Altruism Question: Toward a Scientific Answer,* and Krebs, "Altruism—An Examination of the Concept and a Review of the Literature." Also, Adam Grant finds that when people feel empathy for others, they exert more effort, persist longer, and engage in more helping behaviors (see Grant, "The Significance of Task Significance: Job Performance Effects, Relational Mechanisms, and Boundary Conditions," and Grant, "Employees Without a Cause: The Motivational Effects of Prosocial Impact in Public Service").

13. W. S. Condon, "Cultural Microrhythms," in M. Davis (ed.), *Interaction Rhythms: Periodicity in Communicative Behavior* (New York: Human Sciences Press, 1982), 53–76.

14. S. Albon and C. Marci (2004), "Psychotherapy Process: The Missing Link," *Psychological Bulletin* 130: 664–668.

15. L. Tickle-Degnan and R. Rosenthal (1990), "The Nature of Rapport and Its Nonverbal Correlates," *Psychological Inquiry* 1(4): 285–293.

16. M. Greer (January 2005), "The Science of Savoir Faire," *Monitor on Psychology* 36(1): 28–30.

17. J. E. Dutton and E. D. Heaphy, "The Power of High Quality Connections," in Cameron, Dutton, and Quinn (eds.), *Positive Organizational Scholarship: Foundations of a New Discipline*, 263–278.

18. For more on the physiological effects of a high-quality connection, see J. Panskepp, *Affective Neuroscience: The Foundations of Human and*

Animal Emotions (Oxford: Oxford University Press, 1998); and S. E. Taylor, S. S. Dickerson, and L. C. Klein, "Toward a Biology of Social Support," in C. R. Snyder and S. L. Lopez (eds.), *Handbook of Positive Psychology* (Oxford: Oxford University Press, 2002), 556–572.

19. D. Goleman, *Social Intelligence: The Revolutionary New Science of Human Relationships* (New York: Bantam, 2007).

20. See R. Collins (1981), "On the Micro-Foundations of Macro-Sociology," *American Journal of Sociology* 86: 984–1014; and R. Collins (1993), "Emotional Energy as the Common Denominator of Rational Action," *Rationality and Society* 5(2): 203–230.

21. Baker, Cross, and Wooten, "Positive Organizational Network Analysis and Energizing Relationships," 328–342.

22. W. Baker, *Achieving Success Through Social Capital: Tapping the Hidden Resources in Your Personal and Business Networks* (San Francisco: Jossey Bass, 2000), 22–23.

23. See W. A. Kahn (2001), "Holding Environments at Work," *Journal of Applied Behavioral Science* 37(3): 260–279 for a description of how empathic relations can help adults in working environments increase their felt security.

24. For research examples of how empathic relationships help people be resilient and find courage, see R. Quinn and M. C. Worline (2008), "Enabling Courageous Collective Action: Conversations From United Airlines Flight 93," *Organization Science* 19(4): 497–516, and M. C. Worline, J. E. Dutton, P. Frost, J. Lilius, J. Kanov and S. Maitlis (2008), "Creating Fertile Soil: The Organizing Dynamics of Resilience," paper presented at the *Academy of Management Annual Meeting*, Denver, CO.

25. Rogers, *On Becoming a Person.*

26. See J. D. Hundleby and G. W. Mercer (1987), "Family and Friends as Social Environments and Their Relationship to Young Adolescents' Use of Alcohol, Tobacco, and Marijuana," *Journal of Marriage and the Family* 49: 151–164; B. C. Miller, *Families Matter: A Research Synthesis of Family Influences on Adolescent Pregnancy* (Washington, DC: The National Campaign to Prevent Teen Pregnancy, 1988); and Partnership for a Drug-Free America (2002), *Partnership Attitude Tracking Study.*

27. A sense of security is often needed to trust others because we make ourselves vulnerable when we choose to trust. See D. M. Rousseau, S. B. Sitkin, R. S. Burt, and C. Camerer (1998), "Not So Different After All: A Cross-Disciplinary View of Trust," *Academy of Management Review* 23(3): 393–404.

28. A. C. Edmondson, R. M. Bohmer, and G. P. Pisano (2001), "Disrupted Routines: Team Learning and New Technology Implementation in Hospitals," *Administrative Science Quarterly* 46: 685–716.

29. A. Hargadon, *How Breakthroughs Happen: The Surprising Truth About How Companies Innovate* (Cambridge, MA: Harvard Business School Press, 2003).

30. M. B. Brewer and W. Gardner (1996), "Who Is This 'We'? Levels of Collective Identity and Self-Representations," *Journal of Personality and Social Psychology* 71(1): 83–93.

31. Warner, *Bonds That Make Us Free: Healing Our Relationships, Coming to Ourselves,* 197.

Chapter 9

1. C. S. Dweck, *Mindset: The New Psychology of Success* (New York: Random House, 2006). Dweck uses the phrase "fixed mindset" to describe the belief that one's abilities are relatively unchanging and unchangeable, and the phrase "growth mindset" to describe the belief that one's abilities can be grown and developed with effort and time. We like Dweck's phrases, but in this book we use the terms "internally closed" and "externally open" to describe these psychological states because they capture the idea that competing values are necessary to make *lift* possible. Internally closed and externally open states, then, are the same things as situationally-oriented fixed and growth mindsets.

2. Ibid.

3. C. S. Dweck and N. D. Reppucci (1973), "Learned Helplessness and Reinforcement Responsibility in Children," *Journal of Personality and Social Psychology* 25(1): 109–116.

4. See C. I. Deiner and C. S. Dweck (1978), "An Analysis of Learned Helplessness: Continuous Changes in Performance, Strategy, and Achievement Cognitions Following Failure," *Journal of Personality and Social Psychology* 36(5): 451–462; C. I. Deiner and C. S. Dweck (1980), "An Analysis of Learned Helplessness: II. The Processing of Success," *Journal of Personality and Social Psychology* 39(5): 940–952; R. Wood and A. Bandura (1989), "Impact of Conceptions of Ability on Self-Regulatory Mechanisms and Complex Decision-Making," *Journal of Personality and Social Psychology* 56(3): 407–415; H. Grant and C. S. Dweck (2003), "Clarifying Achievement Goals and Their Impact," *Journal of Personality and Social Psychology* 85(3): 541–553; and P. A. Heslin, G. P. Latham, and D. VandeWalle (2005), "The Effect of Implicit Person Theory on Performance Appraisals," *Journal of Applied Psychology* 90(5): 842–856.

5. Dweck, *Mindset: The New Psychology of Success,* 47.

6. C. M. Mueller and C. S. Dweck (1998), "Praise for Intelligence Can Undermine Children's Intelligence and Performance," *Journal of Personality and Social Psychology* 75(1): 33–52.

7. Although researchers have not examined the explicit link between praise for ability and becoming internally closed, they have found that it is not difficult to induce an internally closed state in adults. There is also quite a bit of anecdotal evidence to support the idea that adults, like children, may be similarly influenced by praise for ability. Citations on inducing an internally closed state in adults include J. Aronson, C. Fried, and C. Good (2002), "Reducing the Effects of Stereotype Threat on African American College Students by Shaping Theories of Intelligence," *Journal of Experimental Social Psychology* 38: 113–125; C.-y. Chiu, Y.-y Hong, and C. S. Dweck (1997), "Lay Dispositionism and Implicit Theories of Personality," *Journal of Personality and Social Psychology* 73: 19–30; and Wood and Bandura, "Impact of Conceptions of Ability on Self-Regulatory Mechanisms and Complex Decision-Making."

8. D. Miller, *The Icarus Paradox: How Exceptional Companies Bring About Their Own Downfall* (New York: HarperCollins, 1992).

9. See, e.g., C. S. Dweck and E. S. Elliott, "Achievement Motivation," in P. H. Mussen (gen. ed.) and E. M. Hetherington (vol. ed.), *Handbook of Child Psychology: Vol. 4. Social and Personality Development* (New York: Wiley, 1983), 643–691.

10. G. H. Seijts, G. P. Latham, K. Tasa, and B. W. Latham (2004), "Goal Setting and Goal Orientation: An Integration of Two Different Yet Related Literatures," *Academy of Management Journal* 47(2): 227–239.

Chapter 10

1. Seijts, Latham, Tasa, et al., "Goal Setting and Goal Orientation: An Integration of Two Different Yet Related Literatures."

2. Dweck, *Mindset: The New Psychology of Success.*

3. See, e.g., R. C. Shank and R. P. Abelson, *Scripts, Plans, Goals, and Understanding* (Hillsdale, NJ: Lawrence Erlbaum Associates, 1977).

4. G. P. Latham and G. H. Seijts (1999), "The Effects of Proximal and Distal Goals on Performance on a Moderately Complex Task," *Journal of Organizational Behavior* 20(4): 421–429.

5. Weick, "Small Wins: Redefining the Scale of Social Problems."

6. C. Moorman and A. S. Miner (1998), "Organizational Improvisation and Organizational Memory," *Academy of Management Review* 23(4): 698–723.

7. M. Csikszentmihalyi, *Flow: The Psychology of Optimal Experience* (New York: Harper Perennial, 1990).

8. Quinn, "Flow in Knowledge Work: High Performance Experience in the Design of National Security Technology."

9. Schön, *The Reflective Practitioner: How Professionals Think in Action.*

10. Csikszentmihalyi, *Flow: The Psychology of Optimal Experience,* 233.

11. Heslin, Latham, and VandeWalle, "The Effect of Implicit Person Theory on Performance Appraisals."

12. P. A. Heslin, D. VandeWalle, and G. P. Latham (2006), "Keen to Help? Managers' Implicit Person Theories and Their Subsequent Employee Coaching," *Personnel Psychology* 59(4): 871–902.

13. Mueller and Dweck, "Praise for Intelligence Can Undermine Children's Intelligence and Performance."

14. J. S. Bunderson and K. M. Sutcliffe (2003), "Management Team Learning Orientation and Business Unit Performance," *Journal of Applied Psychology* 88(3): 552–560.

15. R. Wood and A. Bandura (1989), "Social Cognitive Theory of Organizational Management," *Academy of Management Review* 14(3): 361–384.

16. Schön, *The Reflective Practitioner: How Professionals Think in Action*.

17. Dweck, *Mindset: The New Psychology of Success*.

18. See J. S. Brown and P. Duguid (2001), "Knowledge and Organization: A Social-Practice Perspective," *Organization Science* 12(2): 198–213; W. J. Orlikowski (1996), "Improvising Organizational Transformation Over Time: A Situated Change Perspective," *Information Systems Research* 7(1): 63–92; and Schön, *The Reflective Practitioner: How Professionals Think in Action*.

19. See B. Barnes, "Practice as Collective Action," in T. R. Schatzki, K. K. Cetina, and E. von Savigny (eds.), *The Practice Turn in Contemporary Theory* (London: Routledge, 2001), 17–28; F. J. Barrett (1998), "Creativity and Improvisation in Jazz and Organizations: Implications for Organizational Learning," *Organization Science* 9(5): 605–622; and D. Obstfeld (2005), "Social Networks, the Tertius Iungens Orientation, and Involvement in Innovation," *Administrative Science Quarterly* 50(1): 100–130.

20. See Edmondson, Bohmer, and Pisano, "Disrupted Routines: Team Learning and New Technology Implementation in Hospitals"; Hargadon, *How Breakthroughs Happen: The Surprising Truth About How Companies Innovate*; and W. J. Orlikowski (2002), "Knowing in Practice· Enacting a Collective Capability in Distributed Organizing," *Organization Science* 13(3): 249–273.

21. See Quinn and Worline, "Enabling Courageous Collective Action: Conversations From United Airlines Flight 93," and J. E. Dutton, M. C. Worline, P. J. Frost, and J. Lilius (2006), "Explaining Compassion Organizing," *Administrative Science Quarterly* 51: 59–96.

22. Dweck, *Mindset: The New Psychology of Success*.

23. Bunderson and Sutcliffe, "Management Team Learning Orientation and Business Unit Performance."

24. A. S. Miner, P. Bassoff, and C. Moorman (2001), "Organizational Improvisation and Learning: A Field Study," *Administrative Science Quarterly* 46(2): 304–339.

25. Throughout chapters 9 and 10 we have focused on people's beliefs about whether their abilities can change. We have not discussed the belief that people can change their character or personality. We focus on ability because simply learning that one's abilities can be developed can be a frame-breaking concept for many people. The thought that they can change their character is even harder to grasp. There is, however, significant research literature on character change, which we do not review here. We note that this literature exists and that many—if not most—of the same principles we discuss in chapters 9 and 10 apply to character change as well as to changing one's abilities. This is especially important when we juxtapose the externally open state with the internally directed state. It is important because becoming internally directed involves recognizing our lack of integrity. This is a hard thing for many people to accept, and some people have trouble forgiving themselves when they discover it. But if they accompany a realization that they have gaps in their integrity with a realization that we are all "works in progress" in the development of our moral character—and that it is okay for the development of our moral character to be incomplete, as long as we are striving to improve—(which are externally-open beliefs) then it is much easier to forgive ourselves for our shortcomings.

Chapter 11

1. M. Losada (1999), "The Complex Dynamics of High Performance Teams," *Mathematical and Computer Modeling* 30(10): 179–192.

2. E. Lorenz (1969), "Atmospheric Predictability as Revealed by Naturally Occurring Analogues," *Journal of the Atmospheric Sciences* 26: 636–646.

3. J. M. Gottman, H. Markman, and C. Notarius (1977), "The Topography of Marital Conflict: A Sequential Analysis of Verbal and Nonverbal Behavior," *Marriage and the Family* 39: 461–477.

4. M. Losada and E. Heaphy (2004), "The Role of Positivity and Connectivity in the Performance of Business Teams: A Nonlinear Dynamics Model," *American Behavioral Scientist* 47(6): 740–765.

5. B. Fredrickson (1998), "What Good Are Positive Emotions?" *Review of General Psychology* 2(3): 300–319.

6. B. L. Fredrickson and M. F. Losada (2005), "Positive Affect and the Complex Dynamics of Human Flourishing," *American Psychologist* 60: 678–686.

7. J. M. Gottman, *The Marriage Clinic: A Scientifically-Based Marital Therapy* (New York: W. W. Norton, 1999).

8. Although laypeople usually think of traits as characteristics that are consistent across situations, this is not necessarily how psychologists use the term. For example, people with authoritarian personalities may be domineering when they are in a high-power situation and submissive when they

are in low-power situation. We use the more common (less formal) way of thinking about personality traits here simply to make a distinction between thinking of people as responsive to situations rather than as being repetitive across situations.

9. For a review of the research on intuition, see E. Dane and M. G. Pratt (2007), "Exploring Intuition and Its Role in Managerial Decision Making," *Academy of Management Review* 32(1): 33–54.

A fabulous "flight crew" enabled us to get this book "up the long, delirious blue." First and foremost, we thank our wives, Amy Quinn and Delsa Quinn, for their support, patience, feedback, and inspiration. Our children and siblings—Shauri, Shawn, Lisa, Kristin, Abram, Travis, Garrett, Mason, Katie, Andrew, and Chloe—have also been an inspiration and a support. In particular, Shawn has given essential support throughout the process and Shauri's feedback has been enormously helpful and to the point. Finally, this book would not be complete without the timely support of Ryan's mother-in-law, Ellen Burnside, who arrived to help after Chloe was born—we would not have survived without her.

Steve Piersanti, Jeevan Sivasubramaniam, and the production and marketing folks at Berrett-Koehler have been amazing to work with. Many of the ideas in this book could not have come to life without Steve's mentoring and insight. We are also grateful to those, in addition to Shawn and Shauri, who reviewed the book for us: Carol Metzker, Walter Nord, Barry Johansen, Chris Lee, Adam Grant, Ed Freeman, Peter Heslin, and Gretchen Spreitzer. The quality of their feedback was generous and stunning. Countless others have helped along the way. Both Bob Bruner, dean of the University of Virginia's Darden Graduate School of Business, and the school's trustees have given generous support. Mike Steep, a Darden alumnus and an executive at Microsoft, has also been generous in his support, as have many of our colleagues at Darden, the University of Michigan's Ross School of Business, and other universities. We could go on and on. We have certainly missed many people. Our gratitude exceeds our memory, and we hope you understand. Each of you has lifted us. We hope this book lifts you and many others.

Ryan and Robert (Bob) Quinn decided to pursue careers as professors of business administration because of the opportunities they would have to lift others. Business professors conduct research, teach students, consult with organizations, and serve in the management of the units, committees, and projects of their schools and their professional organizations. Ryan works as an assistant professor in the Leadership and Organizational Behavior area of the University of Virginia's Darden Graduate School of Business. Bob is the Margaret Elliott Tracy Collegiate Professor in the Management and Organizations department at the University of Michigan's Ross School of Business.

Organizational behavior is an interdisciplinary topic, so Ryan and Bob draw on fields such as sociology, psychology, and economics when they do their research. Ryan tries to lift people with his research by studying how people lift others in their communication. He studies verbal and nonverbal communication to see how people increase each other's courage; empower, energize, and learn from one another; and create high-performance experiences. Bob studies effectiveness and change. He developed the competing-values framework, is one of the cofounders of the Center for Positive Organizational Scholarship at the Ross School of business, and has published sixteen books, including *Beyond Rational Management, Becoming a Master Manager, Deep Change, Change the World, Building the Bridge as You Walk on It*, and

Diagnosing and Changing Organizational Culture. Both Bob and Ryan drew on their complementary expertise to write this book.

Ryan and Bob put into practice the things they learn through their research by trying to lift the students they teach and the clients for whom they consult. They have taught students in undergraduate, MBA, and Executive MBA programs, as well in executive education. They have also consulted for Fortune 500 companies, government agencies, and nonprofit organizations throughout the world. They focus their teaching and consulting on leadership and change.

As much as they enjoy their careers and the opportunities to lift people around the world, Ryan and Bob most enjoy trying to lift their families. Ryan has been married to his wife, Amy, for eleven years, and has four children: Mason, Katie, Andrew, and Chloe. Bob has been married to Delsa for thirty-nine years. He has six children, three children-in-law, and eight grandchildren: Shauri, Ryan, Amy, Shawn, Lisa, Kristin, Abram, Travis, Garrett, Mason, Katie, Keely, Max, Andrew, Ben, Aviva, and Chloe.

Berrett-Koehler is an independent publisher dedicated to an ambitious mission: Creating a World That Works for All.

We believe that to truly create a better world, action is needed at all levels—individual, organizational, and societal. At the individual level, our publications help people align their lives with their values and with their aspirations for a better world. At the organizational level, our publications promote progressive leadership and management practices, socially responsible approaches to business, and humane and effective organizations. At the societal level, our publications advance social and economic justice, shared prosperity, sustainability, and new solutions to national and global issues.

A major theme of our publications is "Opening Up New Space." They challenge conventional thinking, introduce new ideas, and foster positive change. Their common quest is changing the underlying beliefs, mindsets, institutions, and structures that keep generating the same cycles of problems, no matter who our leaders are or what improvement programs we adopt.

We strive to practice what we preach—to operate our publishing company in line with the ideas in our books. At the core of our approach is *stewardship*, which we define as a deep sense of responsibility to administer the company for the benefit of all of our "stakeholder" groups: authors, customers, employees, investors, service providers, and the communities and environment around us.

We are grateful to the thousands of readers, authors, and other friends of the company who consider themselves to be part of the "BK Community." We hope that you, too, will join us in our mission.

Visit Our Website

Go to www.bkconnection.com to read exclusive previews and excerpts of new books, find detailed information on all Berrett-Koehler titles and authors, browse subject-area libraries of books, and get special discounts.

Subscribe to Our Free E-Newsletter

Be the first to hear about new publications, special discount offers, exclusive articles, news about bestsellers, and more! Get on the list for our free e-newsletter by going to www.bkconnection.com.

Get Quantity Discounts

Berrett-Koehler books are available at quantity discounts for orders of ten or more copies. Please call us toll-free at (800) 929-2929 or email us at bkp .orders@aidcvt.com.

Host a Reading Group

For tips on how to form and carry on a book reading group in your workplace or community, see our website at www.bkconnection.com.

Join the BK Community

Thousands of readers of our books have become part of the "BK Community" by participating in events featuring our authors, reviewing draft manuscripts of forthcoming books, spreading the word about their favorite books, and supporting our publishing program in other ways. If you would like to join the BK Community, please contact us at bkcommunity@bkpub.com.